PORTRAIT

of

SPAIN

PORTRAIT

of

SPAIN

British *and* American Accounts *of* SPAIN *in the* Nineteenth *and* Twentieth Centuries

<small>SELECTED BY</small> *Thomas·F·McGann*

New York 1963

ALFRED·A·KNOPF

ACKNOWLEDGMENTS

From *Fabled Shore* by Rose Macaulay. Reprinted by permission of the Estate of Rose Macaulay, and Hamish Hamilton, Ltd. Published in the United States by Farrar, Straus & Co., Inc. From *George Ticknor's Travels in Spain,* edited by G. T. Northrup. Reprinted by permission of the University of Toronto Press. From *Don Fernando* by W. Somerset Maugham. Copyright 1935 by W. Somerset Maugham. Reprinted by permission of the author, Doubleday & Co., Inc., and William Heinemann Ltd. From *Familiar Spanish Travels* by William Dean Howells. Reprinted by permission of W. W. Howells. Published by Harper & Brothers. From *Days in Old Spain* by Gertrude Bone. Reprinted by permission of Macmillan & Co. Ltd. From *Heart of Spain* by Georgiana Goddard King, edited by Agnes Mongan. Copyright 1941 by The President and Fellows of Harvard College. Reprinted by permission of Harvard University Press. From *Homage to Catalonia* by George Orwell. Copyright 1952 by Sonia Brownell Orwell. Reprinted by permission of Harcourt, Brace & World, Inc., and Martin Secker & Warburg Limited. From *The Face of Spain* by Gerald Brenan. Reprinted by permission of Farrar, Straus & Co., Inc., and Hamish Hamilton, Ltd. Copyright 1951 by Gerald Brenan. From *Don Gypsy* by Walter Starkie. Copyright 1937 by E. P. Dutton & Co., Inc. Reprinted by permission of E. P. Dutton & Co., Inc., and Christy & Moore, Ltd. From *Virgin Spain* by Waldo Frank. Copyright 1926, 1942 by Waldo Frank. Reprinted by permission of Duell, Sloan & Pearce, Inc. From *Spain* by Sacheverell Sitwell. Reprinted by permission of B. T. Batsford, Ltd., and Hastings House, Publishers, Inc. From *Silk Hats and No Breakfast* by Honor Tracy. © Copyright 1957 by Honor Tracy. Reprinted by permission of Random House, Inc., and Methuen & Co. Ltd. From *Spring in Spain* by MacKinley Helm. Copyright 1952 by MacKinley Helm. Reprinted by permission of the author, and Harcourt, Brace & World, Inc. From *Five Pens in Hand* by Robert Graves. Reprinted by permission of Willis Kingsley Wing. Copyright 1954 International Authors N.V. Published by Doubleday & Co., Inc. From *Death in the Afternoon* by Ernest Hemingway. Copyright 1932 by Charles Scribner's Sons; renewal copyright © 1960 by Ernest Hemingway. Reprinted by permission of Charles Scribner's Sons, and Jonathan Cape Limited.

L. C. catalog card number: 63–9143

THIS IS A BORZOI BOOK,

PUBLISHED BY ALFRED A. KNOPF, INC.

FIRST EDITION

To my wife

FOREWORD

SPAIN is a castle. Proud, remote, a glorious ruin to the world outside, vital and enduring within, its inhabitants are keepers of physical and moral treasures lost in other Western lands, a people, once known, not to be forgotten.

The tapestry which is Spain, woven across its history and land, is brilliant and complex. An area smaller than Texas— once a mere outpost of the Spanish empire—contains matchless diversity. The blond fisherman of Galicia in the misty northwest could be a Breton or a Gael; the dark peasant of Andalucía is a son of the Moors; the pallid Castilian has the commanding grace of ancestors who from their cold central plateau once ruled from the North Sea to North Africa, from California to Tierra del Fuego, from the Philippines to Florida. Among the granite boulders and stone walls of Extremadura in western Spain against the Portuguese border, in a region no larger than Massachusetts or Wales, sprang up a race of conquerors led by Cortés, the Pizarros, Balboa. On the Mediterranean shore, Catalans have built the metropolis of Barcelona and from their cities and villages they go out to fish the green and purple sea or to tend their poppy-strewn vineyards and tight haystacks.

The roots of Spanish diversity are deep, nourished by geographical variety and hardened in a long past. Cádiz, lying white along the hook of its peninsula thrust into the Atlantic west of Gibraltar, is one of the oldest continuously inhabited cities in Europe. From the Straits north to the Pyrenees stretches a dissected, generally arid land which has bred a people also dissected among themselves and arid to alien ways, men and women of inexpungible humanity, versatile, cruel, and lovely.

The tread of history has been heavy on the land. Two centuries before Christ, Roman legions fought there against Carthaginians; nine centuries later, Moorish horsemen swept across the peninsula and nearly broke the Christian world; eleven centuries later, Wellington and Napoleon's generals battled there for Europe; in our century, Russian and German tankmen and fliers practiced their weapons and a million Spaniards died, with Americans and Englishmen, Frenchmen and Italians.

But Spain has always belonged to the Spaniards. Despite their fierce individualism and hectic regionalism, their essence is unity. They are in profound agreement, or disagreement, about central concerns of life: God, death, love. Four centuries of Western science and its by-products of thought and goods have dented the Spanish armor, but the issue of which Spanish values may die and which may survive is far from settled.

Unity born of diversity; diversity within unity: this is the overriding paradox of a paradoxical race. Passionate democrats in their social relations, yet given to the rule of a leader; tenacious defenders of their religious faith, yet at times its violent enemies; scornful of prolonged labor for mere gain, but capable of astounding feats of physical and psychic endurance, Spaniards seem difficult to understand and harder to like, perhaps especially for Englishmen and Americans. To many English, Spain is an old, if now helpless, adversary, whose Armada and religion were defeated four centuries ago. Americans (forgetting the lands south of the Rio Grande) regard Spain as a strange mother who somehow performed an act of birth—

Columbus—and then abandoned his discovery to be reared, eventually, by Great Britain. Such attitudes are a mild version of the Black Legend, which has painted the Spaniards as monsters unfit to rule in the New World or in the Old.

Why, then, have Americans and Englishmen been fascinated by Spain? Why has Spain preoccupied some of the most culti-vated minds among English-speaking people? How is the Spanish obsession to be explained?

A principal answer lies in the fact that Spain appears to be romantic; not artificially, for commercial reasons, nor merely historically, as a museum may contain items which evoke a brilliant and dramatic past, but really, in truth, still romantic. *The Alhambra*, by Washington Irving, and *The Bible in Spain*, by the dynamic, astute English tract-seller, George Borrow, were published in the 1830's. They were widely read on both sides of the Atlantic and they helped to shape this popular image of Spain—a vision of a knight's shield on which are emblazoned in gold and black a castle, a rampant bull, a burn-ing sun, and a cluster of castanets.

Spain has these: and since all are either un-English or un-American, or both, they are sought out by those alien folk. But Spain's attractive mystery runs deeper, for it contains elements of repulsion which seem to season the lure. Mixed with the foreigner's gay first views are antagonisms: dismay at the dirtily cassocked and unshaven priest; alarm over the apparent political incapacity of the Spaniards; mistrust of non-businessmen who carry no clock in their brains, keep no ap-pointments on time—and are not thereby in the least disturbed; disgust at unmitigated poverty; disdain for the excessive for-malism and occasional colossal arrogance of Spanish males.

Spain's defects are indeed as dramatic as her virtues. The chilling smog of a winter morning in Madrid and the pleas of a sniveling Gypsy beggar boy are remote from the dream of the *cante hondo* echoing across the *vega* of Granada while the sun shines on the ice fields of the Sierra Nevada a mile above the Alhambra. But, still, there is no more generous, courteous people, none more tender with children, none more honest and innately noble, gregarious yet dignified. Spaniards know that time is not money, and that one cannot buy the other. They spend time as it was meant to be used, by investing it for itself, in intimate touch with each other and with their children and with death. In politics Spaniards are not unstable; indeed, they are rigid, as is shown by their commitment to monarchy over more than twenty centuries. Yet at intervals their dogmatism polarizes, and as there is no force capable of perpetually reconciling the political ideals of two or more Spaniards, civil violence results.

The Church is another institution to be understood in Spanish terms (if one wishes to understand Spain). It is a Spanish church which was once, under the king (or queen, for the Spanish male knows when to accept the rule of a woman), more powerful and more Catholic than the Papacy in the days of its power. The men and women whose writings make up this book have understood the Spanish religion; some of them, perhaps, because they take a certain pleasure in the fact that many Spaniards have long esteemed anti-clericalism and church-burning.

The cultural greatness of Spain is as certain, yet as equivocal, as other aspects of that country's life. Quality, not quantity, must be accepted as the measure. Cervantes, Quevedo, Goya, Picasso—a few men who have spoken for each passing century in terms wholly Spanish—and therefore universal.

The authors of this book know Spain, but there are others who have brilliantly described its deceptive virtues yet are not here. Richard Ford understood Spain as well as Borrow did—perhaps better. John Dos Passos youthfully took *Rosinante to the Road Again* many decades ago, but he has been excluded, along with V. S. Pritchett, Irving Babbitt, William Cullen Bryant, Roger Fry, and others. As this portrait was painted, its pattern of themes and its dimensions in time and space obliged me to omit even some of my own favorites.

I came to Spain by a rather long route, by way of study of Latin American history and by living in Latin America, before knowing Spain. Despite the profound imprint of Spain upon Spanish America, it is an error to think that Mexico, or Argentina, or Peru are like Spain, or that their people are similar to Spaniards. Latin America is in fact a New World. It stands alone. And so does Spain; alone, as always; strong where other nations are weak, and weak where they are strong.

Spain is a castle. He who gains the castle wins a great victory.

THOMAS F. McGANN

NOTE: Spelling and accentuation of Spanish words remain as in the originals.

I am indebted to Charles Houston Harris III, Helen P. Travis, Ellen Bandler, Gretchen Blackmon, and Colleen Kain for their assistance in the preparation of *Portrait of Spain*.

THE *real permanent and standing cause of Spain's thinly peopled state, want of cultivation, and abomination of desolation, is BAD GOVERNMENT, civil and religious: this all who run may read in her lonely land and silent towns. But Spain, if the anecdote which her children love to tell be true, will never be able to remove the incubus of this fertile origin of every evil. When Ferdinand III captured Seville and died, being a saint he escaped purgatory, and Santiago presented him to the Virgin, who forthwith desired him to ask any favors for beloved Spain. The monarch petitioned for oil, wine, and corn: conceded; for sunny skies, brave men, and pretty women: allowed; for cigars, relics, and bulls: by all means; for a* good government: *"Nay, Nay,"* said the Virgin, *"that never can be granted, for were it bestowed, not an angel would remain a day longer in Heaven.*

RICHARD FORD
Gatherings from Spain (*1846*)

BAY OF BISCAY

ATLANTIC OCEAN

La Coruña
CAPE FINISTERRE
Santiago de Compostela
Lugo
Gijón
Oviedo
ASTURIAS
CANTABRIAN MTS.
Bilbao
VIZCAYA
Vitoria
GALICIA
León
LEÓN
Burgos
OLD CASTILE
Numant
Sori
Vigo
Valladolid
Aranda
DUERO R.
Oporto
DOURO R.
Zamora
Salamanca
Segovia
(La Granja)
SIERRA DE GUADARRAMA
S. Ildefonso
Guadalaj
Avila
El Escorial
Alcalá d
Henare
Coimbra
Yuste
Plasencia
Madrid
Toledo
Aranjuez
S P A
TAJO R. (TAGUS R.)
Alcántara
NEW CASTILE
Cáceres
ESTREMADURA
Toboso
Mérida
GUADIANA R.
La Mancha
Lisbon
Badajoz
Valdepeñas
SIERRA MORENA
La Carolina
Bailén
Córdoba
Ecija
GUADALQUIVIR R.
CAPE ST. VINCENT
A N D A L U C Í A
Sevilla
Luisiana
Carmona
Guadix
Granada
SIERRA NEVADA
GULF OF CÁDIZ
Jerez de la Frontera
Ronda
SIERRA DE RONDA
Málaga
Almer
Cádiz
Algeciras
Gibraltar
STRAIT OF GIBRALTAR
Tangier
SPANISH MOROCCO
PORTUGAL

map by palacios

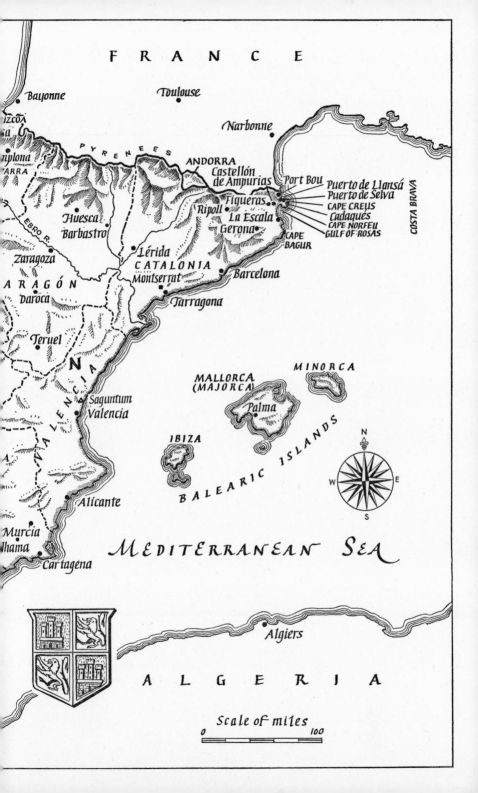

CONTENTS

xvii

CONTENTS

ILLUSTRATIONS

xix

PORTRAIT

of

SPAIN

ROSE MACAULAY

The Costa Brava

A SELECTION FROM *Fabled Shore*

Of the routes by which the traveler may enter the castle that is Spain, two are superb because of the drama of their histories. One route comes up from the south across the Straits, leaving Africa behind as the Moors did twelve centuries ago: by it one enters Spain—Andalucía—from the southern sea, sailing past the Rock of Gibraltar into the Bay of Algeciras. The other route comes from the north, from France, and passes between the Pyrenees and the Mediterranean. At the snug cove of Port Bou the Costa Brava, the Rugged Coast, begins to stretch its tawny length, reaching almost to Barcelona.

The Costa Brava is the eastern fringe of the ancient kingdom of Catalonia; it is the western fringe of the Mediter-

3

ranean. This strip of land fifty-six air miles in length (one hundred miles by the twisting coastal road) embraces antiquity and today, Greece and Rome, Moslem and Visigoth, medieval and modern. The heart of the coast is the Ampurdán, whose Catalan roots run back to the Iberians, and one of whose glories is the battered, golden-hued sea wall, built by the Greeks half a thousand years before Christ, upon which one looks down from the mosaic stone terraces of Roman governors.

Rose Macaulay entered Spain by this route in 1947, when Spain was even more impoverished and isolated than usual, to begin a journey along the "fabled shore" from the Pyrenees to Portugal. A graduate of Oxford and a relative of the nineteenth-century British historian of the same name, Miss Macaulay was a novelist and essayist who also wrote superb travel accounts. Her unquenchable English individualism, deeply cultivated mind, and brilliant prose style combine to make her narrative of Spain a classic of travel literature.

LEAVING the Catalan mountains of Roussillon for those of the Ampurdán, one knows that it is already Spain. The small dark frontier guards in olive-green uniforms and shiny black cocked hats are of another century; they have grace and beauty rather than apprehension; they pore over passports with interest and absorption and apparent surprise at what they find there. "British Subject" . . . is that, they inquire, a name? Perhaps they find the handwriting of British passport officials obscure. It takes time; but they are pleasant and friendly, and when they have digested the passport and driving licence, and, with interest, searched the car, they wish one

4

good fortune and a happy visit to Spain, which they hope one will enjoy, and one is away.

The road, the old Roman road from Gaul to Tarragona, sweeps up from Port Bou in wild and noble curves, lying like a curled snake along the barren mountain flanks of the Alta Ampurdán, climbing dizzily up, darting steeply down into gorges and ravines, above deep rocky inlets where blue water thrusts into rock-bound coves, and small bays of sand where it whispers and croons in its tideless stir. Points and capes jut boldly through thin blue air above a deep cobalt sea; rocky islets lie offshore; the road dips down to the little bay of Culera, where once throve a little fishing port, where now is an almost abandoned village, pounded to pieces by the bombarding naval guns of the civil war, which ranged down the Catalan coast with their capricious thunder. Here, in a quiet valley behind the quiet village of San Miquel de Culera, moulder more ancient ruins, those of a great Benedictine convent, one of those great monasteries to which Ampurdán gave its feudal allegiance through the Middle Ages. There is a cloister left, some broken arches, a few columns and capitals, three Romanesque apses; they and the church are twelfth century, built on the ruins of an older, probably Visigothic, convent and church: they have an air of having been there from the earliest Christian times, brooding, remote, fallen, but still dominating those bare, pine-clad hills where little vines sprout like cabbages out of the stony mountain sides.

The first beach of any size is that of Garbet, shut between two points and much frequented by Catalan *veraneantes*. Cross the Punta de Gates, and there is another wide bay with the road running close above it. On this July day it was very smooth, iridescent, turquoise with bands of cobalt and indigo further out; it is a most lovely bay, or rather a series of tiny bays. These Catalan bays, with the blue and green boats drawn up at the sea's edge and the brown nets spread out on the hot sands to dry, while bare-legged women sit and mend them, have a grace and beauty far more pictorial than the fishing beaches of Provence, or even those of Liguria; they suggest an antiquity still more remote, a tradition more unbroken. So did boats and nets lie, so did Iberian fishermen wade and lounge, Iberian fisherwomen cobble and gossip on the hot sands, before the Greeks sailed down this coast from Phocaea five-and-twenty centuries ago.

The road, bending inland, runs into the old town of Llansá (the Roman Deciana). Llansá is charming. High above its plaza stands its fine Romanesque church, San Vicente, partly destroyed, like so many Catalan churches, by the anarchists in 1936. Two kilometres from the town is the little port, Puerto de Llansá, a crescent of sandy beach full of fishing boats (sardines are the main haul), shut at its southern tip by a rocky island and a castle, so that the little bay is smooth and sheltered like a lake. On the beach just above the nets and boats is a small white inn with green shutters, the Miramar, with tables and benches on the sand outside it. Here I spent the night; from it, on that hot July evening, I bathed in the smooth curve of sea, that lapped about me as cool and warm as silk, while stars came out, and the great rock jutted into still water against a rose-flushed west. Afterwards I dined at one of the little tables on the sandy verandah, among the local fishermen and a few Catalan visitors. The *patrón* and his family were charming. They had seen, it seemed, few British passports; anyhow, they and their acquaintances who were dining there pored over mine with absorbed interest. They sat and gossiped and drank coffee at the little tables till long after midnight; *vieja costumbre española*, shared to the full by Catalans. It includes, naturally, late morning rising; my inn got stirring about half-past eight, and I got my coffee about half-past nine, after an exquisite early bathe in the still, limpid, opal, waveless sea, to which I stepped carefully down the sands between the

6

drying nets. At ten I took the road winding above silver-blue coves and rocky shores round the deeply indented bay that holds Puerto de Selva in its southern crook. Vines, olives, figs, cactus and aloes filled the hot morning with their aromatic breath. Puerto de Selva is, to my mind, almost the most attractive little port of all the Costa Brava. Sheltered by the crook of the point behind it, and by the great jut of the Cadaqués peninsula that pushes out, vine-leaf shaped, north of the Gulf of Rosas, the little port lies on one side of the inner curve of a horse-shoe, facing west to the opposite shore and hauling in nets full of sardines. Above it on both sides of the bay tower great bare mountains, their faint evanescent colours shifting with each turn of light and shadow, so that they are here opal, there transparent indigo, there again faint rust; it is like the shifting colours on a dove's breast. The houses round the port are gaily and freshly painted white, their doors and shutters a vivid blue and green; they wear balconies with tubs of geraniums, blue convolvulus and plump-leaved sprawling shrubs. Some people prefer and would restore the less gaudy rust, moss and ochre colours, with which the town camouflaged itself against bombardment during the civil war, producing an effect of melting into its mountain background; and indeed this must have been very lovely. But so also is the vivid white and blue that dazzles on the luminous air. The camouflage, it seems, was not very effective, for Puerto de Selva suffered much damage from bombs. Like so many Catalan villages, it was bombed by one side and had its church destroyed by the other, thus getting the worst of two worlds. The interior of the church has been rebuilt: over the altar is the legend "Radix salva. Erecta in ruinis A.D. 1944. Salva Porta."

Two miles inland from the port is the still more ancient village of Selva de Dalt. The woods which gave village and port their name have long since been destroyed; now only little

7

vines scramble over the lower slopes of the great hill flanks. Selva was hot, tiny, and smelt of figs. Its little lanes were blocked with donkeys and great loads of grass, and trailed off into hill paths. One of these led up the mountain on whose top towers the great ruined Benedictine abbey of San Pere de Roda. A car, they told me, could get up the mountain to within two kilometres of the monastery, and one would finish the climb on foot. A donkey, said Murray, would make it in an hour and a half. I dare say it would; but I had no donkey; it was very hot, and very steep; I renounced the enterprise and turned my back on Selva.

But the shadow of this mighty ruin haunted me, and haunts me still. I should have seen it. Instead, I read all about it in books by Catalans—how it was one of the major Benedictine foundations, which wielded feudal power over the country for miles round sheltering the villages of Selva and Llansá and encouraging the fishing in the ports because the monks loved fish. The monastery was abandoned in 1798; the monks wearied of their lonely life on the mountains, and came down to the cheerful plains, nearer the fish, moving finally to Besalú. The deserted abbey was sacked and plundered of its doors, windows, pillars and stones; it fell into ruins, long before the dissolution of the monasteries put it into the hands of the State. To-day it broods in sombre Romanesque magnificence, a pile of broken walls, Byzantine arches, square towers, solitary on the bare mountain, looking down over Ampurdán and the sea. Not even Poblet or Ripoll is a more tremendous relic of the monastic grandeur that dominated eastern Spain during the *Edad Media*.

From Selva a rough road jolts inland across the vine-leaf promontory to Cadaqués. The coast, which has here at present no road (it is said there is to be one), is indented by one lovely small bay after another, only accessible by foot; coves, caves, beaches and points, rocky islets, little harbours, none so well sheltered as Puerto de Selva, except Port Lligat, which is shut round by an island and is smooth and still, like a lake; among its three or four fishermen's cottages the square white house of Salvador Dali stands out. Lligat has a fascination not incongruous with Dali, and not quite of this earth.

The first port to be reached by the road from Selva is Cadaqués; a very pleasant and beautiful place, with its wide open plaza on the sea, shaded by mimosas and planes, the white town with deep blue doors and windows, the long curve of beach with the coloured fishing boats drawn up, the magnificent church standing high and sheer on the top of a pile of houses and narrow streets. Cadaqués is an historic port; in its bay the French, through the Count of Foix, met the Catalan admiral, Roger of Laurier, to negotiate peace after the French invasion of 1285. Barbarossa's squadrons took and sacked the town when they raged down that coast in 1543. Cadaqués has always been exposed to the people of the sea, as well as to storms, strong currents and winds that have made the lives of its fishermen hard. It is remote; until the making of the roads from Selva and from Rosas, it lay isolated in its bay at the tip of this easternmost spur of the Pyrenees. It is said to be still archaic, behind the times, in spite of the recent incursions of *veraneantes*. Archaic or not, it is a lovely place, white and clear and curved like a crescent moon. They fish for pearl in the bay. The church, Santa Maria (undamaged both by republicans and rebels), has a fine Romanesque-looking exterior, but inside is dated 1662, and is a gorgeous riot of baroque. It was in the porch of this church that I first read the placards which, all over Spain, warn señoras and señoritas what they must wear in church. "Señora! Señorita! You present yourself without stockings? In a short dress? With short sleeves? You go into church? Stop! Stop! If you go thus into church, you will be turned out. If you go thus indecorously to confession, you will not be given absolution. If you have the audacity to approach the Blessed Sacrament, you will be refused in the presence of all."

Apart from the sex unfairness of this (for it seems that señores may wear what they like), what strikes one is the profound difference of attitude between the Roman and the Anglican Churches, the one making church-going an occasion, a mystery, to be approached *en grande tenue*, in especial clothes, the other easy, casual, laissez-faire, go-as-you-please, come-as-you-are, come in your working and playing clothes, bare headed, bare armed, bare legged, just as you happen to be. (Vain hope, for how seldom do we come at all!) To surround religious devotion with pomp and ceremony, awe, stockings, voluminous ceremonial clothes, has much to be said for it, though the stocking requirement must keep many women from church; in these fishing ports stockings are seldom seen; the women mending nets on the beach and marketing in the town never wear them; they may keep a pair for church, but to go home and put them on when the bell clangs for a service must be difficult. On the other hand, those who do go to church thus decorously attired, thus set apart from their secular workaday selves, must, I suppose, feel very blest and spiritually prepared. As, no doubt, church-goers in Victorian England used to feel, processing churchward on Sunday mornings in top-hats and Sunday frocks. The Anglicans, who have dropped so much, have dropped all that; "come as you are, my dear people," is now the vicar's vain and coaxing plea. What English vicar would dare to placard his church door with "Ladies! Stop! Stop! Change your clothes or you will be turned away!" The same difference in attitudes lies, I think, behind the so careful guarding of Spanish churches, so that between one and four, when caretakers and sacristans are having their midday meal and their siesta, you will find every church and cathedral locked against visitors; very disappointing for those who are passing through in the afternoon and cannot wait. In England, cathedrals and churches stand casually and negligently open to all comers all day until dark; you may wander about them, stockingless, in mid-afternoon. The difference may, in part, be due to fear of the ancient Spanish tradition of ecclesioclasm, which has done in the past such irretrievable hurt to churches. But there is, I think, also a difference in attitude; the Holy Mysteries, the Heavenly Sanctuary, too hallowed for unguarded approach, as against come-and-go-as-you-please.

From outside the Cadaqués church, one looks down a sheer precipice of a wall over the moon-like port and pale blue bay set with fantastic rocks. A flight of steps takes one down into narrow streets, clean and steep, and so into the broad, delicious plaza, which was this afternoon bathed in soft and luminous brightness; it seemed a serene and happy place. At one side is the curve of sea; at the other restaurants and café tables. A waiter came and talked to me in charming American; he had, he said, waited for ten years in New York (and I remembered reading that many Cadaqués men emigrate to America, because life in Cadaqués is hard). "They live very good there," said the waiter, on a wistful note. "Sure thing, they live very good." But it seems to the casual visitor that life in Cadaqués too might be good; the place has an exquisite tranquillity, dignity and grace.

Leaving it reluctantly, I took the coast road for Rosas. It is a good road, winding up and down great olive-grown and rocky mountains, whose rust-coloured slopes sweep down to blue bays. I believe these mountains are the Sierra of Rosas, the eastern end of the Pyrenees. Above the olive zone they tower, barren and noble, in the magnificent uselessness of uncultivated mountain lands.

The road dips down to the sea at the lovely little bay of Montjoi. From here one may—indeed one must—walk to Cape Norfeu, and get, on a clear day, one of the most glorious views of the Costa Brava—all down the Gulf of Rosas as far as the Medas islands and Cape Bagur, and inland across the Ampurdán to the high Pyrenees.

Leaving Montjoi, the road sweeps around the bay of La Pelisa and curls north-west, dropping down from the heights into Rosas Bay, between bamboo groves where the cicadas ziz and churr without stop in the July heat, making the sound of a thousand saws. A great azure gulf opens at one's feet; the Gulf of Rosas; one slides down into the port, along a road where boats are building, smelling of tar and sweet timber; and here is the long bay beneath the mountains, where the Greeks (having lost their southern Spanish marts to the Carthaginians) anchored and traded two thousand and five hundred years ago, and, at the gulf's southerly end, made their settlement of Emporion. The gulf was sheltered—"portus effuse jacet nullisque flabris aequor est obnoxium," wrote Avienus. Yet not so sheltered as all that, for the day I was there a little breeze was ruffling the sea.

There is, it seems, no certain proof that the town now Rosas was founded by the Greeks. The Greek settlement of Rhodus (probably an offshoot from Emporion) may have been not on the site of the present town, but near it, and now buried beneath the silting sands. Traces have been found. "Here too," says Strabo, "is Rhodus, a small town belonging to the Emporitans. . . ." And Scymnus, writing in the fifth century B.C., says that Rhodus was founded by the Massiliots after Emporion. But just where in the gulf it was, both they and other writers leave tantalizingly vague.

Rosas does not emerge much into history until the Middle Ages, when it was part of the domains of the Counts of Ampurias, who kept the Ampurdán in such a continuous bustle, and may well have disturbed and buried ancient sites beneath the weight of the fortifications and castles that they threw up all round Castellón de Ampurias. Under these so militant and

12

enemy-conscious counts, Rosas was a naval port, anchoring
the squadrons that guarded the trade of Castellón and the river
Muga, to which came merchants from far Mediterranean and
Adriatic ports. Rosas lay under the dominion and shadow of
the great Benedictine convent of Santa María, which, greatly
ichthyophagous like all monasteries, encouraged the fishing industry all up the coast to Cape Creus. The city encircled a
walled and fortified abbey citadel, of which remains are still to
be seen. Suchet blew it up in 1814. Fish and coral brought the
town prosperity, and revived it after its many assaults and de-
structions, for through centuries it was a centre of the storms
that always raged over Ampurdán both from within and
without. A tough and adventurous seafaring population was
reared in this dangerous city; often in recent centuries they
have fared, like my Cadaqués waiter, out of their own exquisite sea across the wild dark wastes of the Atlantic to try new
lands. Some, like him, have returned, to talk American to
tourists in the plaza, or to sail their fishing boats about their
blue and jade and silver bay, and to lounge on the sea wall
beneath the trees, as I did now, looking down the long bay
that the sinking sun turned to a great rose, looking at the
white, west-facing town delicately flushed, and across the
bay to the opposite coast, where Castellón de Ampurias
rises on its hill among the shadow-blue plains of Ampurdán.
Rosas is lovely, though it has not the remote outpost charm of
Cadaqués. I drove along the short coast road to the point
where the lighthouse stands, and beyond it to the point of
Poncella (view, as Baedeker would say; and a view indeed it
is). On the hill-side above the faro is the ruined castle of La
Trinitat, smashed up in 1808 by the French. I began to climb
up to it, but was stopped by a sentry; probably it bristles with
guns that foreigners may not see. I returned to the town, and
took the road to Castellón de Ampurias, five miles west.

Once the capital of Ampurdán and the residence of the

counts, Castellón stands on the river Muga, under three miles from the sea, surrounded by reservoirs and marshes. It stands on a hill; a fine mediaeval walled city, with a fourteenth-century church, castle, moat and bridge. The church—or rather cathedral—is magnificent; a tall square pinnacled tower, arcaded in three tiers, with fine buttresses and gargoyles, a broad nave of seven bays, west door sculptured with alabaster apostles, rich retablo and high altar. It is one of the most pleasing Gothic churches I saw in Catalonia. Close to it (I think joined on) is the castle, with its moat and its steep fortress walls brilliant all the way up with flowers and green plants. The streets are fascinating; you come at unexpected corners on some broken arch that may once have been part of a cloister, or of some chapel of ease; in them fig trees grow and goats graze. Coming to Castellón from the shore where the Greeks trafficked and made their settlements, from that golden shore, classical, Mediterranean, pagan, urbane, is to step into feudalism, into the rough, turbulent life of Gothic barbarism, where wild counts and dominating abbots and their retainers fought one another and defended their cities from assault. Everything seems built for defence or for prayer; and even the churches are forts. There is nothing Greek about these walled and castled cities.

I had to get on to Figueras, five miles further, where there would be petrol and oil (both scarce in the country north of Barcelona). Figueras, the capital of Ampurdán, and, after the fall of Barcelona in the last months of the civil war, for a short time capital of Republican Spain, is noisy and crowded, its narrow streets a maze, through which I and my car were guided to a hotel by a kind youth who was studying English and collected stamps; for both these hobbies he found me profitable, though, for all I understood of what he said, he might as well have talked Catalan. He collected and introduced to me his instructress in English, a smiling little spectacled lady who conversed with me in the street, but seemed to understand the remarks she made to me better than those I made to her; with me it was the other way round. She said, "You make long stay in Figueras?" I said, one night only. She said, "You will be a week staying, yes." I said one night. She said, "Yes, one week. You like Figueras." I said it was beautiful. She said, apologetically, that she could not quite understand my English, which was not, was it, of London. She said some more, in the English of Figueras, and we parted with mutual compliments and friendship. I like the people of Figueras. But not the church clock, which made the night unquiet by resononantly striking every quarter. Wakeful and fretful, I began to understand the Spanish passion for church-burning. But, in the case of Figueras, I was mistaken. I saw the church in the morning; a fine fifteenth-century building which had been destroyed by the church-burners and was being very beautifully rebuilt; the new part included the bell tower which so sonorously disturbed the night; the old one, I was told, had not struck the night hours. Perhaps sleepless nights in Figueras had been planned as a form of reparation for sacrilege, and I thought it served Figueras right.

Some of the old church remained; part of the nave, the base of the tower, the sculptured figures over the west door. San Pedro must have been a magnificent church. I was shown over the ruins and over the new building by an intelligent priest; he gave me a booklet about its history, which related also much of the history of the town. Figueras was the Roman Juncaria, and stood on a Roman military road; it was destroyed by Saracens in the early Middle Ages, and rebuilt, further from the road, a plain and humble town which the inhabitants called Tapioles; in the course of time it became Ficerias, Figariae, Figueras. To-day the ancient name is only preserved in one district, called Tapis. Tradition says that St. Paul (so busy in Spain) visited Juncaria, landing at Emporion,

15

and preached the Christian religion there with immense success, which produced later several martyr saints. The Saracens destroyed Figueras and its first (probably Visogothic)
church; after the reconquest it was rebuilt, with the help of
the San Pere de Rosa Benedictines. This Romanesque church
was burnt down, with the whole town, by an incendiary count
of Ampurias. With its indefatigable powers of recuperation,
Figueras built itself and its church up again, the latter in the
purest Catalan Gothic of the fifteenth century; austere and
tremendous, its severity lightened by its graceful *campanario*.
There were later disasters and attacks, and the *campanario*
was scarred by French bullets; but the church remained
standing for nearly five hundred years, its longest period yet.
Then, on July 21st, 1936, the Figuerenses began to set fire to
churches; "surgió la chispa necrosificadora, el espíritu sa-
tánico de destrucción y de ruina . . ."; the mob broke into
the parish church during Mass, seized benches and chairs, and
set them ablaze. What a conflagration! Flames leaped to the
roof. "The faithful, livid with fear, retired into a corner of
the church, believing their last hour to have come," but they
were allowed to go without molestation. The flames con-
sumed nearly everything; what they left was looted or destroyed.

Mysterious madness which ever and anon attacks the Spanish, driving them to these strange pyrrhic frenzies! It seems
the reverse side of religious devotion: in Anglican England
we have little of either; in consequence our churches and
cathedrals remain standing, though somewhat sparsely filled.
It was odd to picture the cheerful Figuerenses at their fiery
work, seeing them so peaceably and gaily employed in their
broad market square on this July morning eleven years later.
Indeed, this morning market was a lovely sight—a brilliant
orchard of gay fruits piled on stalls—oranges, peaches, apricots, greengages, melons, tomatoes; and behind each stall a

smiling buxom woman selling, before it other smiling buxom women buying; had they, I wondered, eleven years ago tossed pictures and images on the bonfire in San Pedro as now they tossed oranges and apricots into straw bags, and with the same zest? From all accounts, yes.

Meanwhile, the new San Pedro goes up apace, and will be beautiful. If it lasts another five hundred years, it will be lucky. The ancient castle of San Fernando, north-east of the town, was blown up in 1939, a last explosion of the Republicans when Franco's army marched in. Figueras is a pleasant capital; it has broad ramblas and narrow streets, and is difficult to find one's way out of. It had no petrol. They told me at the garage that petrol north of Barcelona was chancy; one might find some pump which had just got its quota, or one might not. La Escala, they said, might have some. They spoke as embittered men: the Ampurdán, one gathered, was being starved of petrol to feed Barcelona, which drank it with gluttonous profusion.

My mind was now set on Ampurias; I hurried out of Figueras, with my basket full of fruit and pots bought in the market. It was another hot and shining day. My way to La Escala and the coast ran through fifteen miles of level country, along a jolting road, past little ochre-coloured mediaeval villages and farms, across the river Fluvia, and so through Vilademat to the little port of Escala, at the southern end of the Gulf of Rosas, whence a short road goes through woods to Ampurias. I arrived in La Escala in a propitious hour; petrol had just arrived, and there was a queue of camions at the pump in the street leading down to the shore, and a busy woman working it. (Most petrol pumps in northern Spain, as in France, are worked by women; further south, not; in the south women are not, I think, supposed to meddle with anything to do with motoring; they stick to donkeys.) The little port was crowded with beautiful fishing boats, great and small; I think it was a holiday, for it was gay with music and coloured paper festoons. Fantastically shaped rocks jutted up about the sea. Señor Pla says Escala is the chief fishing centre of the Costa Brava, and that the fishermen have a hard life, for the port faces north, and in winter gets the tramontana and the icy winds from Canigou and Provence. This, says he, has made the *escalanes* a rather sad, pessimistic people. Fortunately it was not winter when I was there; on that July morning La Escala was blue and exquisite, though its rock-strewn bay was ruffled by a breeze. The town did not look sad and grey, as my book said, though it does lack the brilliant whitewash and paint of many of the harbour towns. At night the fishing boats go out with lights, the whole Gulf sparkles as with fireflies, and is very exquisite. Tiny coves of rock and sand surround the town to north and south; that morning they were pale jade and aquamarine, the waves lapping against jagged rocks.

The short road to Ampurias crosses a bridge just outside La Escala and runs through a sandy pine-wood. The ruins lie above the road, back from a bay of delightful sand and jutting rocks, the bay where Gnaeus Cornelius Scipio landed with his squadron to fight the Carthaginians, "at a place in Iberia called Emporium," says Polybius. "Starting from this town, he made descents upon the coast, landing and besieging those who refused to submit to him along the seaboard as far as the Iber. . . ."

The Emporium where Scipio landed in 211 B.C. was already over three centuries old as a Greek settlement, and illimitably older as an Iberian village. Somewhere about 550 B.C. Phocaean sailors and traders from Marseilles, cut off from the southern coast by the iron curtain of the Carthaginian conquest, made here, in the shelter of this Gulf of Rosas, and close to a small native town, a trading settlement. They settled first on what was then an island, where the almost ruined little mediaeval village of San Martí now stands, guarding that

18

buried town of Paleopolis, and a temple of the Ephesian Artemis which must have stood there. This first settlement is still unexcavated. The second, Neapolis, made a few years later, on the side of the little harbour and buried from sight for many centuries, only yielding up occasional treasures to casual searchers, was first systematically excavated by the Barcelona archaeological society forty years ago; interrupted by the civil war, the work is now again in progress. Neapolis has been revealed, layer below layer, each period identifiable by its fragments of pottery and sculpture and its coins, from the Visigothic town superimposed on it by the barbarian invaders, through the Roman city of splendid and ornate buildings, market places, temples and rich villas, the Hellenistic city that preceded and merged with the Roman, the Attic town of the fifth century, down to the earliest levels, the level of the sixth-century Massiliotes who founded the settlement and of the Iberian town joined to it; of those earliest towns there is little to show now.

The remains of the walls, huge and massive, with their single gate, are of the fifth century B.C. By then, Emporion had Greek works of art, Attic vases, the famous statute of Asklepios and other Athenian objects. Emporitans grew richer and more cultivated; by the fourth century, the Hellenistic age, their town was enlarged and beautified, a long, crowded rectangle of crossing streets and open squares, villas with mosaic floors, tombs, temples, statues. There was the temple of Jupiter Serapis, surrounded by a spacious colonnade, the door giving on the sea. There was a stoa, or market-place, with shops within and pillared ambulatory without, where buyers and sellers walked, chaffering and bartering in Greek, Iberian, Latin, all the dialects of the Middle Sea. And through the city the winds from this sea, and the sound of it, murmured always.

The Romans came; Emporion wisely allied itself with

Rome, as a defence against Carthage. Romans colonized the Hellenistic town, making a city behind it far larger, richer, finer, than Emporion itself. There were beautiful houses, grand temples, rich mosaic floors, cisterns, plumbing, baths. The name was now Emporiae, for there were three cities, the Roman, the Greek, the Iberian. Recent excavations of the Roman town have discovered its great wall, built by Caesar, on the base of an older wall of the cyclopean type. There have also been exposed a gymnasium, and a large ellipitical amphitheatre. Emporion under the Romans had advanced far from the early cramped Greek town. In the third century Frankish pirates attacked the coast and destroyed Neapolis; its inhabitants abandoned it, and settled in the Roman city, which was presently Christianized; there was a basilica, and a Christian burial ground. Then, in Rome's decadence, arrived the barbarians, and the Visigothic town superimposed itself on Emporion. It became the seat of a bishopric.

Then, by the ninth century, Ampurias disappears from history; it has been conjectured that it was sacked and destroyed by the Norman pirates who raged up and down the coast, though some historians blame the Saracens. Villanueva, in his *Viaje Literario a las Iglesias de España*, quotes a record from the archives of the monastery of Santa Maria de Roda— "The pagans came and sacked the whole town, and the pirates laid waste the territory; its inhabitants and peasants were in large numbers taken captive, and many others, abandoning their farms during that time because of the oppressions of the wicked pirates, emigrated elsewhere."

A common story all down that perilous coast. Ampurias was apparently abandoned; and, after some attempts by its counts to revive it, they retired inland to Castellón de Ampurias, and the sea town gradually sank deeper beneath the silting sands, and was forgotten, to wait a thousand years for its unburial. The guidebooks of a century ago, such as Ford's, count Emporion a complete loss, but for the "miserable ruined fishing hamlet" on the hill close by; all that the Baedeker of 1901 says is that the name of Castellón de Ampurias "recalls Emporion, an ancient Greek colony on the Gulf of Rosas." Later English guidebooks only give Ampurias a few lines.

Ampurais to-day is a place inexpressibly moving in its beauty and desolation. Along the intricate criss-cross of the streets that run between the vanished houses, cypresses darkly and necropolistically stand, and fig trees sprawl stickily in the sun. The columns of arcaded porticoes and of temples rear broken stumps against sky and sea. You may wander through the city among ghosts of Greek traders, Iberian vendors, Roman gentlemen lounging outside their villas or gossiping in loud Roman voices in the agora, simple Visigoths knocking down heathen statues and drinking deeply of the wines of Ampurdán.

Across a sandy stretch of land to the north the tumbled, ruinous little pile of San Martí climbs its rocky hill; beneath it sleeps forgotten the old, the original Paleopolis. In front of Ampurias the sea whispers and creams; its tang breathes about the ghostly city like a song. Before Herodotus wrote, Greeks lived and traded here; before Rome was a republic, this little Greek mart was doing business on the shores of the gulf that sheltered merchant ships beneath this great spur of the eastern Pyrenees. Now, along the massive wall above the sea road, red oleanders sprawl. A model of the Asklepios statue presides serenely over the broken desert of little streets. In the western corner, close to the Roman city, on the site of a ruined convent, stands the little museum, where some of the Ampurias finds can be seen—mosaics and vases, pottery of all the periods, fragments, some most lovely. Most of the important things are in the Barcelona archaeological museum, and some at Gerona; but this little branch of it has kept some valuable finds, and also some interesting and pleasing model reconstructions of buildings. It is an unpretentious, rather charming little place.

From Ampurias one goes a few hundred yards along the sea road to San Martí, the walled hamlet on the hill that was once an island. It is the quietest mediaeval hamlet imaginable; but for one gay-tiled villa, the houses, inhabited by a few peasants and animals, seem all tumbling or tumbled into ruin. Its square-towered church crowns the steep streets. Why the village is in such dilapidation, and how long it has been so, I was not able to discover. I wandered about its empty streets, and spoke with a few people outside a tumbling house; a peasant was driving a donkey cart piled with grass up the street; by the gate there was an ancient well. The counts of Ampurias used long ago to frequent this fortified town on its hill; but they retired inland to the safer fortress of Castellón, and San Martí was abandoned to peasants and pirates.

I ate my lunch in the pine woods below the high, steep walls, then went back to Ampurias to spend the afternoon among its whispering centuries of ghosts. Leaving it at last, I drove back along the wood road to La Escala. From there a new road, made during the civil war, runs south for a few kilometres down the rocky coast of coves and capes as far as El Milá. But to explore these coves properly one needs a boat. The gnarled grey rocks jut out into a cobalt and azure sea with, in profile, the mute ferocity of couching beasts, sheltering them here and there white coves of sand, above some of which a few cottages sprawl, and in and out of which fishing boats slip. A stormy sea among these fantastic wild-cat rocks must be an affair of sound, foam and fury; that July afternoon the Mediterranean was a suave and cooing murmuration of blue doves.

HAVELOCK ELLIS

The Genius of Spain

AN ARTICLE FROM
The Nineteenth Century and After

*England's leading authority on the psychology of sex, Ellis
was a prolific writer in his field, but he also knew Spain and
wrote so well about its people that he ranks with the talented
band of his countrymen whose work and lives were centered
in England, but whose hearts, one suspects, were usually in
Spain.*

*Ellis visited Spain on several occasions around the turn of
the nineteenth century and later, and his book,* The Soul of
Spain, *is the chief evidence of his regard for the peninsula. The
following selection is an article which Ellis published in a British magazine in 1902. As a general statement about the com-*

plex thing called "Spain," Ellis's article can stand with the most perceptive attempts at synthesis. But his article was not chosen only for its intrinsic value; it is also a demonstration of the enduring, unchanging qualities which make, as they have always made, Spain unique in Europe and, more important, the Spaniards unique among human beings. Ellis's article mentions that vital sameness, the curse and the blessing of Spain. His article is now many decades old: it will well serve the reader who wishes to know how Spaniards fare today.

I

WHEN I attempt to define to myself the special note or mark of the genius of Spain I am faced with contradictions. All nations, like individuals, must have the defects of their qualities, but both the qualities and the defects of the Spanish character are so emphatic, so various, at first sight so unrelated, that it is difficult indeed to fit them into a single formula, however simple, however complex. Whatever can be done by sheer force of genius or the impulse of some ardent passion, whether in the physical world or in the spiritual world, that a Spaniard has done. But in the aptitude or the inclination to organize practical life, or to furnish that basis of efficient mediocrity on which alone man's progress is possible, Spain has always been hopelessly wanting; despots and monks have alone sometimes succeeded in obtaining a temporary factitious unity. In this respect Spain lies at the farthest possible remove from Germany, where plodding pliability, easily accepting the organisation of a strong arm, furnishes results which in the individual are inconspicuous but in the social body overwhelming. There is no end to the audacity or the variety of Spain's achievements in the world. Spaniards and Portuguese penetrated to the furthest seas before any other nation; to Spain, through her recognition and patronage of a Genoese adventurer, belongs the most stupendous discovery that Europe has ever made. Even in the sixteenth century, when England had no empire at all, Spain was in possession of a colonial empire which remained vaster than that of any other country even until the last century. In the spiritual world Spain can show names as great as those of Columbus, Hernan Cortes, and Vasco de Gama in the physical world: St. Teresa, Juan de la Cruz, Xavier, Loyola. There have been no great groups of Spanish novelists or painters, yet a Cervantes stands out as the author of the greatest and most popular novel that Europe has produced, and Velasquez now appears as perhaps the greatest painter of Europe. We are accustomed to say that the Spaniard has no genius for government. And yet no country has ever produced greater rulers, and at one period no country possessed better laws. The Spaniard Balbus was the first barbarian who reached the Roman Consulship; the Spaniard Trajan was the first barbarian elected emperor, while Hadrian was also a Spaniard and Marcus Aurelius was accounted one. So that, as has often been pointed out, Spaniards ruled the world during nearly the greater part of that period—from the death of Domitian to the accession of Commodus—which Gibbon declared to be the happiest in human history. At a later period Aragon and Catalonia possessed extraordinary political and municipal freedom when England was still crushed beneath the mailed hand of the Normans. Against the English Alfred, Spain can place her Alfonso the Wise, and in the long roll of great queens Isabella must always be placed near the top.

Thus a first glance at the history of Spain, and at the great figures Spain has given the world, reveals little but a perplexing series of glaring contrasts. On the one hand no country in

Europe can produce such a series of magnificent achievements; on the other hand we can nowhere find so prolonged a history of misrule and ineffectiveness and failure. From the days of Diodorus down to the present, Spaniards have impressed other nations by their courage and obstinate tenacity; yet of all the great countries of Europe Spain alone has allowed herself to be effaced from the map of the extra-European world.

There is only one assertion that at the outset we can safely make concerning the genius of Spain. Its first characteristic is individualism. Its successes are due to fine personalities; its failures to the lack of concerted and organised action. Its contributions to the world have been the gifts of men who were mostly indifferent to the virtues of association and subordination, who were above all original persons, careless of their environment, daring to assert themselves. Spain, as one of her own children has said, is "the land of holiness and of chivalry"; of all the manifestations of the human spirit there are none in which the personal qualities of the individual count for so much as the knight and the saint.

Both the knight and the saint are really militant personages, and the Spaniard has been from the first a soldier. Even the Romans learnt lessons in the art of warfare from the most skillful and determined enemy they had ever encountered; the national hero of Spain, the Cid, was a soldier of fortune; and down to the middle of the seventeenth century Spanish infantry was unsurpassed in Europe. It is noteworthy that even so peaceful a profession as that of letters has in Spain been throughout associated either with the conduct of affairs or more usually with the profession of arms. It would be tedious to enumerate the examples which Spain offers of this unusual association, found even in the greatest of her writers, for Lope de Vega, who in mere amount wrote more than any Grub Street drudge, was a man whose chief interests were in life, and who was always ready to fight when called upon, while Cervantes was essentially a soldier, a battered veteran who wrote his books in the intervals of life. It is this characteristic more than any other which has given the chief impress to Spanish literature, its special qualities of swift, pungent, picturesque life, of vivid movement and intrigue, as well as its absence of self-consciousness, its carelessness of artistic perfection. The phenomenon can scarcely be met with elsewhere. All the great English poets, for instance, from Chaucer and Spenser onwards, have been dreamers, spectators of the world, vividly interested, indeed, but rarely—as in a slight degree Milton—themselves men of affairs, and never by preference soldiers. Sir Philip Sidney was a soldier, but he occupies only a small niche in English letters. Ben Jonson was once a soldier, but it was merely a youthful episode; it was possibly the same with Chapman, who in some respects recalls the characteristics of Spain. And even if we turn to a southern country like Italy we find that the same holds good, and that from Dante to Carducci there has been no special connection between the sword and the pen. Casanova, certainly, reveals a passion for letters dominated by a still more ardent passion for life, but Casanova was a man of Spanish descent, indeed of most characteristically Spanish ancestry. The predominance in Spain of these special embodiments of independent originality, the knight and the saint—more precisely the soldier, the man of affairs, and the monk—is so complete that every distinguished Spanish writer, down to Valera, may fairly be included in one or the other category.

II

No doubt the fundamental independence and originality of the manifestations of Spanish genius are not wholly inexplicable. One naturally turns in the first place to examine the racial elements composing the Spanish people. But even here the path is far from clear, and though it is no longer necessary to adopt the hasty conclusion of one baffled investigator who decided that the people of Spain had been dropped directly from Heaven, it is only recently that any definite conclusions as to their origin have been generally accepted.

In a study of the genius of France I have elsewhere shown that every province of that country has an intellectual character of its own, and that when we examine French history and apportion the great men of the country to their proper districts, a vast mass of complex phenomena falls into harmonious order. At the first glance we should expect to find the same spiritual diversity in the provinces of Spain as we find in those of France. The obvious differences in the ancient kingdoms of Spain are so marked, and their political histories so distinct, that we look for something radically different in the temperament of their peoples as manifested in their men of genius. For the most part, however, it seems to me that we shall look in vain. We find, speaking generally, that religious fervour is predominant in Castile, practical initiative and commercial aptitude in Aragon and Catalonia, that Galicia and the other northern provinces produce manual workers, while Andalusia and the other southern provinces are marked by a love of the arts. But the distinctions between Norman and Provençal, Breton and Gascon, are far more radical. And when we come to map out Spanish men of genius (as I have before mapped out French men of genius) according to their places of racial origin, the discrepancies are everywhere conspicuous. It is not obvious why the Cid should come from the north-east, the Great Captain from the south-west, why Martial should come from the south-east, and Campoamor— the chief Spanish poet of recent days, with a method of art and an attitude towards art resembling that of Martial after an interval of two thousand years—from the north-west. Nor, so far as I can see, have the great men of any Spanish province characters so distinct as in Great Britain mark off the finest men of Wales from those of the Lowlands, or the Cornish from the East Anglians.

The primitive population of Spain, as far back as we can go, was mainly Iberian. . . . It is fairly clear that the Iberians formed part of a great Mediterranean race which reached Spain from Africa. . . . Spain as the nearest country to Africa became the special European seat of the Eurafrican race and has remained so to the present day, the Basques in their isolated fastnesses, as is now generally recognized, having best preserved, though still with much modification, the primitive Iberian traits. The Celts came at a later date, chiefly to the northern and north-western coast, forming a fringe to the Iberian population, and the Carthaginians, preceded by the Phoenicians, formed a similar fringe along the south and south-western coast. With this southern fringe the Romans mingled their civilisation; and then the Visigoths penetrated to the centre of the country and ruled it for many centuries, to be driven to the north of the peninsula, together with all the most unyielding elements of the population, by the irresistible Arabs and Berbers who developed in the southern half of the country the most exquisite civilisation that Islam has ever attained. Then after five centuries the northern element of the population rolled back with renewed energy to overlay and expel the Mohammedan population. From that time there have been no new immigrations, and so far as the composition of the race has been altered it has been by the more unfortunate methods of banishment, emigration, and destruction. An interesting and probably very significant point about the immigrations is that they were largely constituted by similar elements. Cut off on every side by the Atlantic and the Pyrenees, Spain was chiefly open on the Mediterranean side, and every immigration on this side, probably even to some extent that of the Romans, was mainly composed of some branch, usually African, of the same Mediterranean race. Only the Celts and the Goths brought in new elements, which, however, have failed to modify greatly the general character of the race. The recent researches of anthropologists have shown that the physical characters of the Spanish population reveal a degree of fusion and uniformity which renders them perhaps the purest race in Europe. The absence of fundamental diversity in the racial characteristics of the several provinces, and possibly the general lack of pliability in the whole nation, may be explained by this uniformity of constitution. Both by its physical features and also by the race and temper of its population, Spain is, then, far more than any other European country African in character. I see curious evidence of the affinity between Africa and Spain in the resemblance in literary spirit between the Latin African writers and Spanish writers. Nowhere but in St. Augustine and Tertullian, the most typically African authors, can we find the torrid emotional fervour, the inflexible ethical independence, dominating all other elements of character, which we so often find in the men of Spain.

This moral element, this peculiar independence, sometimes coarsely fibred, more often finely fibred, seems the predominant element of the Spanish mind. The Spanish are not a great artistic race like the French or the North Italians, in spite of isolated achievements in painting and architecture; still less are they a race of abstract thinkers and philosophers, like the southern Italians or the Bretons: not one of the pure thinkers of Europe has been a Spaniard; not one of the great discoveries in science has been made in Spain; the Spanish are not even, in the strict sense, an emotional people like the Germans, and the large emancipating emotional personalities, of whom Luther is the supreme type, are not produced by Spain, whose Luther was a Loyola. But to a greater extent even than England, Spain is the land of character, of originality, of independence. Character and conduct, alike on the grave and the comic sides, from the subtleties of the theologians to the gusto of the picaresque novelist, have ever occupied the Spaniard in a peculiar degree. In a people more than any other impelled to become the prey of their instincts and passions—by no means always ignoble instincts and passions—conduct and character become matters of more vivid interest than they can ever be to a tamer race. One may note the tendency to sententiousness which characterizes this serious and laconic people; no country is so rich in proverbial wisdom. Nor is it by accident that the greatest and most typical of European moralists is Seneca of Cordova.

Although at the first glance the statement may seem paradoxical, it is probable that in this racial tendency to moral fervour we may really find the intimate basis of the chief defect in the Spanish character. Sweet-natured, generous, affectionate, faithful, as the Spanish man or woman can be in personal relationships, that inflexibility of fibre which is the virtue and quality of the race at its best easily becomes cruelty. Indifference to the sufferings of animals seems natural to Spaniards (except perhaps the Basques), though to a far less extent than to the Moors. The bull-fight, though not originally a Spanish institution but apparently the mediaeval development of Moorish boar-baiting, is certainly a true expression of the people, and though it would be unjust to say that the attraction of the bull-fight is its cruelty, it remains true that a people more sensitive to the infliction of pain could not so long have tolerated a sport in which the infliction of pain is at all events more obvious, if not greater, than in the hunting of foxes or the shooting of pheasants. But when we talk of Spanish cruelty we must always remember that a Spaniard can be at least as cruel to himself as he is to others. The Spaniard has ever been ready to apply the lash to others, remorselessly, but never more remorselessly than he has applied it to himself. He is only indifferent to the pain of others because he is indifferent to his own pain. Even Strabo noted this aspect of Spanish cruelty; Spanish mothers, he says, slay their children rather than that they should fall into the hands of the enemy, and he tells how certain Spaniards when taken prisoners by the Romans, and affixed to the cross, still chanted songs of triumph. One may perhaps say that it is on the side of its austerity that Catholicism has appealed so strongly to Spaniards; Spain was always antagonistic to the domination of Rome, but it was Spain that created the counter-Reformation, and saved the Church. It was in Spain that the celibacy of the secular clergy was first declared, a century before it was accepted by the rest of the Christian world. One may recall that the first Christians who were willing to die at the hands of the Church for fidelity to unorthodox opinions, as well as the Churchmen who slew them, were alike Spaniards. At a later date the early Inquisitors were themselves martyrs; and the violent excesses of a Torquemada and a Lucero were the acts of men who had no brutal thirst of blood, but who naturally and habitually subordinated the infliction of pain to the achievement of their fervid and narrow ideals. The atrocities of the Inquisition, committed on Jew and Moor and heretic, become intelligible when we remember that from the days of Saguntum and Numantia unto our own time, the Spaniard has never been surpassed in the capacity for facing calmly and deliberately every form of suffering and death. Nietzsche has preached to a sceptical generation the ennobling virtues that are born of hardness and pain, but that is a lesson that the Spaniard has at no time needed to learn.

III

Not only are the characteristics of the Spanish people, however superficially various, fundamentally the same from Biscay and Asturias to Andalusia and Catalonia, but they have remained the same from the beginning of history. It happens that this opinion is not incapable of verification. When the traveller to-day enters Spain he will, for example, observe that the favourite colour for dresses is black, that the men wear cloaks, while the women are fond of embroidered shawls, their national headdress also being a mantilla coquettishly shading the face, while the hair is done in certain peculiar fashions, especially in an elevated structure. He would also observe that they are fond of the flesh of the goat, that they use oil instead of butter, that they drink water and are extremely frugal and temperate. He might note that the women till the soil and that it is common for two people to ride one horse. He would be struck by the confidence with which the maimed beggars rely on the passer for charity. He would find the inhabitants sometimes urbane, sometimes with a certain ruggedness of character, always brave. And he would find that while not avoiding necessary labour they are very disinclined to unnecessary labour. Now every one of these observations, literally true to-day of the manners and morals of the Spanish people, was made 2,000 years ago by a famous Greek traveller who wrote before the Christian era. If Strabo returned to life to revive his *Geography*, there is probably no part of it which would need so little change as the book on Spain. What ancient writers have told us about Britain is almost wholly meaningless as regards the British to-day; in what they told us of France and Germany we discern a resemblance to the general temper and character of the people still inhabiting those countries. But in what has come down to us concerning Spain we recognize the very accent and gesture of the modern Spaniard, just as the statue of the Gaditanian dancing girl in the Museum at Naples presents the precise pose of the modern Spanish dancer. The bull-ring and the Church have indeed been added to Spanish institutions, but they have only been grafted on to more ancient habits of the people.

33

We realize the singular persistence of the Spanish genius if we trace the history of a single district. We could not take a better example than Cordova. Even the names of cities seem to have changed less in Spain than elsewhere, and Cordova still retains the name by which it has always been known. Before the Christian era the civilisation of which Cordova is the centre was so ancient that Strabo tells us it was thought to possess laws and poems not less than six thousand years old. In any case the inhabitants of the fertile valley of the Guadalquivir, always famed for its olives, were even then regarded as the most polished and urbane people of Spain, and such qualities are the surest index of an ancient civilisation. The first important Roman settlement was at Cordova, and from the time that we first begin to trace its history definitely it has never ceased to produce great men. The first of these—as also the first great Latin author of non-Italian origin—was the elder Seneca, as man and as writer a representative of that mixture of sternness and humour which marked alike the early Roman and the Spaniard, as also, it may be added, in later times the English and the Lowland Scotch. The traditions of Cordova were carried on by the younger Seneca and by Lucan, who with much foreign rhetoric exhibits in full development the arrogant and perfervid independence of the Spanish temper; the sentiment of the well-known line:

VICTRIX CAUSA DIIS PLACUIT, SED VICTA CATONI

represents an attitude which has always been peculiarly Spanish. The establishment of Christianity in no way affected the intellectual position of Cordova, and in the days of Athanasius and Constantine, the greatest of Western ecclesiastics was no Italian, but Hosius, Bishop of Cordova. The Moslems came, but Cordova only flourished the more, and in the fourth century was the most civilized and the most magnificent city in Europe. Almanzor, the greatest statesman

34

and general of Mohammedan Spain, began life as a poor student of Cordova; Ziriab, the most accomplished dilettante and Epicurean of the mediaeval world, also belonged to a city equally pre-eminent in the arts of war and of peace. In its famous mosque Cordova possessed a temple which even now is only exceeded in size, though scarcely in interest, by St. Peter's. Before the institution of universities Cordova was the chief centre of European learning, and Albucasis, Abenzoar, Al Hazen were the chief scientific luminaries of their time, while it was a Cordovan of distinguished Cordovan family, Averroës, who by introducing Aristotle to the modern world led to the revival of learning in Europe. When Cordova again became Christian it played a smaller part in the world but never ceased to be a great city. Gonsalvo, "the great Captain," one of the glories of Spain and of Europe in the fifteenth century, was of old Cordovan family. Even to the present Cordova has maintained its reputation as a city to be born in, and Valera, the best novelist and the finest prose-writer of modern Spain, is a son of Cordova. To-day as we wander through the ever-delightful streets of the ancient city we are far from conscious of the gloom that broods over the dead cities of Europe; the grass may grow on the streets that were first in Europe to be paved, but we everywhere feel the presence of a race of unconquerable fibre. It is a climate of extremes, like that of Florence, and the men of Cordova and the men of Florence alike possess a peculiar intellectual energy, separating them, as an elect people, from their fellows. But while the energy of Florence has been mainly compressed into a few centuries, that of Cordova has been spread over a period that cannot be measured.

I V

What is the cause of the sudden extinction of the finest intellectual elements in a civilisation that flourished during so vast

a period? Before we attempt to answer that question we have
to go beyond the characteristics of the Spanish people and to
consider the special conditions under which the nation has
evolved.

A fact which seems of the most fateful significance in the
history of Spain is the ultimate domination of Castile. When at
the end of the fifteenth century the masterful, fervent, bigoted Isabella united Aragon to Castile and drove the Moslems
of Granada out of the country, she at once laid the foundations of Spain as a great power in the world and insured its
speedy overthrow. A country that is dominated by its most
central region is sure to be badly dominated. The centre may
possibly contain the strongest race, but it will certainly be unprogressive and conservative to a dangerous extent. In the
centre the race will be most homogeneous, with least of that
pliability tending to civilisation which comes from a fine
blending of races, and the centre is necessarily more impreg-
nable to external influences. If we could imagine France dominated by the pure and unprogressive Celts of Auvergne we
should have to picture a wholly different France. Peter the
Great knew well what he was about when he transferred the
capital of Russia from Moscow to St. Petersburg; and it may
be doubted whether the domination of the German Empire
by its most remote and least civilized region will eventually
prove an unmixed advantage. There can be little doubt that the
pre-eminence of Castile has exerted an unhappy influence on
Spain. The special inflexibility and fervour of the Spanish people is more unmixed in Castile than elsewhere; in Castile also
there was a conflict between the ruling classes and the people,
who, while marked by more excellent qualities than their
rulers have usually possessed, have seldom shown any desire
or aptitude to take the reins into their own hands. Their activities have chiefly run into religious or literary channels, and
how great a race they were in temper and capacity we may be

36

content to find witness in the tongue they fashioned, a speech which for the special qualities of strength and beauty can only be equalled by English among the living tongues of Europe. As a people they deserved the highest admiration; as rulers they were utterly unfit to govern an empire. That intense racial fervour, which in the spiritual sphere produced results we may sometimes admire and sometimes deplore, when turned into a practical direction produced only the gloomiest and most suicidal results.

Until the days of Ferdinand and Isabella, the history of Spain, though sanguinary and confusing, is on the whole cheerful and certainly picturesque, full of freedom and fine energy, of variegated activities in every field. From the sixteenth century onward it is a record of intense and unrelieved gloom. It was no doubt the influence of Isabella, perhaps the most masterful and powerful woman who ever sat on a throne—in harmony with her wily and rapacious husband, Ferdinand—that finally moulded the temper of Spain, such as it existed when the first great world-power of the modern world, such as we now know it in its decay. Without Isabella there would have been no Ximenez and no Torquemada; without the protection afforded by her great personal character and wifely devotion Ferdinand could not have corrupted the Spanish spirit so safely and so thoroughly. Up to the end of the fifteenth century Spain had for 2,000 years been a land of great men, but it had never been a great nation. Even under the rule of wiser kings and better laws than were elsewhere to be found in Europe, the people had preserved a sturdy distrust both of kings and laws. The task that was too great even for Alfonso the Wise was accomplished by the quiet, beautiful, inflexible, remorseless girl who once and for all dominated the firm and stubborn men of Spain; henceforth they were chained to the car of a great state, obedient to the crack of the whip. But that result was attained not only at terrible ultimate cost, but with an effort that would have been impossible to monarchs less bigoted than Isabella, less greedy and unscrupulous than Ferdinand. These qualities were required not only to build up the financial prosperity of United Spain, but to wield the fearful instrument of the Inquisition, by which, above all, Spain was moulded into a homogeneous whole, a great State without great men. Hitherto Spaniards had been the least intolerant peoples; not only were they natively opposed to any interference with individual freedom, but intercourse with the cultured Moors had made bigotry difficult, and Spain had taken no part in the Crusades. The Inquisition met at first with opposition from clergy and laity alike, and not a few early Inquisitors were slain or grievously injured. Torquemada only became possible in Spain because the religious Isabella and the greedy Ferdinand saw in the Inquisition a marvellous device for the double purpose of exterminating the heretic and appropriating his gold. So, in spite of all pledges, in spite of the Pope himself, it was set up throughout the kingdom. A great Inquisitor cannot, however, be manufactured by royal mandate, and just as there is something in the Spanish character which makes the bull-fight, though not originally Spanish, the most characteristic of Spanish institutions, so we can see how, when once his humanity and independence had been crushed, the terrible fervour and inflexibility of the Castilian, that power of ferocious concentration on a single aim, lent itself peculiarly to the skilful and thorough manipulation of this awful instrument. It has often been pointed out, and it is needless here to repeat, how the Spanish character was modified by the Inquisition, not merely by the direct elimination of the most independent elements of the population, such as at a later date the revocation of the Edict of Nantes effected for the spiritual impoverishment of France, but by the modification of traditions. On the one hand bigotry, greed, bribery, indolence became habits of the governing class, parasitism and servility habits of the governed classes; on the other hand, the reserve and gloom, of which the germs lay in the Spanish character from the first, were intensified in days when the only sure way to be a free man—and that open to but few—was to become oneself a familiar of the Holy Office. Thus was formed the typical Spanish don of the seventeenth century, well known throughout Europe. The free-thinking, free-speaking, free-acting Cid had always been the national hero of Spain, henceforth the Cid had no more relation to Spanish life than Robin Hood to English life. The last great Spaniard in practical affairs belonging to old Spain was Gonsalvo, the "Gran Capitán," a great soldier, a great diplomatist, a great gentleman; and even he was not wholly untouched at the last by the methods of his master, Ferdinand. From that time it was not in life but in art, in novels, in drama, in poetry, in painting—and sometimes in religion—that Spain could claim any unmixed reverence. Cervantes, Calderón, Lope de Vega, and Velasquez nobly filled the seventeenth century, together with a group of great religious mystics, above all, St. Teresa, the chief of European woman saints. Since they died Spain has not given the world one manifestation of supreme original genius in any field.

V

. . . I have already pointed out how, even in such minute peculiarities as those of costume, usually so fleeting, the Spaniards of to-day resemble the Spaniards who lived before the Christian era. It is one of the results of this racial conservatism, that of all European countries except Russia—which has not yet emerged from those ages—Spain alone presents to us something of the aspect of the Middle Ages. The piety of Spain is mediaeval; in the cathedral of Saragossa the unaffected dramatic attitudes of the ecstatic worshippers belong to a time when the religious attitude was natural to all men. Not less mediaeval when, within the walls of the Troitsa monastery of Central Russia, I noted the peasants on a great feast day crowding into the church as into their own homes, to rest and talk and eat. In the modern world men and women have learnt to fear both God and their neighbours, and march into their sacred temples with such decent, self-conscious uniformity, that a church nowadays is the last place in which a lover of human nature would seek to observe his fellows. It is such points as these that indicate the profound but subtle difference in the atmosphere to which in Spain, as in Russia, we are brought back. As in sacred, so in secular things, Spain clings to the old ways. Everywhere one may see the signs of British and, more especially of late years, Belgian enterprise and industry in Spain, but of Spanish rarely indeed. The Italians have become showmen and restaurant keepers and waiters, to exploit their country as a comfortable and well-kept museum of antiquities. The Spaniard, neither anxious to attract nor to repel the foreigner, calmly maintains his ancient traditions, and in his manners and customs we may still read those generous and chivalric traits which delight us in mediaeval Spain.

In the modern world as we know it to-day, and above all in the English-speaking world, there is nothing that seems to the great mass of the population so worthy of pursuit and so satisfactory as a standard of progress, as the cultivation of commerce, education and politics. Among the common people of Spain these things are dead or have never existed. Commerce, except in Catalonia, is treated with indifference or contempt; education is so neglected that in no European country is there so large a proportion of individuals who can neither read nor write; while the experience of many centuries has shown the people the futility of politics, and there is no motive power to renovate political life. . . .

When we live with the Spaniard, however, we learn to recognize that the modern method of compressing the maximum of feverish haste into the day's work—"and for life's sake losing the reasons for living"—is perhaps less wholly desirable than we have sometimes imagined. There is no need to haste after wealth in a land where men are agreed that poverty is not contemptible, and that the best things cannot be bought for money. The only worthy social end that can be reached by money is democratic equality, and that has already been attained more perfectly in Spain than in any newer civilisation is even conceivable. There is no new country where equality of social intercourse, courtesy, and sympathy are more general among all classes of the population, and where the habits of an instinctive fine breeding may be found even among the poorest. The sense of personal dignity and consideration for others has already bought all that the *mirage* of wealth only promises. Again, while the absence of education is doubtless a real loss—and certainly to those who measure the civilisation of a country by the magnitude of its newspaper press Spain must indeed be contemptible—it is a vast mistake to suppose that there is no education in Spain. The traditions of the old civilisation diffused throughout the country constitute an atmosphere in which every boy or girl grows up naturally and which cannot by any effort be produced in the most vigorous and progressive of newer and cruder civilisations. The woman who can with difficulty write her name shows an unfailing instinct where the essentials of good breeding are concerned; the fine-fibred *toreador*, brutal as his occupation may seem to us, need fear no comparison either in physical or mental qualities with the athlete of the English-speaking world. That hideous laugh which rings out in the night air of London—as pathetic in its reckless vacuity as any cry of sorrow—is never heard in the lowest quarters of any Spanish city, not because there is no mirth there, or any forced re-

41

straint, but because the gracious traditions of an old civilisation are part of the lives of the commonest people. Thus it is that in Spain, unlike those centres in which civilisation has ripened too quickly, vulgarity and prudery are alike absent. We have indeed left behind our own civilisation and the virtues that belong to it: but we have entered another civilisation in which virtues that we vainly and ineffectively strive after are the common possession of the common people.

VI

It is usually the women of the country who present most clearly its fundamental racial character. Certainly it is so in Spain; and whatever the reputation of Spain in other respects Spanish women at all events have never lacked fervent admirers. Even here, however, the admiration of the foreigner has more often been remarkable for its enthusiasm than for its insight. Far from being the gaily dressed beauty who raises her skirts and ostentatiously flirts behind her fan, the typical daughter of Spain is grave, quiet, unfailingly dignified, simple and home-loving, singularly affectionate in her domestic relationships. Passionate she can doubtless be, but passion to a Spanish woman is a matter of life and death, far too serious a matter to be played with, and flirting is unknown to her. That is the secret of that simple, direct bearing and speech of the Spanish woman, so free from the embarrassing consciousness of sex, which renders a Spanish woman so charming, with a charm in this and in many other respects so unlike that of the Frenchwoman; and the poorest of Spanish women, however gracious she may be, has no difficulty in conveying an assurance of the fact that she belongs to herself. The saying of Pope that "most women have no character at all" would at all events not have suggested itself in Spain, where the sense of almost self-sufficing self-possession seems to be the rule among the women of the ordinary population, who often retain both vitality and charm of manner into old age. There is no class of the population of whom this is not true, perhaps least of all that class (on the verge of gipsydom) which still keeps up the dances of old Spain for the joy of an ever smaller circle. . . . In the near East a dance is a rhythm of the body alone, in the far East dancing is all done with the arms, in the North with the legs. The most ancient and famous art of dancing in the Western world is a rhythmic and harmonious motion of the whole person, a motion in which body and limbs, even head and eyes, all play their measured part. It is this above all that marks the dances of Spain as attaining the highest point which the poetry of movement has ever reached. Even when the dance becomes, as in its essence it often really is, the conventionalized physical expression of the most profound emotion of human passion, it never loses its reserve or dignity in its added intensity of meaning, nor passes beyond the bounds of art. It is Spain alone which justifies the saying of Nietzsche, that dancing is the highest symbol of perfected human activity.

Every dance-tune in Spain may be a song-tune, and when the dance passes into a song, and we hear that soul-stirring extraordinary chant that is partly Moorish, partly gipsy, wholly Spanish, we begin to understand why its dancing is so peculiarly attractive to all those who are held by the fascination of Spain. In this dying and neglected art we reach the last stronghold in which the spirit of the race has entrenched itself. Dancing is the final embodiment of the genius of Spain, the epitome of its great and sorrowful history.

George Ticknor's Travels in Spain

A SELECTION FROM HIS JOURNAL
University of Toronto Studies

(*edited by G. T. Northup*)

George Ticknor, who was born in 1791, spent the years from 1815 to 1819 traveling and studying in Europe. He was the first scholar from the new United States to steep himself (sixteen hours a day, in Germany) in European languages and literatures.

The most formative part of Ticknor's lengthy Wanderjahre *were the months spent in Spain in 1818, and this despite the fact that Spain was at one of its chronic nadirs, having been battered by its long war against Napoleon, which had ended a few years earlier. The country was suffering under the reactionary and obscene despotism of Ferdinand VII. Yet this land and people, so barren intellectually at first acquaintance, had had a brilliant literary past, and this became the chief concern of America's first European-trained intellectual. Ticknor returned home, to dedicate himself principally to the study and teaching of Spanish literature—perhaps to his own surprise, and certainly to the consternation of Boston, where Spanish was a language quite as unknown and, no doubt, considered to be quite as pagan as Swahili. Ticknor's career was marked by his classic* History of Spanish Literature *and by his tenure as the first Smith Professor of Romance Languages at Harvard, a chair in which he was followed by Henry Wadsworth Longfellow, and the latter by James Russell Lowell.*

The founder of Hispanic studies in the United States came into Spain—into Catalonia—from Perpignan, through the Pyrenees and down to Barcelona. Travel was hard enough in those years in any part of the world (even between Richmond, Va., and Washington, D.C., as Ticknor recalls with some sourness), but of all the main roads in the "civilized" world, perhaps the four hundred miles between Barcelona and Madrid were the most wearying to body and soul. It was a Spanish journey.

BETWEEN May 11 and May 23, I was all the time on the road between Barcelona and Madrid, and a journey of such weariness, want, and suffering I have never before made, not even one which I cannot easily forget that I made between

Washington and Richmond in January, 1815. My conveyance now was different from that between Perpignan and Barcelona, but no less characteristick. It was an enormous coach without springs, such as we see in pictures that preserve the style of Queen Elizabeth's times, narrow at the bottom and spreading out at the top, painted in vermilion and gilt profusely; in short, in all respects awkward, clumsy, and antiquated. It was drawn by six mules, conducted by a *calesero* and two *zagales*. We were four passengers, a very good-natured man of the noble guard of the king; a genuine young rogue, and I had almost said swindler, belonging to Madrid, but who ran off from it the same afternoon we arrived; and Madrazo, the king's painter, who has lived the last seventeen years at Rome, and has just received his appointment, a man of talent, knowledge, and taste, and one of the most kind, true-hearted gentlemen I have known, a man, in short, always to be most depended on when you most need him, as I often found in this journey.

We set off early in the morning, and I soon found how different were to be the means and comforts of my journey from what they had been in Catalonia, or rather the eastern part of it, for we were still in this active and fertile province. Even in that portion I had passed through the inns are bad, very bad, but here they begin to be abominable, and, what is worse, to disappear altogether.

The houses on which travellers are to descend for the meagre, dirty fare they can hope to get on the roads in this part of Spain are of three kinds: 1. *Fondas*, or what we call inns, though poor and filthy. They are common in Catalonia, but very rare everywhere else, and in some parts of the country unknown, as in Aragon, where there is not a single one. When you find them, however, you are sure of meeting with a bed and something to eat, for they are obliged by law to keep it. 2. *Posadas*, almost always private establishments, though sometimes established by the government. They are in towns or villages, furnish you houseroom and a bed perhaps, but keep no provisions, which you are obliged to go out and buy. 3. *Ventas*, houses like the last where you find only a room and fire, but, what is worse, situated in the open country, so that you are obliged to bring everything with you. We stopped at these, I think, about three-quarters of the time between Barcelona and Madrid, and whoever wishes to have an idea of the squalid filth and rude manners of those who keep them has only to read *Don Quixote*, where the descriptions are still as faithful as nature. Poor, however, as they are, they would not exist at all if the government did not build the houses, and sometimes even hire the people to keep them.

And what is the reason of this? For no custom gets general currency in a whole people without one. The reason is that there is almost no travelling in Spain. Between Barcelona and Madrid, in a journey of thirteen days, we met only a few muleteers, a few carts, and one single coach like our own, not half a dozen in all; and yet the road was the main highway between the capital and one of the principal cities of the kingdom. Of course, there is not the least encouragement or means for supporting good taverns, good roads, or anything that tends only to facilitate intercourse, for generally speaking no intercourse exists.

With these means, however, and these prospects, we commenced our journey. The first night we slept at a very miserable *venta*, dirty, poor, and of most inhospitable manners, at the foot of Montserrat. I amused myself with my friend the painter, in walking up and down in the valley and on the side of the hill, admiring the rude masses and bold cones of this grand mountain, which has long been famous in the religious history of Spain and in the books of all travellers, and especially of Laborde, who in his *Voyage pittoresque* gives many fine views of the venerable convent. He was just in season,

47

for the French have since nearly ruined it by changing it to a fortification as one of the few means they had of maintaining a footing in Catalonia.

The next day I came to Cervera. My friend Vega had given me some letters here, but I did not make use of them, for there was nothing to see, nothing to know that interested me. It has a university, I should rather say an enormous dark stone barrack, built in 1718 by Philip V in gratitude for the fidelity this city alone from all Catalonia observed towards him, and he did it, too, by abolishing all the universities in the province. It would not do, however, and Cervera is now, like all the other universities of Spain, *nominis umbra*.

On the 14th we came to Lerida. This city, fallen as it now is, has, nevertheless, a long, glorious history, for it is the very Lerida where Scipio, in A.U.C. 537, gained a splendid victory over Hanno, and where Julius Caesar in 705 defeated the adherents of Pompey. After this it went through all the changes that have marked the fortune of this part of Spain, became Gothick when the Goths were there, Moorish under the Arabs, and was rescued by Count Raymond in 1149. True to the archduke, it was taken by assault in 1707, and, equally true in its hatred of the French now as in the last century, it made a brave resistance in the last war, the marks of which are still visible. With all this glory, it is falling to ruins, with hardly 15,000 inhabitants, and has nothing to verify the beautiful description Lucan gives of it but its fine situation on the western bank of the Segra.

The next day, the fourth of our journey, we entered into the heavy wastes which begin in Catalonia and extend far up into Aragon. Everything here is dry, uncultivated, and cheerless; everything looks as if it had been burnt up by a scorching sun or wasted by some hidden principle of desolation. The trees disappear with the habitations of man and the flocks with the masters; and if perchance a small village does occur,

48

it is, like all the other productions of this hard, unfriendly soil, meagre and miserable. We soon passed the little village of Alcaraz, and, immediately afterwards, entered Aragon and came to dine at Fraja, which, squalid and ruined as it is now, with a population of but 2,000 souls, had once an independent king who reigned over the wastes around him. Through miserable villages like this, the residence only of poverty and suffering, and across such wastes, where a few flocks are barely preserved from starving by their half savage shepherds, who look like Shumelites from the desert, we continued to pass on for a day and a half, until on the 16th in the morning, we saw the towers of Zaragoza on the horizon before us and were refreshed on our left hand by the prospect of the culti-vated country that borders the Ebro. We passed the Gallego, and entered a fine avenue which must have been magnificent before everything was laid waste by the late siege, and, traversing the scene of the famous battle of August 20, 1710, which had nearly proved fatal to the pretensions of Philip V, we came to the very entrance of this extraordinary city.

I have no words to express what I saw there, for these are achievements that have no parallel. Characters which, as they stand alone in the history of man and leave behind them monuments such as all antiquity has not sent down to us, have no means or hopes of being rightly understood and justly ex-plained. For where are the models by which they are to be judged or the rivals by whom they are to be estimated? In my feelings, Leipzig, Lützen, and Waterloo are ordinary fields of battle compared with Zaragoza; for I understand how human nature could be screwed up to the sticking place for such enterprises and be kept there one day, or two, or three. But how this could be done for months, indeed, almost for a year, as happened at Zaragoza, of this I have no example, and am able to form no just or satisfactory idea.

As we approached the city, the sides of the road were

marked everywhere by lines of ruin which appeal equally to the heart and to the imagination. I got out of the carriage and walked on. Just at that moment we came to the remains of a large convent which had served as a fortification, and I went across to see it. The peasants were ploughing round it, and, as I passed over the fresh mould, I trod at every step on pieces of leather, fragments of arms and helmets, and sometimes saw human bones which still remained undecayed and unhidden after the cultivation of nine summers, so terrible was the carnage and so little the respect for the dead! The bridge by which you enter the city was broken up during the siege, and is still imperfectly repaired. The houses next it are nearly all demolished, and the next more or less injured. We entered the city. In many parts whole streets still remain in ruins, and great squares are made and making where once lived a crowded and busy population.

As the city was entirely without walls, convents and churches became fortresses, and, as not an inch was yielded but to a force that could not be resisted, the two armies often fought for several days from opposite sides of the same street. Two streets were shown me where the Spaniards, obliged to retire, did it by breaking down the back walls of the houses, and then continued to fire for above twenty-four hours from the other side where they could still be supported, so that it cost the French three days of uninterrupted fighting to drive them out of the front apartments of a range of houses when they were already in possession of the street; and afterwards another day to compel them to retreat through the walls into the next range, where all they had to do was to recommence the same warfare. And how is it possible that human nature can have such force and resolution? I can understand that an individual may be so happily constituted in his moral and physical character as to be able to do this, but here it was not one man or a hundred, but 60,000 where there was not only no traitor and no coward, but none that was not sure and unshaken in his mind and unfatigued and invincible in his body. How is this to be accounted for?

I do all honour to the spirit that defended Zaragoza, but still I am aware other than moral causes must be sought to explain such a phenomenon. It is the same spirit which in 535 A.U.C. surrendered only a heap of ruins at Saguntum to Hannibal, and in 621 at Numancia, after three sieges, surrendered nothing but a slaughtered population to Scipio. And it is a spirit, too, which I am satisfied has always existed in Spain, and never existed anywhere else. It is apparent in their wars with the Romans, the Goths, and the Moors. It showed itself decidedly and often in the War of the Succession, and every Spaniard who knew his country calculated on it the moment the Revolution broke out in 1808. This is the moral spirit of the people, who, however humble and abject they may be to their domestick rulers, never submit to foreign usurpation, whatever form it may assume. But this is not enough. How comes it that they have the physical force necessary to support this unrelenting spirit? I do all honour to the Spanish character, and especially to the Aragonese, for to an Aragonese of the lower class I would trust my purse or my life without hesitation; but his physical hardihood comes from his want of civilization. He has, as yet, learned little of the conveniences and nothing of the comforts of life. He is nearly as well off in this respect during the sufferings of a siege as he was in his cheerless, barren wastes, where he often wants the sufficient means of subsistence nearly half a year. In short, he is so accustomed to privations and sufferings of all sorts that he can afford to be beaten where an army formed in a more civilized nation cannot sustain even the privations that follow a victory. He has, therefore, only to avoid discouragement, and who ever saw a Spaniard discouraged? Who that knows the history of the sieges of Saguntum, Numancia and Zaragoza can ever suspect him of becoming so?

The day we passed here I could do nothing but walk round among these awful ruins, for I felt that I had not seen either in Germany or Italy anything to mark such a character as this. There are, however, many things worthy to be seen at Zaragoza. My friend Madrazo, who has an excellent taste and judgment, carried me to them almost in spite of myself. In the first place, there is the New Tower, as it is called, built, however, in the year 1504, which is, as it seems to me, quite as much out of the perpendicular as the famous tower of Pisa, of which everybody has read and talked. It is in one point more remarkable, since it is built of bricks. I do not know how high it is, but it is so high that 284 steps are necessary to bring you to the top, where you are repaid by a magnificent view of the immense plain of Zaragoza, bounded by the hills and mountains of the east and south, traversed by the Tagus [sic] and its canal. Everywhere it was rich and abundant, forming a singular contrast with the desolation I had hardly left, and which was still almost in sight.

The cathedral, called, I know now why, the *seu*, is, on the inside, one of the nobler specimens of Gothick architecture, and would be perfect in its kind if it were a little longer in proportion to its width. The splendour of its ornaments and the wealth and splendour that were everywhere apparent, together with the very manner in which vespers were sung and heard, the pomp of the canons, and the submission and reverence of the people, proved to me that such a church is here no useless appendage of the religion it professes, as it generally is even in Italy. It was the same spirit I had seen at Gerona and Barcelona, and which has accompanied me every step of the way to Madrid.

The finest thing, however, that I saw at Zaragoza for the

arts is the church of Nuestra Señora del Pilar, which, excepting the mixture of a little Gothick at one end of more ancient architecture, is one that would certainly be numbered among the most remarkable churches in Italy, if it were on the other side of the Alps. The proportions are inimitable. The whole effect is one of wealth and splendour. The French found this church so much reverenced that they were obliged to respect it themselves. It is full of paintings and sculpture that put my friend Madrazo into ecstasies at every step. Under the grand vault is a building of the same kind with the house at Loretto, but of much more beauty, I think, whose roof is painted in fresco by Velasquez, and whose sides are covered with bas-reliefs of the best age and style of the Spanish school. Indeed, the whole church is a mangificent monument, the marbles are rich and splendid, the paintings fine, the architecture imposing, the pavilion of the Virgin noble, pure, and grand, so that I know not where, out of Italy, I should go to find its parallel. I almost forgot the ruins of Zaragoza as I was admiring it.

Zaragoza was the native city of Prudentius, and there must have been the object most in his thoughts when he pronounced those touching adieux to his country that still remain to us. I felt hardly less regret, though of a different sort, when the next morning we passed out of this extraordinary city whose devotion and suffering has reduced it from about 43,000 inhabitants to less than 30,000, a fact hardly less remarkable than the unparalleled one that without walls or fortifications of any kind it defended itself against a vastly superior force of regular troops, the Spanish being chiefly undisciplined, during the whole of the tremendous siege of 1809.

We traversed the beautiful plain that surrounds the city, and stopped an instant to see the canal of Aragon, which was commenced by Charles V in 1529, and, though brought to a state to be very useful under Philip II in 1566 and Charles III in 1770–1775, is still unfinished. If it ever should be completed, it would much change the situation and character of the countries through which it passes.

From this moment, I can truly say, our journey became a journey of suffering. Excepting Daroca, we passed for six days through no place that deserved to be called a town, and even this just comes up to the requisite conditions. All the rest of the way was through dreary wastes where the guidebook coolly and laconically informs you from time to time that there is danger of robbery; and if perchance there was a village, it was too squalid, miserable, and poor to afford anything but bread and wine, while at the *ventas* that now grew rarer and worse, nothing was to be hoped. From Barcelona to Madrid I did not once sleep upon a bed, and several times merely rolled myself up in my great coat and lay down on the floor, which was badly paved. Twice I dined in the same apartment with our mules, who were not two steps from me. Two days we had no meat and one day only a breakfast at twelve o'clock, given to us at a *venta* by an Aragonese, who, to do it, parted, for money, with more than half of what he had for his family. In this account of the miseries of our journey I say nothing of the filth, which was so great that I generally preferred staying in the carriage when we stopped rather than go into their squalid houses, where, as there is no fireplace other than a hearth in the centre of the building, your eyes are put out with smoke, and where, as the stable, the pigstye, and the house are all one establishment, the smell is intolerable and the fleas so numerous that I brought a full colony upon me to Madrid. However, we all got through it, and never for a moment lost our gaiety and good humour, though poor Madrazo, who had left his country very young and had lived out of it seventeen years, sometimes felt a little sinking of the heart at the thought of having abandoned an income of three or four thousand dollars a year to come and re-establish himself here for a second time.

The first symptom we had of our approach to a more civilized region was near Guadalaxara. We had come out of Aragon between Used and Embid del Marqués, and often on the road found ruined villages where many sad, striking, and horrible tales were told of the circumstances under which they were destroyed, and of the strange obstinacy of the inhabitants in not yielding when resistance was idle; and of the cruelty of the French, who thought to punish thus a bravery and resolution they ought to have respected.

At Guadalaxara I hoped to find something again for the arts, and went to see the famous pantheon of the family of the Infantado, one of the first houses in Spain; but, like the barbarians in the Middle Ages at Rome, the French had made fortifications even of the tombs, and everything here was in ruins. The same day, May 22, we came on through the rich fields of Castile, abounding in grain just ready for the harvest. We slept at Alcalá de Henares, the Complutum of the Romans, the place where the famous Polyglot was printed, and, what is more to me than all this, the birthplace of Cervantes, the unimitated, the inimitable Cervantes. The epoch of the splendour of Alcalá is that of the reigns of Ferdinand and Isabella and of Charles V, and of the administration of Cardinal Ximenes, who founded and peculiarly protected the university here. For nearly a century it was famous, and often numbered 4,000 students on its rolls; but now it is entirely fallen, has many fine buildings commenced about that period but never finished; churches for 20,000 souls, and a population of hardly 5,000; a great college and a few students; and an abundance of fat, ignorant professors without more than 400 hearers; in short, everything that announces a decayed and falling city.

On the morning of the twenty-third, a bright, fine day,

such as I always like to have for entering a great city, we set out early for Madrid. The villages did not increase, and in fact rather diminished, for in seven leagues, which are about thirty miles, there were but two. The cultivation did not increase, for I very often noticed fields bare and uncultivated; and the passing did not increase, for we met only one *calesina* and a few muleteers. Nothing, in short, indicated our approach to the capital. On the contrary, I should rather have thought we were more removed into the deserts than we had been yet, for as this is the season of the emigration of the flocks from Estremadura to the mountains, we met eight all marshaled so exactly in the form of an army that it no longer seemed to me ridiculous that Don Quixote should have mistaken them for one, with their shepherds at the head, the dogs as a rear-guard and a reserve behind of the lame and sick, accompanied by the asses that carried the baggage of the whole establishment. It seemed as if the days of the Ishmaelites were returned, and I were in the desert of Arabia witnessing one of their emigrations with all their flocks, so open and bare was the country, and so little marked by the diligence of cultivation; and yet the towers of Madrid were full before us in the horizon. In the midst of the astonishment this desolation would naturally awake in one who had entered London, Paris, and Naples, we came to the very city. No suburb preceded it; hardly a house, indeed, was to be seen. All was as still as the grave; and yet I was in the principal street of the capital of Spain at eleven o'clock in the forenoon.

Longfellow in Spain

A SELECTION FROM THE
Life of Henry Wadsworth Longfellow

(edited by Samuel Longfellow)

A few years after Ticknor's visit, another, and younger, traveler from the United States, also destined to become a world-famed man of letters, crossed the Pyrenees almost by accident—and fell in love with Spain.

In his lengthy career (too long, poetically, some may say today), America's most famous nineteenth-century poet gave first place, after those of his native land, to Spain's principal language and literature. Spain was a fresh fountain, exhilarating to a man not long out of Bowdoin College, and despite his travels in other parts of Europe. Longfellow set to work, hard, on his Spanish studies.

57

Ferdinand VII, who had once, in the resistance to Napoleon, been called the Well-Beloved by his people, continued to make life grim in his domain in 1827, as he had almost a decade earlier, in Ticknor's time. Travel had not in the least improved even for those who, like Longfellow, came into the country and on to the capital along the most used route, by way of French Bayonne and Spanish Irún. Longfellow later went on from Madrid, south through La Mancha, and into Andalucía, recording his journey in letters to his family and in his journal.

Hardships of the road did not dim the poet's memories of his eight months in Spain, nor did they dull his scholarly labors there or in later years when, for a time, he became Ticknor's successor in the Smith chair at Harvard. Sitting in his study or perhaps in the garden of Craigie House in Cambridge, he wrote: "It is a beautiful morning in June;—so beautiful that I almost fancy myself in Spain."

Longfellow made three trips to Europe in the years after his student travels. He did not go again to Spain for he did not wish, wisely no doubt, to risk breaking the spell which had been put upon him when he was twenty.

BAYONNE is a little city, worthy of no description but such as you will find in guide-books and gazetteers. I was forced to drag out one dull day there, and on the morrow was on my way for the Spanish frontier, through the Basques.

The Basque girls are very beautiful; they are literally "nut-brown maidens." They appear to be very industrious, and several of them earn a livelihood by conducting travellers on horseback from Bayonne to Irun. This is a very singular and very agreeable mode of travelling. At the gate of Bayonne you find these girls stationed, with their horses. The saddle is constructed with a large frame-work, extending two feet on each side of the horse and covered with a cushion, so that the traveller and the guide sit balancing each other, with their feet hanging down in front by the horse's neck. We saw a great many persons travelling in this way, and I wished myself out of the *diligence* a thousand times.

I said that the Basque girls were handsome. They have most beautiful dark eyes, fine teeth, a sun-burnt complexion, and glossy, black hair parted over the forehead, gathered behind the ears, and falling down to the knees in a large, beautiful braid. The first I saw were those travelling in the way described; one, in particular, whose image haunts me still,— a most cheerful-looking girl in the dress of the peasantry, her hair braided, and a large gypsy straw-hat thrown over her shoulders; and then that comfortable way of jogging on together! . . .

South from Bayonne, the scene suddenly changes from the waste sands to a broken and mountainous country. On this road I caught glimpses of the sea, as it came tumbling in among the rocks. It was the first time I had seen it for nearly a twelvemonth. I was glad to hear its old familiar voice; and you can hardly imagine what feelings it awakened within me. I thought I was quite near you again. It seemed but a step— a little step—from one shore to the other; and with my mind's eye I saw White Head looming through the mists that gathered on the horizon,—White Head, Bangs's Island, the Lighthouse, and old Freeman, all as usual.

The little river Bidassoa is the boundary between France and Spain, and you cross it to Irun, on the Spanish side. We passed it at night, and when the morning broke we were high up amongst the mountains of St. Salvador, the continuation of the chain of the Pyrénées. In the little of Pyrenean scenery which I saw in thus passing there was nothing remarkably bold or striking. The mountain sides were neither rugged nor precipitous, and the trace of the plough-share was occasionally seen quite to their summits. Besides, there was no forest scenery to cheer the eye, and as the season of vegetation had not commenced, the huge outline of the mountains lay black and barren and uninviting. What alone gave romance to the scene was the dashing of a little mountain-brook that we followed for miles through the valley, now breaking into a cascade, now foaming under a rural bridge.

One of the first things which attract the attention of the traveller on entering the northern provinces of Spain is the poverty-stricken appearance of everything around him. The country seems deserted. There are no herds in the fields, no flocks by the wayside. The villages are half depopulated, the cottages ruinous and falling away piecemeal, whilst the people have nothing left them but rags and religion. Of these, such as they are, they have enough. Among the bleak and barren mountains, the traveller will frequently find a little chapel, with a cluster of not more than six cottages around it, where, as soon as the bell sounds for noonday, all within hearing fall to prayer; and whenever you stop on the road, the village children come about the doors of the carriage with little crucifixes, curiously ornamented and set off with many-colored ribbons. As you pass through the towns, too, you see an idle and ragged population, lounging about at the corners, and, wrapped in tattered brown cloaks, sunning themselves on the south sides of the houses and walls. Everybody in Spain wears a cloak; rich or poor, high or low, old or young. To be sure, this in the poorer classes sometimes dwindles down to a blanket, but it is always gracefully worn, and you see the muleteers sitting on their saddles with their cloaks wrapped round them and the corner thrown over the left shoulder, and riding along with all the dignity of dons and nobleman.

But throughout Biscay and the northern provinces, such as Old and New Castile, the poor are clad with brown rags.

The route I pursued on leaving Irun lay through Tolosa, Victoria, and Burgos; thence directly south through Aranda to Madrid. Part of the distance an armed guard accompanies the *diligence*. This sounds very formidable; but happening to be alone in the carriage the first night of my journey, this guard consisted of a mere scare-crow of a soldier with a flannel jacket and a gun, who slept as soundly as was becoming to a good sentinel,—and so we kept guard over each other. But to be guarded in this way was rather irritating, for it only kept me sensible of the danger I was in, when I most wished to forget it.

In broad daylight, too, one who travels in this country has always something to remind him of the perilous ways he is treading. The cold, inhospitable, uncultivated look of the country itself, the dark, fiendish countenances which peep at him from the folds of the Spanish cloak in every town and village, but more than all, the little black crosses which one comes upon at almost every step, standing by the roadside, in commemoration of a murder or other violent death which has taken place upon the spot,—these keep his fancy busy.

Besides these general remarks, I have little to say of my journey to Madrid. I was hurrying on, night and day, with all possible speed, and regretted only that I could not tarry a little at Burgos, the capital of Old Castile, to see the tomb of Cid, the Campeador, so celebrated in the Moorish wars. Thus my journey was by no means fruitful in adventures, I being neither robbed and pillaged, nor having the honor of a little black cross by the roadside.

I have already so overrun all bounds in this letter of mine that I must postpone to another occasion the description of my ride to Segovia and the Escorial. Behold me then in Madrid, most happily situated and with most brilliant prospects before me. I must not forget to mention that I have immediately taken a Spanish instructor, and feel enough enthusiasm about the language to make good progress in it.

The withered leaves were already dropping, and the immense plains, as far as the eye could reach, looked brown, barren, and sunburnt. I have never seen a country that wore so desolate a look. You trace the road for miles before you, with neither cottage nor green tree. In some parts, when you start on your journey in the morning, you may see in a direct line before you the village in which you are to pass the night. As I dislike to be hurried through a country, however sad and solitary it may be, without seeing its peculiarities, I took a seat in the wagon of a carrier from Castile to Andalusia. You cannot imagine with what fear and trembling one travels at the present day in Spain. The whole country is overrun with robbers. Every village in La Mancha has its tale to tell of atrocities committed in its neighborhood. At night, in the capacious inn-kitchen, my fellow-travellers would huddle together and talk of the dangers we were to pass through on the morrow, and converse for hours in that mysterious undertone which always fills the mind with phantoms. But fortunately, we passed through all unmolested. It was undoubtedly owing to that *poor-gentleman* look which every one of us carried about him. A poverty-stricken country; everywhere in the roofless cottages and ruined walls we trace the footsteps of the Peninsular War. A lapse of ten years has not changed the scene. As you approach the wretched habitations of the peasantry, a troop of half-starved children, some absolutely naked, others with but a fragment of a shirt, or a tattered jacket, will come shouting forth, begging, dancing, and tumbling along the road, with such strange gambols that it raises a smile at the same time that it makes your heart ache. One circumstance which much surprised me in La Mancha was the cleanliness of the inn-kitchens. A paved carriage-road generally passes directly through the centre of the inn, and upon each side of it are the rooms and bed-chambers of the family. I recollect one that had two crossroads in it, it somewhat resembled four cottages under one large roof. In this thoroughfare you always find the heavy baggage of muleteers and wagoners; and in some nook the fire glances upon the whitewashed walls of the kitchen. The kitchen of a country inn is seldom a separate room; it is rather a large alcove, with its fire in the middle of the floor, benches built against the walls on each side and covered with mats, on which sleeps the tired muleteer, wrapped in his cloak. Above is a great tunnel of a chimney which embraces the whole ceiling. One may well wonder how there can be much neatness in such an arrangement; but the glitter of brazen pans, and a goodly show of crockery arranged with care against the white walls have such a neat, comely look, that they appeal as feelingly and persuasively to a man's stomach as the tidy kitchen-maid with nicely braided hair, to his heart.

The traveller is occasionally cheered by green olive fields; and as you approach the village of Val-de-Peñas, celebrated for its wines, the hills are covered with vineyards. South of Val-de-Peñas, the country wears a more cheerful aspect. The landscape breaks into hill and dale; you catch glimpses of whitewashed villages sheltered in the hollows of the mountains. In the Sierra Morena the chain of mountains which separates La Mancha from Andalusia, there is a wild narrow pass called Despeñaperros. It is the thoroughfare of all travellers from Madrid to Seville,—the most bold and picturesque scenery I have yet met with in Spain. Just as the entrance of the pass stands the Venta of Cadenas,—the inn at which the poor knight-errant suffered so many misfortunes. It is a long, low house, with paved cart-road passing through the centre; the kitchen a mere nook, and within it a strapping wench busy among pots and kettles. She was the very counterpart of the faithful Maritornes, whose midnight assignment with the muleteer began the melancholy history of Don Quixote's adventures at the inn, when faithful to the laws of chivalry, he guarded at midnight the gates of the enchanted castle and listened to the lament of the captive princess. Immediately on leaving the inn, you enter the wild mountain scenery. It becomes wilder and wilder. The wood runs along near the summit of the mountains,—on one side huge overhanging rocks, on the other a precipice of immense depth covered with rugged forest, shrubs, and wild vines. At the bottom of the ravine wind the silver waters of a little stream. You pursue this road for miles, now skirting the brow of the hills, and now winding down into shadowy hollows. The scene resembles that of the White Mountains, but it is not so fine. . . . At the close of the day we reached a little village called La Carolina, the first Spanish village I saw which had anything of rural beauty about it. The bloom of Andalusia opens before you there.

WASHINGTON IRVING

The Alhambra

A SELECTION FROM *The Alhambra*

The Spanish flair, or curse, of making explicit the paradoxes of existence shows in the fact that the most famous place in Spain is not Spanish. In the south, in Andalucía (Land of the Vandals, or, perhaps, Land of the West), in the city of Granada, stands the Moorish fortress-palace, the Ahlambra. Built during the thirteenth and fourteenth centuries by the Arabic-African conquerors of almost all of Spain, it rises from a steep-sided hill which juts above the fertile vega *or plain of Granada. The citadel was surrendered to Ferdinand and Isabella on January 2, 1492, by the last Moorish ruler in Spain. 1492 was Spain's supreme year of glory: the Reconquista ended, and a new world was discovered by Columbus.*

It is appropriate that the first famed American man of letters, Washington Irving, lived many years in Spain and found there themes for several of his books, including the first worthy biography of Columbus, and The Alhambra. *To Irving is due, perhaps, the salvation of the Alhambra, which in the 1820's, when Irving first lived in Spain, was disintegrating under the two burdens which Spaniards often impose upon their historic buildings: absolute neglect combined with commonplace daily use of the premises.*

Irving knew Spain better than any other American traveler of the nineteenth century, because he was more than a traveler: he lived in Spain from 1826 to 1829 and again, as United States Minister, from 1842 to 1846. And what other American has dwelt in the Alhambra, as Irving did, in the apartment which still carries his name above the door?

No longer the first man of American letters in any but a chronological sense, Irving was a person of charm and sentiment, a romantic figure, yet a hardy traveler who withstood the grim realities of Spanish roads and inns while capturing the spirit of adventure and legend which pervades the air. He was the first American to tell of his love for Spain, and he caught forever the essence of the Alhambra, "a rugged fortress without, a voluptuous palace within; war frowning from its battlements, poetry breathing throughout the fairy architecture of its halls."

THE ancient kingdom of Granada, into which we were able to penetrate, is one of the most mountainous regions of Spain. Vast sierras, or chains of mountains, destitute of shrub or tree, and mottled with variegated marbles and granites, elevate their sunburnt summits against a deep-blue sky; yet in their rugged bosoms lie ingulfed verdant and fertile valleys, where the desert and the garden strive for mastery, and the very rock is, as it were, compelled to yield the fig, the orange, and the citron, and to blossom with the myrtle and the rose.

In the wild passes of these mountains the sight of walled towns and villages, built like eagles' nests among the cliffs, and surrounded by Moorish battlements, or of ruined watch-towers perched on lofty peaks, carries the mind back to the chivalric days of Christian and Moslem warfare, and to the romantic struggle for the conquest of Granada. In transversing these lofty sierras the traveller is often obliged to alight, and lead his horse up and down the steep and jagged ascents and descents, resembling the broken steps of a staircase. Sometimes the road winds along dizzy precipices, without parapet to guard him from the gulfs below, and then will plunge down steep and dark and dangerous declivities. Sometimes it struggles through rugged *barrancos*, or ravines, worn by winter torrents, the obscure path of the *contrabandista;* while, ever and anon, the ominous cross, the monument of robbery and murder, erected on a mound of stones at some lonely part of the road, admonishes the traveller that he is among the haunts of banditti, perhaps at that very moment under the eye of some lurking *bandolero*. Sometimes, in winding through the narrow valleys, he is startled by a hoarse bellowing, and beholds above him on some green fold of the mountain a herd of fierce Andalusian bulls, destined for the combat of the arena.

The day was without a cloud. The heat of the sun was tempered by cool breezes from the mountains. Before us extended the glorious Vega. In the distance was romantic Granada surmounted by the ruddy towers of the Alhambra, while far above it the snowy summits of the Sierra Nevada shone like silver.

67

Our repast finished, we spread our cloaks and took our last *siesta al fresco*, lulled by the humming of bees among the flowers and the notes of doves among the olive trees. When the sultry hours were passed we resumed our journey. After a time we overtook a pursy little man, shaped not unlike a toad, and mounted on a mule. He fell into conversation with Sancho, and, finding we were strangers, undertook to guide us to a good *posada*. He was an *escribano* (notary), he said, and knew the city as thoroughly as his own pocket. "*Ah, dios, señores!* what a city you are going to see. Such streets! such squares! such palaces! and then the women—*ah, Santa Maria purísima*—what women!"—"But the *posada* you talk of," said I, "are you sure it is a good one?"

"Good! *Santa Maria!* the best in Granada. *Salones grandes —camas de luxo—colchones de pluma* (grand saloons, luxurious sleeping-rooms—beds of down). Ah, Señores, you will fare like King Chico in the Alhambra."

"And how will my horse fare?" cried Sancho.

"Like King Chico's horses. *Chocolate con leche y bollos para almuerza*" (chocolate and milk with sugar cakes for breakfast), giving the squire a knowing wink and a leer.

After such satisfactory accounts, nothing more was to be desired on that head. So we rode quietly on, the squab little notary taking the lead, and turning to us every moment with some fresh exclamation about the grandeurs of Granada and the famous times we were to have at the *posada*.

Thus escorted, we passed between hedges of aloes and Indian figs, and through that wilderness of gardens with which the Vega is embroidered, and arrived about sunset at the gates of the city. Our officious little conductor conveyed us up one street and down another, until he rode into the courtyard of an inn where he appeared to be perfectly at home. Summoning the landlord by his Christian name, he committed us to his care as two *cavalleros de mucho valor*, worthy of his best

68

apartments and most sumptuous fare. We were instantly reminded of the patronizing stranger who introduced Gil Blas with such a flourish of trumpets to the host and hostess of the inn at Pennaflor, ordering trouts for his supper, and eating voraciously at his expense. "You know not what you possess," cried he to the innkeeper and his wife. "You have a treasure in your house. Behold in this young gentleman the eighth wonder of the world—nothing in this house is too good for Señor Gil Blas of Santillane, who deserves to be entertained like a prince."

Determined that the little notary should not eat trouts at our expense, like his prototype of Pennaflor, we forebore to ask him to supper: nor had we reason to reproach ourselves with ingratitude, for we found before morning the little varlet, who was no doubt a good friend of the landlord, had decoyed us into one of the shabbiest *posadas* in Granada.

To the traveller imbued with a feeling for the historical and poetical, so inseparably intertwined in the annals of romantic Spain, the Alhambra is as much an object of devotion as is the Caaba to all true Moslems. How many legends and traditions, true and fabulous,—how many songs and ballads, Arabian and Spanish, of love and war and chivalry, are associated with this Oriental pile! It was the royal abode of the Moorish kings, where, surrounded with the splendors and refinements of Asiatic luxury, they held dominion over what they vaunted as a terrestrial paradise, and made their last stand for empire in Spain. The royal palace forms but a part of a fortress, the walls of which, studded with towers, stretch irregularly round the whole crest of a hill, a spur of the Sierra Nevada or Snowy Mountains, and overlook the city; externally it is a rude congregation of towers and battlements, with no regularity of plan nor grace of architecture, and giving little promise of the grace and beauty which prevail within.

In the time of the Moors the fortress was capable of containing within its outward precincts an army of forty thousand men, and served occasionally as a stronghold of the sovereigns against their rebellious subjects. After the kingdom had passed into the hands of the Christians, the Alhambra continued to be a royal demesne, and was occasionally inhabited by the Castilian monarchs. The emperor Charles V commenced a sumptuous palace within its walls, but was deterred from completing it by repeated shocks of earthquakes. The last royal residents were Philip V and his beautiful queen, Elizabetta of Parma, early in the eighteenth century. Great preparations were made for their reception. The palace and gardens were placed in a state of repair, and a new suite of apartments erected, and decorated by artists brought from Italy. The sojourn of the sovereigns was transient, and after their departure the palace once more became desolate. Still the place was maintained with some military state. The governor held it immediately from the crown, its jurisdiction extended down into the suburbs of the city, and was independent of the captain-general of Granada. A considerable garrison was kept up; the governor had his apartments in the front of the old Moorish palace, and never descended into Granada without some military parade. The fortress, in fact, was a little town of itself, having several streets of houses within its walls, together with a Franciscan convent and a parochial church.

The desertion of the court, however, was a fatal blow to the Alhambra. Its beautiful halls became desolate, and some of them fell to ruin; the gardens were destroyed, and the fountains ceased to play. By degrees the dwellings became filled with a loose and lawless population: *contrabandistas*, who availed themselves of its independent jurisdiction to carry on a wide and daring course of smuggling, and thieves and rogues of all sorts, who made this their place of refuge whence they might depredate upon Granada and its vicinity. The strong arm of government at length interfered, the whole community was thoroughly sifted; none were suffered to remain but such as were of honest character, and had legitimate right to a residence; the greater part of the houses were demolished and a mere hamlet left, with the parochial church and the Franciscan convent. During the recent troubles in Spain, when Granada was in the hands of the French, the Alhambra was garrisoned by their troops, and the palace was occasionally inhabited by the French commander. With that enlightened taste which has ever distinguished the French nation in their conquests, this monument of Moorish elegance and grandeur was rescued from the absolute ruin and desolation that were overwhelming it. The roofs were repaired, the saloons and galleries protected from the weather, the gardens cultivated, the watercourse restored, and fountains once more made to throw up their sparkling showers; and Spain may thank her invaders for having preserved to her the most beautiful and interesting of her historical monuments.

On the departure of the French they blew up several towers of the outer wall, and left the fortifications scarcely tenable. Since that time the military importance of the post is at an end. The garrison is a handful of invalid soldiers, whose principal duty is to guard some of the outer towers, which serve occasionally as a prison of state; and the governor, abandoning the lofty hill of the Alhambra, resides in the centre of Granada, for the more convenient despatch of his official duties. . . .

Leaving our *posada*, and traversing the renowned square of the Vivarrambla, once the scene of Moorish jousts and tournaments, now a crowded market-place, we proceeded along the Zacatin, the main street of what, in the time of the Moors, was the Great Bazaar, and where small shops and narrow alleys still retain the Oriental character. Crossing an open place in front of the palace of the captain-general, we ascended a confined and winding street, the name of which reminded us of the chivalric days of Granada. It is called the Calle, or street of the Gomeres, from a Moorish family famous in chronicle and song. This street led up to the Puerta de las Granadas, a massive gateway of Grecian architecture, built by Charles V, forming the entrance to the domains of the Alhambra.

At the gate were two or three ragged super-annuated soldiers, dozing on a stone bench, the successors of the Zegris and the Abencerrages; while a tall, meagre varlet, whose rusty-brown cloak was evidently intended to conceal the ragged state of his nether garments, was lounging in the sunshine and gossiping with an ancient sentinel on duty. He joined us as we entered the gate, and offered his services to show us the fortress.

I have a traveller's dislike to officious ciceroni, and did not altogether like the garb of the applicant.

"You are well acquainted with the place, I presume?"

"*Ninguno mas; pues, señor, soy hijo de la Alhambra.*"— (Nobody better, in fact, sir, I am a son of the Alhambra!)

The common Spaniards have certainly a most poetical way of expressing themselves. "A son of the Alhambra!" the appellation caught me at once; the very tattered garb of my new acquaintance assumed a dignity in my eyes. It was emblematic of the fortunes of the place, and befitted the progeny of a ruin.

I put some further questions to him, and found that his title was legitimate. His family had lived in the fortress from generation to generation ever since the time of the Conquest. His name was Mateo Ximenes. "Then, perhaps," I said, "you may be a descendant from the great Cardinal Ximenes?" "*Dios sabe!* God knows, señor! It may be so. We are the oldest family in the Alhambra,—*Christianos viejos*, old Christians, without any taint of Moor or Jew. I know we belong to some great family or other, but I forget whom. My father knows all about it; he has the coat-of-arms hanging up in his cottage, up in the fortress." There is not any Spaniard, however poor, but has some claim to high pedigree. The first title of this ragged worthy, however, had completely captivated me, so I gladly accepted the services of the "son of the Alhambra."

We now found ourselves in a deep, narrow ravine, filled with beautiful groves, with a steep avenue, and various foot-paths winding through it, bordered with stone seats, and ornamented with fountains. To our left we beheld the towers of the Alhambra beetling above us; to our right, on the opposite side of the ravine, we were equally dominated by rival towers on a rocky eminence. These, we were told, were the *torres vermejos*, or vermilion towers, so called from their ruddy hue. No one knows their origin. They are of a date much anterior to the Alhambra: some suppose them to have been built by the Romans; others, by some wandering colony of Phoenicians. Ascending the steep and shady avenue, we arrived at the foot of a huge square Moorish tower, forming a kind of barbican, through which passed the main entrance to the fortress. Within the barbican was another group of veteran invalids, one mounting guard at the portal, while the rest, wrapped in their tattered cloaks, slept on the stone benches. This portal is called the Gate of Justice, from the tribunal held within its porch during the Moslem domination, for the immediate trial of petty causes—a custom common to the Oriental nations, and occasionally alluded to in the sacred Scriptures. "Judges and officers shalt thou make thee *in all the gates*, and they shall judge the people with just judgment."

The great vestibule, or porch of the gate, is formed by an immense Arabian arch, of the horseshoe form, which springs to half the height of the tower. On the keystone of this arch is engraven a gigantic hand. Within the vestibule, on the keystone of the portal, is sculptured, in like manner, a gigantic key. Those who pretend to some knowledge of Mohammedan symbols affirm that the hand is the emblem of doctrine, the five fingers designating the five principal commandments of the creed of Islam, fasting, pilgrimaging, almsgiving, ablution, and war against infidels. The key, say they, is the emblem of the faith or of power; the key of Daoud, or David, transmitted to the prophet. "And the key of the house of David will I lay upon his shoulder; so he shall open and none shall shut, and he shall shut and none shall open." (Isaiah xxii., 22.) The key we are told was emblazoned on the standard of the Moslems in opposition to the Christian emblem of the cross, when they subdued Spain or Andalusia. It betokened the conquering power invested in the prophet. "He that hath the key of David, he that openeth and no man shutteth; and shutteth and no man openeth." (Rev. iii., 7.)

A different explanation of these emblems, however, was given by the legitimate son of the Alhambra, and one more in unison with the notions of the common people, who attach something of mystery and magic to everything Moorish, and have all kinds of superstitions connected with this old Moslem fortress. According to Mateo, it was a tradition handed down from the oldest inhabitants, and which he had from his father and grandfather, that the hand and key were magical devices on which the fate of the Alhambra depended. The Moorish king who built it was a great magician, or, as some believed, had sold himself to the devil, and had laid the whole fortress under a magic spell. By this means it had remained standing for several years, in defiance of storms and earthquakes, while almost all other buildings of the Moors had fallen to ruin and disappeared. This spell, the tradition went on to say, would last until the hand on the outer arch should reach down and grasp the key, when the whole pile would tumble to pieces, and all the treasures buried beneath it by the Moors would be revealed.

Notwithstanding this ominous prediction, we ventured to

pass through the spellbound gateway, feeling some little assurance against magic art in the protection of the Virgin, a
statue of whom we observed above the portal.

After passing through the barbican, we ascended a narrow
lane, winding between walls, and came on an open esplanade
within the fortress, called the Plaza de los Algibes, or Place of
the Cisterns, from great reservoirs which undermine it, cut in
the living rock by the Moors to receive the water brought by
conduits from the Darro, for the supply of the fortress. Here,
also, is a well of immense depth, furnishing the purest and cold-
est of water,—another monument of the delicate taste of the
Moors, who were indefatigable in their exertions to obtain that
element in its crystal purity.

In front of this esplanade is the splendid pile commenced by
Charles V, and intended, it is said, to eclipse the residence of
the Moorish kings. Much of the Oriental edifice intended for
the winter season was demolished to make way for this massive pile. The grand entrance was blocked up, so that the present entrance to the Moorish palace is through a simple and almost humble portal in a corner. With all the massive grandeur
and architectural merit of the palace of Charles V, we regarded it as an arrogant intruder, and, passing by it with a feeling almost of scorn, rang at the Moslem portal.

While waiting for admittance, our self-imposed cicerone,
Mateo Ximenes, informed us that the royal palace was entrusted to the care of a worthy old maiden dame called Doña
Antonia Molina, but who, according to Spanish custom, went
by the more neighborly appellation of Tia Antonia (Aunt
Antonia), who maintained the Moorish halls and gardens in
order and showed them to strangers. While we were talking,
the door was opened by a plump little black-eyed Andalusian
damsel, whom Mateo addressed as Dolores, but who, from
her bright looks and cheerful disposition, evidently merited a
merrier name. Mateo informed me in a whisper that she was

the niece of Tia Antonia, and I found she was the good fairy who was to conduct us through the enchanted palace. Under her guidance we crossed the threshold, and were at once transported, as if by magic wand, into other times and an Oriental realm, and were treading the scenes of Arabian story. Nothing could be in greater contrast than the unpromising exterior of the pile with the scene now before us. We found ourselves in a vast *patio* or court, one hundred and fifty feet in length, and upwards of eighty feet in breadth, paved with white marble, and decorated at each end with light Moorish peristyles, one of which supported an elegant gallery of fretted architecture. Along the mouldings of the cornices and on various parts of the walls were escutcheons and ciphers, and cufic and Arabic characters in high relief, repeating the pious mottoes of the Moslem monarchs, the builders of the Alhambra, or extolling their grandeur and munificence. Along the centre of the court extended an immense basin or tank (*estanque*,) a hundred and twenty-four feet in length, twenty-seven in breadth, and five in depth, receiving its water from two marble vases. Hence it is called the Court of the Alberca (from *al beerkah*, the Arabic for a pond or tank). Great numbers of gold-fish were to be seen gleaming through the waters of the basin, and it was bordered by hedges of roses.

Passing from the Court of the Alberca under a Moorish archway, we entered the renowned Court of Lions. No part of the edifice gives a more complete idea of its original beauty than this, for none has suffered so little from the ravages of time. In the centre stands the fountain famous in song and story. The alabaster basins still shed their diamond drops; the twelve lions which support them, and give the court its name, still cast forth crystal streams as in the days of Boabdil. The lions, however, are unworthy of their fame, being of miserable sculpture, the work probably of some Christian captive. The court is laid out in flower-beds, instead of its

ancient and appropriate pavement of tiles or marble; the alteration, an instance of bad taste, was made by the French when
in possession of Granada. Round the four sides of the court
are light Arabian arcades of open filigree work, supported by
slender pillars of white marble, which it is supposed were
originally guilded. The architecture, like that in most parts of
the interior of the palace, is characterized by elegance rather
than grandeur, bespeaking a delicate and graceful taste, and a
disposition to indolent enjoyment. When one looks upon the
fairy traces of the peristyles, and the apparently fragile fret-
work of the walls, it is difficult to believe that so much has survived the wear and tear of centuries, the shocks of earthquakes, the violence of war, and the quiet, though no less
baneful, pilferings of the tasteful traveller; it is almost sufficient to excuse the popular tradition that the whole is protected by a magic charm.

On one side of the court a rich portal opens into the Hall
of the Abencerrages: so called from the gallant cavaliers of
that illustrious line who were here perfidiously massacred.
There are some who doubt the whole story, but our humble
cicerone Mateo pointed out the very wicket of the portal
through which they were introduced one by one into the
Court of Lions, and the white marble fountain in the centre of
the hall beside which they were beheaded. He showed us also
certain broad ruddy stains on the pavement, traces of their
blood, which, according to popular belief, can never be effaced.

V

Immediately opposite the Hall of the Abencerrages, a portal, richly adorned, leads into a hall of less tragical associations. It is light and lofty, exquisitely graceful in its architecture, paved with white marble, and bears the suggestive name
of the Hall of the Two Sisters. Some destroy the romance of

the name by attributing it to two enormous slabs of alabaster which lie side by side, and form a great part of the pavement: an opinion strongly supported by Mateo Ximenes. Others are disposed to give the name a more poetical significance, as the vague memorial of Moorish beauties who once graced this hall, which was evidently a part of the royal harem. This opinion I was happy to find entertained by our little bright-eyed guide, Dolores, who pointed to a balcony over an inner porch, which gallery, she had been told, belonged to the women's apartment. "You see, señor," she said, "it is all grated and latticed, like the gallery in a convent chapel where the nuns hear mass; for the Moorish kings," added she, indignantly, "shut up their wives just like nuns."

The latticed "jalousies," in fact, still remain, whence the dark-eyed beauties of the harem might gaze unseen upon the *zambras* and other dances and entertainments of the hall below.

On each side of this hall are recesses or alcoves for ottomans and couches, on which the voluptuous lords of the Alhambra indulged in that dreamy repose so dear to the Orientalists. A cupola or lantern admits a tempered light from above and a free circulation of air; while on one side is heard the refreshing sound of waters from the Fountain of the Lions, and on the other side the soft splash from the basin in the garden of Lindaraxa.

It is impossible to contemplate this scene, so perfectly Oriental, without feeling the early associations of Arabian romance, and almost expecting to see the white arm of some mysterious princess beckoning from the gallery, or some dark eye sparkling through the lattice. The abode of beauty is here as if it had been inhabited but yesterday; but where are the two sisters, where the Zoraydas and Lindaraxas!

An abundant supply of water, brought from the mountains by old Moorish aqueducts, circulates throughout the palace, supplying its baths and fish-pools, sparkling in jets within its halls or murmuring in channels along the marble pavements. When it has paid its tribute to the royal pile, and visited its gardens and parterres, it flows down the long avenue leading to the city, tinkling in rills, gushing in fountains, and maintaining a perpetual verdure in those groves that embower and beautify the whole hill of the Alhambra.

Those also who have sojourned in the ardent climates of the South can appreciate the delights of an abode combining the breezy coolness of the mountain with the freshness and verdure of the valley. While the city below pants with the noontide heat, and the parched Vega trembles to the eye, the delicate airs from the Sierra Nevada play through these lofty halls, bringing with them the sweetness of the surrounding gardens. Everything invites to that indolent repose, the bliss of southern climes; and while the half-shut eye looks out from shaded balconies upon the glittering landscape, the ear is lulled by the rustling of groves and the murmur of running streams.

Dizzy in Andalucía

A SELECTION FROM *Home Letters Written*
by the Late Earl of Beaconsfield
in 1830 and 1831

Another man of letters (and in the future rather more of a po-
litical figure than Irving) arrived in Spain in 1830. Benjamin
Disraeli was twenty-six years old and had embarked during an
uncertain period of his career, and for his health, on a lengthy
tour. In Andalucía, the only region of Spain which he visited,
he had brushes with brigands, saw "more than one bullfight"
(although he thought the affairs marred by the killing of so
many horses, his judgment was that "the sight is magnifi-
cent"), and enjoyed the hospitality of the British government
on the Rock of Gibraltar.

One may imagine that the Spaniards saw some of their own
flair for life in the garishly dressed young man with the care-

*fully tended black ringlets and the demanding ways, who al-
ternated between vast energy and well-cultivated lassitude.
Sparkling egotism was the guise and evidence of the genius by
which this seemingly unlikely person converted himself into
Queen Victoria's Prime Minister. The reader of Disraeli's letters from Spain may learn something about Spain, and about
Gibraltar, and about British gentlemen abroad; he will also
learn a good deal about Benjamin Disraeli. The letters are, as
his brother wrote in the preface to* Home Letters, *strictly that.
Who but Dizzy could visit Cádiz for the first time and forget
to describe the city in his letters home? But he liked Spain, and
understood it, and well he might, for he was of Spain: the
Earl of Beaconsfield was a Sephardic Jew.*

Gibraltar: July 1.

My dear Father,

I write to you from a country where the hedges consist of
aloes all in blossom: fourteen, sixteen feet high. Conceive the
contrast to our beloved and beechy Bucks. I say nothing of
geraniums and myrtles, bowers of oranges and woods of
olives, though the occasional palm should not be forgotten for
its great novelty and uncommon grace. We arrived here after
a very brief and very agreeable passage, passed in very agreeable society. You have already heard of our detention at Fal-
mouth for a week. As from the change of my plans Gib has
become to me what I had intended Malta to have been, conceive the awkwardness of my situation, when the only person
to whom I had a letter, Colonel Falla, is in England; but the
introduction to Broadfoot has counteracted all inconvenience.
He is here really a person of the first importance, and has

treated us with the most marked consideration, so I could not have been better off if I had had letters to all the authorities. This rock is a wonderful place, with a population infinitely diversified. Moors with costumes radiant as a rainbow or an Eastern melodrama; Jews with gaberdines and skull caps; Genoeses, Highlanders, and Spaniards, whose dress is as picturesque as that of the sons of Ivor. There are two public libraries—the Garrison Library, with more than 12,000 volumes; and the Merchants', with upward of half that number. In the garrison are all your works, even the last edition of the "Literary Character;" in the Merchants' the greater part. Each possesses a copy of another book, supposed to be written by a member of our family, and which is looked upon at Gibraltar as one of the masterpieces of the nineteenth century. You may feel their intellectual pulse from this. At first I apologised and talked of youthful blunders and all that, really being ashamed; but finding them, to my astonishment, sincere, and fearing they were stupid enough to adopt my last opinion, I shifted my position just in time, looked very grand, and passed myself off for a child of the Sun, like the Spaniard in Peru.

We were presented by B. to the Governor, Sir George Don, a general and G.C.B., a very fine old gentleman, of the Windsor Terrace school, courtly, almost regal in his manner, paternal, almost officious in his temper, a sort of mixture of Lord St. Vincent and the Prince de Ligne, English in his general style, but highly polished and experienced in European society. His palace, the Government House, is an old convent, and one of the most delightful residences I know, with a garden under the superintendence of Lady Don, full of rare exotics, with a beautiful terrace over the sea, a berceau of vines, and other delicacies which would quite delight you. Besides this, Sir George has a delightful pavilion, modestly called The Cottage, at the extreme point of the Rock, and a villa at San

Roque, in Spain, about ten miles off. Thus, by a constant change of residence, he counteracts the monotony of his situation. He possesses a large private fortune, all of which he here disburses, and has ornamented Gibraltar as a lover does his mistress. The Alameda here is superior to that at Cadiz, with banks of pink geraniums, truly delicious. But Gibraltar is a limited theatre for his Excellency, and he has civilised Spain for twenty miles round, by making roads at his own expense, building bridges, and reforming posadas. He behaved to us with great kindness, asked us to dine, and gave us a route himself for an excursion to the Sierra da Ronda, a savage mountain district, abounding in the most beautiful scenery and bugs! We returned from this excursion, which took us a week, yesterday, greatly gratified. The country in which we travelled is a land entirely of robbers and smugglers. They commit no personal violence, but lay you on the ground and clean out your pockets. If you have less than sixteen dollars they shoot you; that is the tariff, and is a loss worth risking. I took care to have very little more, and no baggage which I could not stow in the red bag which my mother remembers making for my pistols. We travelled on horseback, rising at four and stopping, on account of the heat, from ten till five in the evening, and then proceeding for three hours more. There are a number of little villages in this Sierra, entirely inhabited by robbers and smugglers, all of which boast a place called a posada. This is in fact a caravansara. The same room holds the cattle, the kitchen, the family, and boards and mats for travellers to sleep on; one or two have small rooms with beds, for the chance of an officer from the garrison, and these were always clean; indeed nothing is more remarkable than the delicacy and the cleanliness of the lower orders in this country, and the precautions which they universally take, by frequent whitewashing, to guard against vermin; but nothing can succeed against this generating sun, and I have suffered severely, though not as much as I expected. These posadas are, I say, mere caravansaras; they afford no provisions, and you must cater as you proceed, and, what is more, cook when you have catered, for that is a science not understood in Spain, or known only as an abomination. You will wonder how we managed to extract pleasure from a life which afforded us hourly peril for our purses and perhaps for our lives, which induced fatigue greater than I ever experienced, for here are no roads, and we were never less than eight hours a day on horseback, picking our way through a course which can only be compared to the steep bed of an exhausted cataract, and with so slight a prospect of attaining for a reward either food or rest.—I will tell you. The country was beautiful, the novelty of the life was great, and above all we had Brunet. What a man! Born in Italy of French parents, he has visited, as the captain of a privateer, all the countries of the Mediterranean: Egypt, Turkey, Syria. Early in life, as valet to Lord Hood, he was in England, and has even been at Guinea. After fourteen years' cruising he was taken by the Algerians, and was in various parts of Barbary for five or six years, and at last he obtains his liberty and settles at Gibraltar, where he becomes Caçador to the Governor, for he is, among his universal accomplishments, a celebrated shot. He can speak all languages but English, of which he makes a sad affair—even Latin, and he hints at a little Greek. He is fifty, but light as a butterfly and gay as a bird; in person not unlike English at Lyme, if you can imagine so insipid a character with a vivacity that never flags, and a tongue that never rests. Brunet did everything, remedied every inconvenience, and found an expedient for every difficulty. Never did I live so well as among these wild mountains of Andalusia, so exquisite is his cookery. Seriously, he is an artist of the first magnitude, and used to amuse himself by giving us some very exquisite dish among these barbarians; for he affects a great contempt of the Spaniards, and an equal admiration of the Moors. Whenever we complained he shrugged his shoulders with a look of ineffable contempt, exclaiming, "Nous ne sommes pas en Barbarie!" Recalling our associations with that word and country, it was superbly ludicrous.

Alas! my sheet has already disappeared, and I have said nothing. I will write you another letter by this post.

Gibraltar: July 1.

My dear Father,

I have already written to you by this post, and although I do not think that I have sufficient intelligence to warrant me in sending you another letter, nevertheless by doing so I err on the right side. To conclude the slight character which I gave you of Brunet in my last, let me tell you that he is at present making me a travelling suit of stuff, for he is a very good tailor. I heard only of one traveller among the Sierra da Ronda, and he was of course an Englishman. I made his acquaintance at Ronda, our ultimate point, and a town on the other side of the mountains, a town with a garrison and some slight marks of civilisation. The traveller was Colonel Batty, sketching, a gentlemanly person and very courteous: he wished me to join him to Granada. I never knew anyone sketch with such elegance, precision, and accuracy; long practice has made him unrivalled in this art, and far superior I should think to any professional artist. In the Sierra every man was armed. We returned through a country which reminded me of the Apennines; the rest was unlike anything I had seen and decidedly characteristic. Here at Castellar we slept in the very haunt of the banditti, among the good fellows of José Maria, the Captain Rolando of this part, and were not touched. In fact we were not promising prey, though picturesque enough in our appearance. Imagine M. and myself on two little Andalusian mountain horses with long tails and jennet necks, followed by a larger beast of burthen with our baggage, and the inevitable Brunet cocked upon its neck with a white hat and slippers, lively, shrivelled and noisy as a pea dancing upon tin. Our Spanish guide, tall, and with a dress excessively *brodé* and covered with brilliant buttons, walking by the side and occasionally adding to the burthen of our sumpter steed. The air of the mountains, the rising sun, the rising appetite, the variety of picturesque persons and things we met, and the impending danger, made a delightful life, and had it not been for the great enemy I should have given myself up entirely to the magic of the life, but that spoiled all. It is not worse; sometimes I think it lighter about the head, but the palpitation about the heart greatly increases, otherwise my health is wonderful. Never have I been better; but what use is this when the end of all existence is debarred me? I say no more upon this melancholy subject, by which I am ever and infinitely depressed, and often most so when the world least imagines it; but to complain is useless, and to endure almost impossible; but existence is certainly less irksome in the mild distraction of this various life. You and all I trust are well and happy. Let me hear from you a great deal at Malta. I shall not be there I dare say till the middle of August, so you can write by that packet, and indeed you had better always direct your letters to me at Malta, and they shall be forwarded to me from that place, which is a fine central position.

Well, to return. In spite of our frequent inquiries after the robbers, my being told "that is one of them," or that "José Maria was here two nights ago," or "is expected here to-night," I was a little disappointed, I confess, to return quite safe, and really began to believe we had been half mystified. Judge then our feelings when, on re-entering the hotel, the first sight that meets us and the first news that greets us, are two Englishmen just arrived from Cadiz, utterly rifled and stripped. They were attacked near a village at which we had been, not far from Gibraltar, by nine men in buckram. The robbers did not even ask for their keys, but *cut* open their portmanteaus and sacks, literally ripped them open, divided their new Geoghegans [1] on the spot, took even their papers, and with barely clothes to cover them, dismissed them in the most courteous manner with two dollars for their journey. "Quelle aventure!" as Parry says. They are now, poor devils, inmates of Griffiths' hotel, Gibraltar, where they are about to be again plundered, if I may judge from my own experience, though not professionally.

Meredith maintains the high character he won in former days in Germany, and is a most admirable travelling companion. I have had more than one offer of that sort at this place, which allows me to pay him a compliment publicly, etc.

Tell my mother that as it is the fashion among the dandies of this place—that is, the officers, for there are no others—not to wear waistcoats in the morning, her new studs come into fine play, and maintain my reputation of being a great judge of costume, to the admiration and envy of many subalterns. I have also the fame of being the first who ever passed the Straits with two canes, a morning and an evening cane. I change my cane as the gun fires, and hope to carry them both on to Cairo. It is wonderful the effect these magical wands produce. I owe to them even more attention than to being the supposed author of—what is it—I forget!

These Straits, by the bye—that is, the passage for the last ten miles or so to Gib, between the two opposite coasts of Africa and Europe, with the ocean for a river, and the shores all mountains—is by far the sublimest thing I have yet seen. We are now preparing for another and longer trip into Spain.

[1] Geoghegan, the shirtmaker of the day.

The part we intend to visit is the South of Spain, that celebrated Andalusia of which you have heard so much, comprising all the remains of the once famous kingdoms of the Moors. We propose returning to Cadiz to our friend Alava, who turned out to be a person of much distinction; ascending the Guadalquivir to Seville, thence to Cordova, Granada, and Malaga. Look at the map and get W. I.'s Chronicle.[2] I do not think much of it as a literary production, for the character he has assumed too much restrains him, though his humor sometimes breaks out; but you will find it most interesting when you remember I am wandering among the scenes. When I beg you to write, I mean my beloved Sa, because I know you think it a bore; but do all as you like. To her and to my dearest mother a thousand kisses. Tell Ralph I have not forgotten my promise of an occasional letter; and my dear pistol-cleaner, that he forgot to oil the locks, which rusted in conveyance. I thank the gods daily I am freed of Louis Clement, who would have been an expense and a bore. Tell Irving he has left a golden name in Spain. Few English visit Gibraltar. Tell Lord Mahon, inquiries made after his health. Adieu, my beloved padre,

Your most affectionate Son,

B. D. . . .

Cadiz: July 14, 1830.

My dear Father,

H.M.S. "Messenger," in which I went out, is, I hear, expected at Cadiz to-day on its return from Corfu, and therefore I send you this letter, though I doubt whether anything justifies me writing except the circumstance of your so speedily receiving it. We passed a very pleasant week at Gibraltar,

---

[2] *Chronicle of the Conquest,* by Washington Irving, 1829.

after our return from Ronda. We dined with the Governor at his cottage at Europa, a most charming pavilion, and met a most agreeable party. Lady Don was well enough to dine with us, and did me the honour of informing me that I was the cause of the exertion, which though of course a fib, was nevertheless flattering. She is, though very old, without exception one of the most agreeable personages that I ever met, excessively acute and *piquante*, with an aptitude of detecting character, and a tact in assuming it, very remarkable. To listen to her you would think you were charming away the hour with a blooming beauty in Mayfair; and though excessively infirm, her eye is so brilliant and so full of *moquerie* that you quite forgot her wrinkles. Although the scene very much resembled a small German Court. There was his Excellency in uniform covered with orders, exactly like the old Grand Duke of Darmstadt, directing everything; his wife the clever Prussian Princess that shared his crown; the aides-de-camp made excellent chamberlains, and the servants in number and formality quite equalled those of a Residenz. The repast was really elegant and *recherché* even for this curious age. Sir George will yet head his table and yet carve, recommend a favourite dish, and deluge you with his summer drink, half champagne and half lemonade. After dinner Lady Don rode out with the very pretty wife of Colonel Considine, and the men dispersed in various directions. It was the fate of Meredith and myself to be lionized to some cave or other with Sir George. What a scene, and what a procession! First came two grooms on two barbs; then a carriage with four horses; at the window at which H. E. sits, a walking footman, and then an outrider, all at a funeral pace. We were directed to meet our host at the cave, ten minutes' walk. During this time Sir G. tries one of the Arabians, but at the gentlest walk, and the footman changes his position in consequence to his side; but it is windy, our valiant but infirm friend is afraid of being blown off, and when he reaches the point of destination, we find him again in the carriage. In spite of his infirmities he will get out to lionize; but before he disembarks, he changes his foraging cap for a full General's cock with a plume as big as the Otranto one; and this, because the hero will never be seen in public in undress, although we were in a solitary cave looking over the ocean, and inhabited only by monkeys. The cave is shown, and we all get in the carriage, because he is sure we are tired; the foraging cap is again assumed, and we travel back to the Cottage, Meredith, myself, the Governor, and the cocked hat, each in a seat. In the evening he has his rubber, which he never misses, and is surprised I do not play "the only game for gentlemen! You should play; learn." However I preferred the conversation of his agreeable lady, although the charms of Mrs. Considine were puzzling, and I was very much like Hercules between—you know the rest.

I am sorry to say my hair is coming off, just at the moment it had attained the highest perfection, and was universally mistaken for a wig, so that I am obliged to let the women pull it to satisfy their —— curiosity. Let me know what my mother thinks. There are no wigs here that I could wear. Pomade and all that is quite a delusion. Somebody recommends me cocoanut oil, which I could get here; but suppose it turns it grey or blue or green! . . .

Your most affectionate Son,
B. D.

I have quite forgotten to say a word about Cadiz, which is charming! Brilliant beyond description. "Fair Florence" is a very dingy affair compared with it. The white houses and the green jalousies sparkle in the sun. Figaro is in every street; Rosina in every balcony.

GEORGE BORROW

The Bible in Spain

A SELECTION FROM
The Bible in Spain

*George Borrow was perhaps the best-equipped and at the
same time the most unlikely of all travelers to succeed in pre-
senting to readers the essential flavor of life in Spain—a flavor
compounded of danger, violent contrasts among people and
scenery, pathos, high humanity, and mystery. Yet, of all the
accounts of Spanish travel which have been written, Borrow's
is the one most nearly indispensable for understanding and
appreciating some of the more exotic traits of the Spanish
people.*

*Borrow came to Spain to peddle Bibles. He believed that
he had God on his side; but he knew right well that his God*

was the Spanish devil. Borrow had British character on his side; but he had such an excess of individualism that it might well have cost him his life: few Spaniards lack character and they do not easily endure alien dogmatists.

But the Bible seller swept back and forth across Spain between 1835 and 1840 with enormous élan. He captivated his audience, his servants, his traveling companions and even the extraordinary horses which bore him on his hazardous rides. A linguistic genius, one of whose feats consisted of translating the Gospel according to St. Luke into the Gypsy tongue while in Spain, Borrow's great strength was in his unrelenting individualism. "My favourite, I might say my only study, is man," he wrote, and it was, of course, precisely his mastery of his subject matter which gives the key to his remarkable success in interpreting, or at least describing unforgettably, the Spanish people.

Not every fact that he writes is gospel truth: he was not writing a guide to Spain, nor explaining the country. His vitality, his impassioned dogmatism checked only by a consummate awareness of life's variety, his courage, bear out what someone wrote about him: "Since Luther there has hardly been such a Protestant as Borrow."

IT WAS the commencement of February when I reached Madrid. After staying a few days at a posada, I removed to a lodging which I engaged at No. 3, in the Calle de la Zarza, a dark dirty street, which, however, was close to the Puerta del Sol, the most central point of Madrid, into which four or five of the principal streets debouch, and which is, at all times of the year, the great place of assemblage for the idlers of the capital, poor or rich.

It was rather a singular house in which I had taken up my abode. I occupied the front part of the first floor; my apartments consisted of an immense parlour, and a small chamber on one side in which I slept; the parlour, notwithstanding its size, contained very little furniture: a few chairs, a table, and a species of sofa, constituted the whole. It was very cold and airy, owing to the draughts which poured in from three large windows, and from sundry doors. The mistress of the house, attended by her two daughters, ushered me in. "Did you ever see a more magnificent apartment?" demanded the former; "is it not fit for a king's son? Last winter it was occupied by the great General Espartero."

The hostess was an exceedingly fat woman, a native of Valladolid, in Old Castile. "Have you any other family," I demanded, "besides these daughters?" "Two sons," she replied; "one of them an officer in the army, father of this urchin," pointing to a wicked but clever-looking boy of about twelve, who at that moment bounded into the room; "the other is the most celebrated national in Madrid: he is a tailor by trade, and his name is Baltasar. He has much influence with the other nationals, on account of the liberality of his opinions, and a word from him is sufficient to bring them all out armed and furious to the Puerta del Sol. He is, however, at present confined to his bed, for he is very dissipated, and fond of the company of bull-fighters and people still worse."

As my principal motive for visiting the Spanish capital was the hope of obtaining permission from the government to print the New Testament in the Castilian language, for circulation in Spain, I lost no time, upon my arrival, in taking what I considered to be the necessary steps.

I was an entire stranger at Madrid, and bore no letters of introduction to any person of influence, who might have assisted me in this undertaking, so that notwithstanding I entertained a hope of success, relying on the assistance of the Almighty, this hope was not at all times very vivid, but was frequently overcast with the clouds of despondency.

Mendizabal was at this time Prime minister of Spain, and was considered as a man of almost unbounded power, in whose hands were placed the destinies of the country. I therefore considered that if I could by any means induce him to favour my views, I should have no reason to fear interruption from other quarters, and I determined upon applying to him.

Before taking this step, however, I deemed it advisable to wait upon Mr. Villiers, the British ambassador at Madrid; and with the freedom permitted to a British subject, to ask his advice in this affair. I was received with great kindness, and enjoyed a conversation with him on various subjects before I introduced the matter which I had most at heart. He said that if I wished for an interview with Mendizabal, he would endeavour to procure me one, but, at the same time, told me frankly that he could not hope that any good would arise from it, as he knew him to be violently prejudiced against the British and Foreign Bible Society, and was far more likely to discountenance than encourage any efforts which they might be disposed to make for introducing the gospel into Spain. I, however, remained resolute in my desire to make the trial, and before I left him, obtained a letter of introduction to Mendizabal.

Early one morning I repaired to the palace, in a wing of which was the office of the Prime minister; it was bitterly cold, and the Guadarama, of which there is a noble view from the palace-plain, was covered with snow. For at least three hours I remained shivering with cold in an ante-room, with several other aspirants for an interview with the man of power. At last his private secretary made his appearance, and after putting various questions to the others, addressed himself to me, asking who I was and what I wanted. I told him that I was an Englishman, and the bearer of a letter from the

British Minister. "If you have no objection, I will myself deliver it to His Excellency," said he; whereupon I handed it to him, and he withdrew. Several individuals were admitted before me; at last, however, my own turn came, and I was ushered into the presence of Mendizabal.

He stood behind a table covered with papers, on which his eyes were intently fixed. He took not the slightest notice when I entered, and I had leisure enough to survey him; he was a huge athletic man, somewhat taller than myself, who measure six foot two without my shoes; his complexion was florid, his features fine and regular, his nose quite aquiline, and his teeth splendidly white; though scarcely fifty years of age, his hair was remarkably grey; he was dressed in a rich morning gown, with a gold chain around his neck, and morocco slippers on his feet.

His secretary, a fine intellectual-looking man, who, as I was subsequently informed, had acquired a name both in English and Spanish literature, stood at one end of the table with papers in his hands.

After I had been standing about a quarter of an hour, Mendizabal suddenly lifted up a pair of sharp eyes, and fixed them upon me with a peculiarly scrutinizing glance.

"I have seen a glance very similar to that amongst the Beni Israel," thought I to myself. . . .

My interview with him lasted nearly an hour. Some singular discourse passed between us: I found him, as I had been informed, a bitter enemy to the Bible Society, of which he spoke in terms of hatred and contempt, and by no means a friend to the Christian religion, which I could easily account for. I was not discouraged, however, and pressed upon him the matter which brought me thither, and was eventually so far successful, as to obtain a promise, that at the expiration of a few months, when he hoped the country would be in a more tranquil state, I should be allowed to print the Scriptures.

95

As I was going away, he said, "Yours is not the first application I have had: ever since I have held the reins of government I have been pestered in this manner by English calling themselves Evangelical Christians, who have of late come flocking over into Spain. Only last week a hunchbacked fellow found his way into my cabinet whilst I was engaged in important business, and told me that Christ was coming. . . . And now you have made your appearance, and almost persuaded me to embroil myself yet more with the priesthood, as if they did not abhor me enough already. What a strange infatuation is this which drives you over lands and waters with Bibles in your hands. My good sir, it is not Bibles we want, but rather guns and gunpowder, to put the rebels down with, and above all, money, that we may pay the troops; whenever you come with these three things you shall have a hearty welcome; if not, we really can dispense with your visits, however great the honour."

Myself.—There will be no end to the troubles of this afflicted country until the gospel have free circulation.

Mendizabal.—I expected that answer, for I have not lived thirteen years in England without forming some acquaintance with the phraseology of you good folks. Now, now, pray go; you see how engaged I am. Come again whenever you please, but let it not be within the next three months.

"Don Jorge," said my hostess, coming into my apartment one morning, whilst I sat at breakfast with my feet upon the brasero, "here is my son Baltasarito, the national; he has risen from his bed, and hearing that there is an Englishman in the house, he has begged me to introduce him, for he loves Englishmen on account of the liberality of their opinions; there he is, what do you think of him?"

I did not state to his mother what I thought; it appeared to me, however, that she was quite right in calling him Baltasarito, which is the diminutive of Baltasar, forasmuch as that

96

ancient and sonorous name had certainly never been bestowed on a more diminutive personage: he might measure about five feet one inch, though he was rather corpulent for his height; his face looked yellow and sickly, he had, however, a kind of fanfaronading air, and his eyes, which were of dark brown, were both sharp and brilliant. His dress, or rather his undress, was somewhat shabby: he had a foraging cap on his head, and in lieu of a morning gown, he wore a sentinel's old great-coat.

"I am glad to make your acquaintance, Señor nacional," said I to him, after his mother had departed, and Baltasar had taken a seat, and of course lighted a paper cigar at the brasero. "I am glad to have made your acquaintance, more especially as your lady mother has informed me that you have great influence with the nationals. I am a stranger in Spain, and may want a friend; fortune has been kind to me in procuring me one who is a member of so powerful a body."

Baltasar.—Yes, I have a gread deal to say with the other nationals; there is none in Madrid better known than Baltasar, or more dreaded by the Carlists. You say you may stand in need of a friend; there is no fear of my failing you in any emergency. Both myself and any of the other nationals will be proud to go out with you as padrinos, should you have any affair of honour on your hands. But why do you not become one of us? We would gladly receive you into our body.

Myself.—Is the duty of a national particularly hard?

Baltasar.—By no means; we have to do duty about once every fifteen days, and then there is occasionally a review, which does not last long. No! the duties of a national are by no means onerous, and the privileges are great. I have seen three of my brother nationals walk up and down the Prado of a Sunday, with sticks in their hands, cudgelling all the suspicious characters, and it is our common practice to scour the streets at night; and then if we meet any person who is ob-

97

noxious to us, we fall upon him, and with a knife or a bayonet generally leave him wallowing in his blood on the pavement: no one but a national would be permitted to do that.

Myself.—Of course none but persons of liberal opinions are to be found among the nationals?

Baltasar.—Would it were so! There are some amongst us, Don Jorge, who are no better than they should be; they are few, however, and for the most part well known. There is no pleasant life, for when they mount guard with the rest they are scouted, and not infrequently cudgelled. The law compels all of a certain age either to serve in the army or to become national soldiers, on which account some of these Godos are to be found amongst us.

Myself.—Are there many in Madrid of the Carlist opinion?

Baltasar.—Not among the young people; the greater part of the Madrilenian Carlists capable of bearing arms departed long ago to join the ranks of the factious in the Basque provinces. Those who remain are for the most part greybeards and priests, good for nothing but to assemble in private coffee-houses, and to prate treason together. Let them prate, Don Jorge; let them prate; the destinies of Spain do not depend on the wishes of ojalateros and pasteleros, but on the hands of stout gallant nationals like myself and friends, Don Jorge.

Myself.—I am sorry to learn from your lady mother that you are strangely dissipated.

Baltasar.—Ho, ho, Don Jorge! she has told you that, has she; what would you have, Don Jorge? I am young, and young blood will have its course. I am called Baltasar the gay by all the other nationals, and it is on account of my gaiety and the liberality of my opinions that I am so popular among them. When I mount guard I invariably carry my guitar with me, and then there is sure to be a function at the guard-house. We send for wine, Don Jorge, and the nationals become wild, Don Jorge, dancing and drinking through the night, whilst Baltasarito strums the guitar, and sings then songs of Germania,—

> *"Una romi sin pachi*
> *Le peno á su chindomar,"* etc., etc.

That is Gitáno, Don Jorge; I learnt it from the toreros of Andalusia, who all speak Gitáno, and are mostly of gipsy blood. I learnt it from them; they are all friends of mine, Montes Sevilla and Poquito Pan. I never miss a function of bulls, Don Jorge. Baltasar is sure to be there with his amiga. Don Jorge, there are no bull-functions in the winter, or I would carry you to one, but happily to-morrow there is an execution, a function de la horca; and there we will go, Don Jorge.

We did go to see this execution, which I shall long remember. The criminals were two young men, brothers; they suffered for a most atrocious murder, having in the dead of night broke open the house of an aged man, whom they put to death, and whose property they stole. Criminals in Spain are not hanged as they are in England, or guillotined as in France, but strangled upon a wooden stage. They sit down on a kind of chair with a post behind, to which is affixed an iron collar with a screw; this iron collar is made to clasp the neck of the prisoner, and on a certain signal it is drawn tighter and tighter by means of the screw, until life becomes extinct. After we had waited amongst the assembled multitude a considerable time, the first of the culprits appeared; he was mounted on an ass, without saddle or stirrups, his legs being allowed to dangle nearly to the ground. He was dressed in yellow sulphur-coloured robes, with a high-peaked conical red hat on his head, which was shaven. Between his hands he held a parchment, on which was written something, I believe the confession of faith. Two priests led the animal by the bridle; two others walked on either side chanting litanies, amongst which

I distinguished the words of heavenly peace and tranquility, for the culprit had been reconciled to the Church, had confessed and received absolution, and had been promised admission to heaven. He did not exhibit the least symptom of fear, but dismounted from the animal and was led, not supported, up the scaffold, where he was placed on the chair, and the fatal collar put around his neck. One of the priests then in a loud voice commenced saying the Belief, and the culprit repeated the words after him. On a sudden, the executioner, who stood behind, commenced turning the screw, which was of prodigious force, and the wretched man was almost instantly a corpse; but, as the screw went round, the priest began to shout, "*Pax et misericordia et tranquillitas*," and still as he shouted, his voice became louder and louder till the lofty walls of Madrid rang with it: then stooping down, he placed his mouth close to the culprit's ear, still shouting, just as if he would pursue the spirit through its course to eternity, cheering it on its way. The effect was tremendous. I myself was so excited that I involuntarily shouted "*misericordia*," and so did many others. God was not thought of; Christ was not thought of; only the priest was thought of, for he seemed at that moment to be the first being in existence, and to have the power of opening and shutting the gates of heaven or of hell, just as he should think proper. A striking instance of the successful working of the Popish system, whose grand aim has ever been to keep people's minds as far as possible from God, and to centre their hopes and fears in the priesthood. The execution of the second culprit was precisely similar; he ascended the scaffold a few minutes after his brother had breathed his last.

I have visited most of the principal capitals of the world, but upon the whole none have ever so interested me as this city of Madrid, in which I now found myself. I will not dwell upon its streets, its edifices, its public squares, its fountains, though some of these are remarkable enough; but Petersburg has finer streets, Paris and Edinburgh more stately edifices, London far nobler squares, whilst Shiraz can boast of more costly fountains, though not cooler water. But the population! Within a mud wall, scarcely one league and a half in circuit, are contained two hundred thousand human beings, certainly forming the most extraordinary vital mass to be found in the entire world; and be it always remembered that this mass is strictly Spanish. The population of Constantinople is extraordinary enough, but to form it twenty nations have contributed; Greeks, Armenians, Persians, Poles, Jews, the latter, by-the-bye, of Spanish origin, and speaking amongst themselves the old Spanish language; but the huge population of Madrid, with the exception of a sprinkling of foreigners, chiefly French tailors, glove-makers, and peruquiers, is strictly Spanish, though a considerable portion are not natives of the place. Here are no colonies of Germans, as at St. Petersburg; no English factories, as at Lisbon; no multitudes of insolent Yankees lounging through the streets, as at the Havannah, with an air which seems to say, the land is our own whenever we choose to take it; but a population which, however strange and wild, and composed of various elements, is Spanish, and will remain so as long as the city itself shall exist. Hail, ye aguadores of Asturia! who, in your dress of coarse duffel and leathern skull-caps, are seen seated in hundreds by the fountain sides, upon your empty water casks, or staggering with them filled to the topmost stories of lofty houses. Hail, ye caleseros of Valencia! who, lolling lazily against your vehicles, rasp tobacco for your paper cigars whilst waiting for a fare. Hail to you, beggars of La Mancha! men and women, who, wrapped in coarse blankets, demand charity indifferently at the gate of the palace or the prison. Hail to you, valets from the mountains, mayordomos and secretaries from Biscay and Guipuscoa, toreros from Andalusia, riposteros from Galicia, shopkeepers from Catalonia! Hail to ye, Castilians, Estremenians, and Aragonese, of whatever calling! And lastly, genuine sons of the capital, rabble of Madrid, ye twenty thousand manolos, whose terrible knives, on the second morning of May, worked such grim havoc amongst the legions of Murat!

And the higher orders—the ladies and gentlemen, the cavaliers and señoras; shall I pass them by in silence? The truth is I have little to say about them; I mingled but little in their society, and what I saw of them by no means tended to exhalt them in my imagination. I am not one of those who, wherever they go, make it a constant practice to disparage the higher orders, and to exalt the populace at their expense. There are many capitals in which the high aristocracy, the lords and ladies, the sons and daughters of nobility, constitute the most remarkable and the most interesting part of the population. This is the case at Vienna, and more especially at London. Who can rival the English aristocrat in lofty stature, in dignified bearing, in strength of hand, and valour of heart? Who rides a nobler horse? Who has a firmer seat? And who more lovely than his wife, or sister, or daughter? But with respect to the Spanish aristocracy, the ladies and gentlemen, the cavaliers and señoras, I believe the less that is said of them on the points to which I have just alluded the better. I confess, however, that I know little about them; they have, perhaps, their admirers, and to the pens of such I leave their panegyric. Le Sage has described them as they were nearly two centuries ago. His description is anything but captivating, and I do not think that they have improved since the period of the sketches of the immortal Frenchman. I would sooner talk of the lower class, not only of Madrid but of all Spain. The Spaniard of the lower class has much more interest for me, whether manolo, labourer, or muleteer. He is not a common being; he is an extraordinary man. He has not, it is true, the amiability and generosity of the Russian mujik, who will give his only rouble rather than the stranger shall want; nor his placid courage, which renders him insensible to fear, and at the command of his Tsar, sends him singing to certain death. There is more hardness and less self-devotion in the disposition of the Spaniard; he possesses, however, a spirit of proud independence, which it is impossible but to admire. He is ignorant, of course; but it is singular, that I have invariably found amongst the low and slightly educated classes far more liberality of sentiment tham amongst the upper. It has long been the fashion to talk of the bigotry of the Spaniards, and their mean jealousy of foreigners. This is true to a certain extent; but it chiefly holds good with respect to the upper classes. If foreign valour or talent has never received its proper meed in Spain, the great body of the Spaniards are certainly not in fault. I have heard Wellington calumniated in this proud scene of his triumphs, but never by the old soldiers of Aragon and the Asturias, who assisted to vanquish the French at Salamanca and the Pyrenees. I have heard the manner of riding of an English jockey criticised, but it was by the idiotic heir of Medina Celi, and not by a picador of the Madrilenian bull ring.

Apropos of bull-fighters:—Shortly after my arrival, I one day entered a low tavern in a neighbourhood notorious for robbery and murder, and in which for the last two hours I had been wandering on a voyage of discovery. I was fatigued, and required refreshment. I found the place thronged with people, who had all the appearance of ruffians. I saluted them, upon which they made way for me to the bar, taking off their sombreros with great ceremony. I emptied a glass of val de peñas, and was about to pay for it and depart, when a horrible-looking fellow, dressed in a buff jerkin, leather breeches, and jackboots, which came halfway up his thighs, and having on his head a white hat, the rims of which were at least a yard and a half in circumference, pushed through the crowd, and confronting me, roared,—

"Otra copita! vamos Inglesito: Otra copita!"

"Thank you, my good sir, you are very kind, you appear to know me, but I have not the honour of knowing you."

"Not know me!" replied the being. "I am Sevilla, the torero. I know you well; you are the friend of Baltasarito, the national, who is a friend of mine, and a very good subject."

Then turning to the company, he said in a sonorous tone, laying a strong emphasis on the last syllable of every word, according to the custom of the gentle rufianesca throughout Spain,—

"Cavaliers, and strong men, this cavalier is the friend of a friend of mine. *Es mucho hombre*. There is none like him in Spain. He speaks the crabbed Gitáno though he is an Inglesito."

"We do not believe it," replied several grave voices. "It is not possible."

"It is not possible, say you? I tell you it is. Come forward, Balseiro, you who had been in prison all your life, and are always boasting that you can speak the crabbed Gitáno, though I say you know nothing of it—come forward and speak to his worship in the crabbed Gitáno."

A low, slight, but active figure stepped forward. He was in his shirt sleeves, and wore a montero cap; his features were handsome, but they were those of a demon.

He spoke a few words in the broken gipsy slang of the prison, inquiring of me whether I had ever been in the condemned cell, and whether I knew what a Gitána was?

"Vamos Inglesito," shouted Sevilla, in a voice of thunder; "answer the monro in the crabbed Gitáno."

I answered the robber, for such he was, and one, too, whose name will live for many years in the ruffian histories of

Madrid; I answered him in a speech of some length, in the dialect of the Estremenian gipsies.

"I believe it is the crabbed Gitáno," muttered Balseiro. "It is either that or English, for I understand not a word of it."

"Did I not say to you," cried the bull-fighter, "that you knew nothing of the crabbed Gitáno? But this Inglesito does. I understood all he said. Vaya, there is none like him for the crabbed Gitáno. He is a good ginete, too; next to myself there is none like him, only he rides with stirrup leathers too short. Inglesito, if you have need of money, I will lend you my purse. All I have is at your service, and that is not a little; I have just gained four thousand chulés by the lottery. Courage, Englishman! Another cup. I will pay all. I, Sevilla!"

And he clapped his hand repeatedly on his breast, reiterating, "I, Sevilla! I ——"

This nocturnal journey endured so long that I almost lost all hope of reaching the town, and had closed my eyes in a doze, though I still trudged on mechanically, leading the horse. Suddenly a voice at a slight distance before me roared out, *"Quien vive?"* for I had at last found my way to Villafranca. It proceeded from the sentry in the suburb, one of those singular half soldiers half guerillas, called Migueletes, who are in general employed by the Spanish government to clear the roads of robbers. I gave the usual answer, "España," and went up to the place where he stood. After a little conversation, I sat down on a stone, awaiting the arrival of Antonio, who was long in making his appearance. On his arrival, I asked if any one had passed him on the road, but he replied that he had seen nothing. The night, or rather the morning, was still very dark, though a small corner of the moon was occasionally visible. On our inquiring the way to the gate, the Miguelet directed us down a street to the left, which we followed. The street was steep, we could see no gate, and our progress was soon stopped by houses and wall. We knocked at the gates of two or three of these houses, (in the upper stories of which lights were burning,) for the purpose of being set right, but we were either disregarded or not heard. A horrid squalling of cats, from the tops of the houses and dark corners, saluted our ears, and I thought of the night arrival of Don Quixote and his squire at Toboso, and their vain search amongst the deserted streets for the palace of Dulcinea. At length we saw light and heard voices in a cottage at the other side of a kind of ditch. Leading the horses over, we called at the door, which was opened by an aged man, who appeared by his dress to be a baker, as indeed he proved, which accounted for his being up at so late an hour. On begging him to show us the way into the town, he led us up a very narrow alley at the end of his cottage, saying that he would likewise conduct us to the posada.

The alley led directly to what appeared to be the market-place, at a corner house of which our guide stopped and knocked. After a long pause an upper window was opened, and a female voice demanded who we were. The old man replied that two travellers had arrived who were in need of lodging. "I cannot be disturbed at this time of night," said the woman; "they will be wanting supper, and there is nothing in the house; they must go elsewhere." She was going to shut the window, but I cried that we wanted no supper, but merely a resting place for ourselves and our horses—that we had come that day from Astorga, and were dying of fatigue. "Who is that speaking?" cried the woman. "Surely that is the voice of Gil, the German clock-maker from Pontevedra. Welcome, old companion; you are come at the right time, for my own is out of order. I am sorry I have kept you waiting, but I will admit you in a moment."

The window was slammed to, presently a light shone

through the crevices of the door, a key turned in the lock, and we were admitted.

"Ave Maria," said the woman; "whom have we here? This is not Gil the clock-maker?" "Whether it be Gil or Juan," said I, "we are in need of your hospitality, and can pay for it." Our first care was to stable the horses, which were much exhausted. We then went in search of some accommodations for ourselves. The house was large and commodious, and having tasted a little water, I stretched myself on the floor of one of the rooms on some mattresses which the woman produced, and in less than a minute was sound asleep.

The sun was shining bright when I awoke. I walked forth into the market-place, which was crowded with people. I looked up, and could see the peaks of tall black mountains peeping over the tops of the houses. The town lay in a deep hollow, and appeared to be surrounded by hills on almost every side. *"Quel pays barbare!"* said Antonio, who now joined me; "the farther we go, my master, the wilder everything looks. I am half afraid to venture into Galicia; they tell me that to get to it we must clamber up those hills: the horses will founder." Leaving the market-place I ascended the wall of the town, and endeavoured to discover the gate by which we should have entered the preceding night; but I was not more successful in the bright sunshine than in the darkness. The town in the direction of Astorga appeared to be hermetically sealed.

I was eager to enter Galicia, and finding that the horses were to a certain extent recovered from the fatigue of the journey of the preceding day, we again mounted and proceeded on our way. Crossing a bridge, we presently found ourselves in a deep gorge amongst the mountains, down which rushed an impetuous rivulet, overhung by the high road which leads into Galicia. We were in the far-famed pass of Fuencebadon.

It is impossible to describe this pass or the circumjacent region, which contains some of the most extraordinary scenery in all Spain; a feeble and imperfect outline is all that I can hope to effect. The traveller who ascends it follows for nearly a league the course of the torrent, whose banks are in some places precipitous, and in others slope down to the waters, and are covered with lofty trees, oaks, poplars, and chestnuts. Small villages are at first continually seen, with low walls, and roofs formed of immense slates, the eaves nearly touching the ground; these hamlets, however, gradually become less frequent as the path grows more steep and narrow, until they finally cease at a short distance before the spot is attained where the rivulet is abandoned, and is no more seen, though its tributaries may yet be heard in many a gully, or described in tiny rills dashing down the steeps. Everything here is wild, strange, and beautiful: the hill up which winds the path towers above on the right, whilst on the farther side of a profound ravine rises an immense mountain, to whose extreme altitudes the eye is scarcely able to attain, but the most singular feature of this pass are the hanging fields and meadows which cover its sides. In these, as I passed, the grass was growing luxuriantly, and in many the mowers were plying their scythes, though it seemed scarcely possible that their feet could find support on ground so precipitous: above and below were driftways, so small as to seem threads along the mountain side. A car, drawn by oxen, is creeping round yon airy eminence; the nearer wheel is actually hanging over the horrid descent; giddiness seizes the brain, and the eye is rapidly withdrawn. A cloud intervenes, and when again you turn to watch their progress, the objects of your anxiety have disappeared. Still more narrow becomes the path along which you yourself are toiling, and its turns more frequent. You have already come a distance of two leagues, and still one-third of the ascent remains unsurmounted. You are not yet in Galicia;

and you still hear Castilian, coarse and unpolished, it is true, spoken in the miserable cabins placed in the sequestered nooks which you pass by in your route.

Shortly before we reached the summit of the pass thick mists began to envelop the tops of the hills, and a drizzling rain descended. "These mists," said Antonio, "are what the Gallegans call bretima; and it is said there is never any lack of them in their country." "Have you ever visited the country before?" I demanded. "Non, mon maître; but I have frequently lived in houses where the domestics were in part Gallegans, on which account I know not a little of their ways, and even something of their language." "Is the opinion which you have formed of them at all in their favour?" I inquired. "By no means, mon maître; the men in general seem clownish and simple, yet they are capable of deceiving the most clever filou of Paris; and as for the women, it is impossible to live in the same house with them, more especially if they are Camareras, and wait upon the Señora; they are continually breeding dissensions and disputes in the house, and telling tales of the other domestics. I have already lost two or three excellent situations in Madrid, solely owing to these Gallegan chambermaids. We have now come to the frontier, mon maître, for such I conceive this village to be."

We entered the village, which stood on the summit of the mountain, and as our horses and ourselves were by this time much fatigued, we looked round for a place in which to obtain refreshment. Close by the gate stood a building which, from the circumstance of a mule or two and a wretched pony standing before it, we concluded was the posada, as in effect it proved to be. We entered: several soldiers were lolling on heaps of coarse hay, with which the place, which much resembled a stable, was half filled. All were exceedingly ill-looking fellows, and very dirty. They were conversing with each other in a strange sounding dialect, which I supposed to be Gallegan. Scarcely did they perceive us when two or three of them, starting from their couch, ran up to Antonio, whom they welcomed with much affection, calling him *companheiro*. "How came you to know these men?" I demanded in French. "*Ces messieurs sont presque tous de ma connoissance*," he replied, "*et, entre nous, ce sont des véritables vauriens;* they are almost all robbers and assassins. That fellow with one eye, who is the corporal, escaped a little time ago from Madrid, more than suspected of being concerned in an affair of poisoning; but he is safe enough here in his own country, and is placed to guard the frontier, as you see; but we must treat them civilly, mon maître; we must give them wine, or they will be offended. I know them, mon maître—I know them. Here, hostess, bring an azumbre of wine."

Whilst Antonio was engaged in treating his friends, I led the horses to the stable; this was through the house, inn, or whatever it might be called. The stable was a wretched shed, in which the horses sank to their fetlocks in mud and puddle. On inquiring for barley, I was told that I was now in Galicia, where barley was not used for provender, and was very rare. I was offered in lieu of it Indian corn, which, however, the horses ate without hesitation. There was no straw to be had; coarse hay, half green, being the substitute. By trampling about in the mud of the stable my horse soon lost a shoe, for which I searched in vain. "Is there a blacksmith in the village?" I demanded of a shock-headed fellow who officiated as ostler.

Ostler.—Si, Senhor; but I suppose you have brought horse-shoes with you, or that large beast of yours cannot be shod in this village.

Myself.—What do you mean? Is the blacksmith unequal to his trade? Cannot he put on a horse-shoe?

Ostler.—Si, Senhor; he can put on a horse-shoe if you give it him; but there are no horse-shoes in Galicia, at least in these parts.

Myself.—Is it not customary then to shoe the horses in Galicia?

Ostler.—Senhor, there are no horses in Galicia, there are only ponies; and those who bring horses to Galicia, and none but madmen ever do, must bring shoes to fit them; only shoes of ponies are to be found here.

Myself.—What do you mean by saying that only madmen bring horses to Galicia?

Ostler.—Senhor, no horse can stand the food of Galicia and the mountains of Galicia long, without falling sick: and then if he does not die at once, he will cost you in farriers more than he is worth; besides, a horse is of no use here, and cannot perform amongst the broken ground the tenth part of the service which a little pony mare can. By-the-bye, Senhor, I perceive that yours is an entire horse; now out of twenty ponies that you see on the roads of Galicia, nineteen are mares; the males are sent down into Castile to be sold. Senhor, your horse will become heated on our roads, and will catch the bad glanders, for which there is no remedy. Senhor, a man must be mad to bring any horse to Galicia, but twice mad to bring an entero, as you have done."

"A strange country this of Galicia," said I, and went to consult with Antonio.

It appeared that the information of the ostler was literally true with regard to the horse-shoe; at least the blacksmith of the village, to whom we conducted the animal, confessed his inability to shoe him, having none that would fit his hoof: he said it was very probable that we should be obliged to lead the animal to Lugo, which, being a cavalry station, we might perhaps find there what we wanted. He added, however, that the greater part of the cavalry soldiers were mounted on the ponies of the country, the mortality amongst the horses brought from the level ground into Galicia being frightful. Lugo was ten leagues distant: there seemed, however, to be no remedy at hand but patience, and, having refreshed ourselves, we proceeded, leading our horses by the bridle.

We were now on level ground, being upon the very top of one of the highest mountains in Galicia. This level continued for about a league, when we began to descend. Before we had crossed the plain, which was overgrown with furze and brushwood, we came suddenly upon half-a-dozen fellows armed with muskets and wearing a tattered uniform. We at first supposed them to be a banditti: they were, however, only a party of soldiers who had been detached from the station we had just quitted to escort one of the provincial posts or couriers. They were clamorous for cigars, but offered us no farther incivility. Having no cigars to bestow, I gave them in lieu thereof a small piece of silver. Two of the worst looking were very eager to be permitted to escort us to Nogales, the village where we proposed to spend the night. "By no means permit them, mon maître," said Antonio, "they are two famous assassins of my acquaintance; I have known them at Madrid; in the first ravine they will shoot and plunder us." I therefore civilly declined their offer and departed. "You seem to be acquainted with all the cut-throats in Galicia," said I to Antonio, as we descended the hill.

"With respect to those two fellows," he replied, "I knew them when I lived as cook in the family of General Q——, who is a Gallegan: they were sworn friends of the repostero. All the Gallegans in Madrid know each other, whether high or low, makes no difference; there, at least they are all good friends, and assist each other on all imaginable occasions; and if there be a Gallegan domestic in a house, the kitchen is sure to be filled with his countrymen, as the cook frequently knows to his cost, for they generally contrive to eat up any little perquisites which he may have reserved for himself and family."

Somewhat less than halfway down the mountain we reached

a small village. On observing a blacksmith's shop, we stopped, in the faint hope of finding a shoe for the horse, who, for want of one, was rapidly becoming lame. To our great joy we found that the smith was in possession of one single horse-shoe, which some time previously he had found upon the way. This, after undergoing much hammering and alteration, was pronounced by the Gallegan vulcan to be capable of serving in lieu of better; whereupon we again mounted, and slowly continued our descent.

Shortly ere sunset we arrived at Nogales, a hamlet situate in a narrow valley at the foot of the mountain, in traversing which we had spent the day. Nothing could be more pictur-esque than the appearance of this spot; steep hills, thickly clad with groves and forests of chestnuts, surrounded it on every side; the village itself was almost embowered in trees, and close beside it ran a purling brook. Here we found a tolerably large and commodious posada.

I was languid and fatigued, but felt little desire to sleep. Antonio cooked our supper, or rather his own, for I had no appetite. I sat by the door, gazing at the wood-covered heights above me, or on the waters of the rivulet, occasionally listen-ing to the people who lounged about the house, conversing in the country dialect. What a strange tongue is the Gallegan, with its half-singing half-whining accent, and with its con-fused jumble of words from many languages, but chiefly from the Spanish and Portuguese. "Can you understand this conver-sation?" I demanded of Antonio, who had by this time re-joined me. "I cannot, mon maître," he replied; "I have ac-quired at various times a great many words amongst the Gallegan domestics in the kitchens where I have officiated as cook, but am quite unable to understand any long conversation. I have heard the Gallegans say that in no two villages is it spoken in one and the same manner, and that very frequently they do not understand each other. The worst of this language is, that everybody on first hearing it thinks that nothing is more easy than to understand it, as words are continually occurring which he has heard before; but these merely serve to bewilder and puzzle him, causing him to misunderstand every thing that is said; whereas, if he were totally ignorant of the tongue, he would occasionally give a shrewd guess at what was meant, as I myself frequently do when I hear Basque spoken, though the only word which I know of that language is *jaunguicoa*."

As the night closed in I retired to bed, where I remained four or five hours, restless and tossing about, the fever of Leon still clinging to my system. It was considerably past midnight when, just as I was sinking into a slumber, I was aroused by a confused noise in the village, and the glare of lights through the lattice of the window of the room where I lay; presently entered Antonio, half-dressed. "Mon maître," said he, "the grand post from Madrid to Coruña has just arrived in the village, attended by a considerable escort, and an immense number of travellers. The road they say, between here and Lugo, is infested with robbers and Carlists, who are committing all kinds of atrocities; let us, therefore, avail ourselves of the opportunity, and by midday to-morrow we shall find ourselves safe in Lugo." On hearing these words, I instantly sprang out of bed and dressed myself, telling Antonio to prepare the horses with all speed.

We were soon mounted and in the street, amidst a confused throng of men and quadrupeds. The light of a couple of flambeaux, which were borne before the courier, shone on the arms of several soldiers, seemingly drawn up on either side of the road; the darkness, however, prevented me from distinguishing objects very clearly. The courier himself was mounted on a little shaggy pony; before and behind him were two immense portmanteaus, or leather sacks, the ends of which nearly touched the ground. For about a quarter of an hour there was much hubbub, shouting, and trampling, at the end of which period the order was given to proceed. Scarcely had we left the village, when the flambeaux were extinguished, and we were left in almost total darkness; for some time we were amongst woods and trees, as was evident from the rustling of leaves on every side. My horse was very uneasy and neighed fearfully, occasionally raising himself bolt upright. "If your horse is not more quiet, cavalier, we shall be obliged to shoot him," said a voice in an Andalusian accent; "he disturbs the whole cavalcade." "That would be a pity, sergeant," I replied, "for he is a Cordovese by the four sides; he is not used to the ways of this barbarous country." "Oh, he is a Cordovese," said the voice, "vaya, I did not know that; I am from Cordova myself. Pobrecito! let me pat him—yes, I know by his coat that he is my countryman—shoot him, indeed! vaya, I would fain see the Gallegan devil who would dare to harm him. Barbarous country, *io lo creo!* neither oil nor olives, bread nor barley. You have been at Cordova. Vaya; oblige me, cavalier, by taking this cigar."

In this manner we proceeded for several hours, up hill and down dale, but generally at a very slow pace. The soldiers who escorted us from time to time sang patriotic songs, breathing love and attachment to the young queen Isabel, and detestation of the grim tyrant Carlos. One of the stanzas which reached my ears, ran something in the following style,—

> "Don Carlos is a hoary churl,
> Of cruel heart, and cold;
> But Isabel's a harmless girl,
> Of only six years old."

At last the day began to break, and I found myself amidst a train of two or three hundred people, some on foot, but the greater part mounted either on mules or the pony mares: I could not distinguish a single horse except my own and Antonio's. A few soldiers were thinly scattered along the road. The country was hilly, but less mountainous and picturesque than the one which we had traversed the preceding day; it was for the most part partitioned into small fields, which were planted with maize. At the distance of every two or three leagues we changed our escort, at some village where was stationed a detachment. The villages were mostly an assemblage of wretched cabins; the roofs were thatched, dank, and moist, and not unfrequently covered with rank vegetation. There were dunghills before the doors, and no lack of pools and puddles. Immense swine were stalking about, intermingled with naked children. The interior of the cabins corresponded with their external appearance: they were filled with filth and misery.

We reached Lugo about two hours past noon: during the last two or three leagues, I became so overpowered with weariness, the result of want of sleep and my late illness, that I was continually dozing in my saddle, so that I took but little notice of what was passing. We put up at a large posada without the wall of the town, built upon a steep bank, and commanding an extensive view of the country towards the east. Shortly after our arrival, the rain began to descend in torrents, and continued without intermission during the next two days, which was, however, to me but a slight source of regret, as I passed the entire time in bed, and I may also say in slumber. On the evening of the third day I arose.

There was much bustle in the house, caused by the arrival of a family from Coruña; they came in a large jaunting car, escorted by four carabineers. The family was rather numerous, consisting of a father, son, and eleven daughters, the eldest of whom might be about eighteen. A shabby-looking fellow, dressed in a jerkin and wearing a high-crowned hat, attended as domestic. They arrived very wet and shivering, and all seemed very disconsolate, especially the father, who was a well-looking middle-aged man. "Can we be accommodated?" he demanded in a gentle voice of the man of the house; "can we be accommodated in this fonda?"

"Certainly, your worship," replied the other; "our house is large. How many apartments does your worship require for your family?"

"One will be sufficient," replied the stranger.

The host, who was a gouty personage and leaned upon a stick, looked for a moment at the traveller, then at every member of his family, not forgetting the domestic, and, without any farther comment than a slight shrug, led the way to the door of an apartment containing two or three flock beds, and which on my arrival I had objected to as being small, dark, and incommodious; this he flung open, and demanded whether it would serve.

"It is rather small," replied the gentleman; "I think, however, that it will do."

"I am glad of it," replied the host. "Shall we make any preparation for the supper of your worship and family?"

"No, I thank you," replied the stranger, "my own domestic will prepare the slight refreshment we are in need of."

The key was delivered to the domestic, and the whole family ensconced themselves in their apartment: before, however, this was effected, the escort were dismissed, the principal carabineer being presented with a peseta. The man stood surveying the gratuity for about half-a-minute, as it flittered in the palm of his hand; then with an abrupt *Vamos!* he turned upon his heel, and without a word of salutation to any person, departed with the men under his command.

"Who can these strangers be?" said I to the host, as we sat together in a large corridor open on one side, and which occupied the entire front of the house.

"I know not," he replied, "but by their escort I suppose

they are people holding some official situation. They are not of this province, however, and I more than suspect them to be Andalusians."

In a few minutes the door of the apartment occupied by the strangers was opened, and the domestic appeared, bearing a cruise in his hand. "Pray, Señor Patron," demanded he, "where can I buy some oil?"

"There is oil in the house," replied the host, "if you want to purchase any; but if, as is probable, you suppose that we shall gain a cuarto by selling it, you will find some over the way. It is as I suspected," continued the host, when the man had departed on his errand, "they are Andalusians, and are about to make what they call gaspacho, on which they will all sup. Oh, the meanness of these Andalusians! They are come here to suck the vitals of Galicia, and yet envy the poor inn-keeper the gain of a cuarto in the oil which they require for their gaspacho. I tell you one thing, master, when that fellow returns, and demands bread and garlic to mix with the oil, I will tell him there is none in the house: as he bought the oil abroad, so he may the bread and garlic; ay, and the water too, for that matter."

FRANCES ERSKINE INGLIS
CALDERÓN DE LA BARCA

The Interment
of the Infanta and
a Trip to Aranjuez

A SELECTION FROM *The Attaché in Madrid*

*In mid-nineteenth-century Spain the life of society, that is,
court life, was a pale but feverish imitation of what it had been
in preceding centuries. Madrid was the center of a net of
petty intrigue, deadly gossip, and military-political coups*

*which brought down individuals and governments with dread-
ful monotony. The luxurious existence of a few did not conceal but rather set in high relief the traditional poverty of the
Spanish people. The capital, for most visitors unlovely because it was in many ways an un-Spanish city, was dominated
by nobles and aristocrats desperately attempting to live in
the past. Thus, two of its appendages were still of importance.
One was the Escorial, the vast monastery-palace-mausoleum
constructed by Philip II in the sixteenth century thirty miles
from Madrid. The Eighth Wonder of the World it has often
been called in centuries past, and so indeed it may seem today
to our own century, which knows death well. It stands starkly
magnificent (and rich in books and art) at the foot of the
Guadarrama Mountains facing across the stony plain of
Castile toward Madrid. Under the altar of the massive church
within the Escorial is the Pantheon of the Kings of Spain.*

*Thirty miles on the other side of Madrid—toward the
south, of course—is a gayer place, to which kings and queens
went to live, not to die, in the palaces in the verdant valley
of the Tajo—Aranjuez.*

*Fanny Inglis Calderón de la Barca was a Scotswoman who
married a Spanish diplomat and politician, lived in America,
and wrote a fine account of life in Mexico. In the heavy air of
Madrid society she had good reason to hide her authorship
of* The Attaché in Madrid *under the anonymous pretense of
being a young German diplomat.*

THREE DAYS have elapsed since my visit to the Escorial,
and I have not yet thawed. All was on a gigantic scale; the
ceremonies, the building, the cold. The coldness of the day,

one of the most severe we have had in Madrid, was almost un-
bearable within the precincts of the Escorial, but it was a
scene which I can never forget. All my day-dreams of old
Spain were realized, or rather surpassed. I was about to write
you a description of all the pomp and circumstance with
which the poor little scion of royalty was conveyed to the
tombs of her fathers; but an official statement published this
day in the *Gaceta*, is so characteristic and so accurate in its
details, that I think you will find it more curious to read a
translation of it, than were I to give you a less circumstantial
and less accurate account of what I saw.

"Act of the delivery and conveyance of the dead body of
her serene highness the Ynfanta of Spain to the Royal Pantheon of the Escorial." "I, Don Raphael Ramirez de Arellano,
secretary of her majesty, subsecretary of the ministry of grace
and justice, appointed by royal order of the 9th of this month,
to execute as delegate of the minister of that department, the
office of chief notary of these kingdoms, and consequently to
assist at the delivery of the royal body of her serene highness
the Ynfanta of Spain (now in glory), daughter of the most
illustrious sovereigns of Spain, Doña Ysabel II, and Don
Francis of Assissium Maria, born in the royal palace of Madrid
on the 5th day of the present month, and baptised on the
following day, the 6th, by the hands of his excellency, Senor
Don Thomas Yglesias y Barones, patriarch of the Indies, without any pomp or solemnity, but in the manner usual in cases
of necessity:

"Do certify and bear witness: that her royal highness
having died of a natural illness in the said royal palace, at ten
minutes past eleven, on the morning of the 8th, I repaired in
fulfilment of the duties of my office, on the morning of the
9th, to the said royal palace, and saw with respect in one of
the saloons, upon a table, the face entirely exposed, the dead
body of her royal highness, dressed in a robe of white cambric,

richly embroidered and trimmed with lace, and placed upon a plateau of silver.

"Her excellency Doña Maria de Carmen Alvarez, de las Asturias Bohorgues, widowed Marchioness of Povar, grandee of Spain, lady of honor to the queen our lady, and governess of her serene highness Princess of the Asturias, who stood at the head of the royal body, accompanied by the ladies of the royal household, addressed herself in a clear voice to his excellency Señor Don Antonio Agüera y Mollinado, Marquis de los Llanos, mayordomo of the week to her majesty, named by her order, to transport the body to the Pantheon of the Royal Chapel of St. Lorenzo of the Escorial, formerly the monastery of that name, saying to him:

" 'I deliver over to your excellency, in compliance with the order of their majesties, the royal body of her serene highness the Ynfanta of Spain, their august daughter. Does your excellency undertake the charge of it?'

"And the mayordomo of the week, Marquis de los Llanos, replied: 'I do undertake the charge of it.'

"Then the aforesaid marquis addressed the royal body of monteros (*chasseurs*), then and there represented by Don Matthew Madrazo, Don Maximus Merino, Don James Fernandez Gil, and Don Sandalio Villasante, and said:

" 'Monteros of the royal chamber and guard; do you recognize the royal body of her serene highness, the Ynfanta of Spain?'

"The monteros replied: 'Yes, we do recognize it.'

" 'Do you take charge of the body of her royal highness?'

" 'Yes, we do take charge of it.'

"Then the mayordomo of the week, his excellency the Count of Casa Flores, his excellency Don Manuel Rosales, Don Fernando Trujillo, and Don Luis Garcini y Castilla, took up the plateau on which the body of her royal highness was placed, and preceded by the other mayordomos of the week and by the *Gentilhombres de Casa y Boca*, Don Pedro José de Mendoza, Don Francisco Aguirre y Mollinedo, Don José Paspati y Bracho, and Don Pedro Juan Cuenca, the procession continued through the principal gallery to the royal chapel.

"At the door was his excellency the patriarch of the Indies, clad in his semi-pontifical robes, with the chaplains of honor" (whose names are here enumerated), "and the other individuals belonging to the said chapel royal.

"The royal body was placed in the centre of the chapel on an imperial bed, hung and covered with rich stuffs of yellow satin, embroidered in colors, with raised work of silver.

"Two monteros of the royal chamber and guard watched at the head and at the sides, and at the foot of the imperial bed two guards of the queen.

"At the right of the head was placed the standard of the royal brotherhood of the servants of their majesties and highnesses, with two individuals of the same, and in the enclosure of the chapel the corresponding lights.

"The procession surrounding the royal body entoned the hymn *Laudate pueri Dominum*, all holding the lights usual in these ceremonies.

"At half-past eleven the royal chapel was opened for the public, until six in the evening, and remained open the two following days, during which three days an extraordinary concourse of persons assembled to see the royal body, giving unequivocal proofs of sorrow and regret. On the 11th, a solemn mass of the angels was sung in the royal chapel, at which his eminence the Cardinal Archbishop of Toledo officiated in his pontifical vestments, and at which assisted his excellency the patriarch and the chaplains of honor.

"Amongst the numerous concourse of persons who had the entry into the said chapel, were his excellency the *Mayordomo Mayor*, the chiefs of the palace, and the grandees of Spain, lords in waiting on her majesty.

"At eight in the evening, with all necessary precautions and security, the Marquis de los Llanos ordered that the royal body should be placed, and it was placed, in an inner case of lead, covered on the upper part by a glass, the act being performed in the presence of the aforesaid monteros of the royal chamber and guard of various individuals of the royal household, and of the royal corps of the queen's guards.

"The leaden case being placed in an exterior one, lined with silver tissue and golden lace, and the coffin containing the royal body being guarded from that hour as it had hitherto been, the Marquis de los Llanos arrived at the royal chapel at seven, on the morning of the 12th, accompanied by me, and we proceeded to verify and did verify, the identity of the royal body through the crystal.

"His excellency, the patriarch of the Indies, then presented himself in semi-pontifical robes, preceded by the cross of the royal chapel, with the chaplains of honor (here enumerated), and with the corresponding chaplains of the altar, the psalmists, singers, and musicians of the said chapel royal.

"The usual prayers being chanted, the coffin was raised from its burial bed. After being locked, and covered with a cloth and cushion of golden tissue, by the mayordomos de Semana (their names enumerated), and carried by them through the midst of all the assistants to the head of the staircase, where it was received by the lords of the bedchamber of her majesty (Señores, &c. &c.), who delivered it over to the equerries, Don Francisco Villavicencia and Don Gabriel Sanchez del Cid, in order to have it placed in a beautiful *estufa* (a kind of carriage), belonging to the *Caballerizas Reales*, of massive mahogany, all adorned with branches and garlands of artificial flowers, and hangings of white satin, with embroidery and borders, arrows, cords and tassels of gold.

"The coffin being placed there in my presence, in that of the Marquis de los Llanos, and of the individuals belonging to the royal corps of the noble Monteros de Espinosa, above mentioned, the funeral procession set off at eight in the morning, preceded in front by a picquet of cavalry, two trumpeters, the officers riding in two lines, two horses with rich housings, the standards and members of the royal confraternity, the cross of the royal chapel, the clerk, psalmists and singers of the same, the chaplains of honor, lords of the bedchamber and household, mayordomos of the week, two life guards, the carriage containing the body of her royal highness, by the side of which rode four lords of the chamber and household, and two masters of the horse with torches, two monteros of the royal chamber by the coach-steps, and two footmen behind. Behind the carriage followed the Marquis de los Llanos, who, with my assistance, presided over the procession, having on his left his excellency Don Nicholas Louis de Lega, archbishop of Seleucia, abbot of San Ildefonso, the march being closed by a piquet of the queen's guards, under the command of Colonel Don Felix Ortega, with an escort of cavalry, commanded by an officer of equal rank. Don José Maria Colarte; bodies of all the regiments in Madrid being drawn out on parade, under the orders of the military governor of the city.

"In this order the funeral procession arrived at San Antonio de la Florida, amidst a numerous assemblage of people collected in spite of the inclemency of the weather, to witness the funeral ceremony. Here, those persons for whom carriages were prepared, got in, and the procession continued in the same order as before, &c."

Here I shall take leave of the veracious chronicler, whom I have followed so far, because my account could not vie in accuracy with that of the royal secretary, and also because the manners and customs of Spain are so unchanging in certain ceremonials, that it might form a pendant to an old MS. shown me by ——, describing the nuptials of Philip II with Mary of England. But having arrived at San Antonio, where, though

I cannot say that a carriage was *prepared* for me, a place in one was permitted, I found myself forming part of the procession, in a comfortable coach, drawn by four sleek mules, with three other young men, who accompanied the cortège in an official capacity. The morning being bitterly cold, we drew up the windows, wrapped ourselves in our cloaks, ventured to light our cigars, and proceeded, of course at a very slow pace, behind the magnificent car containing the remains of the little Ynfanta.

In the villages of Las Rozas, Galapagar, and what is called the *Escorial de Abajo,* long delays were made. The clergy of the parish churches came out to meet the procession, and again the beautiful psalm, *Laudate pueri Dominum,* was entoned in solemn accents, under the clear blue cold sky. It was dusk long before we arrived at the Escorial, at nearly half-past six. I strained my eyes in the darkness to distinguish this wonderful monument of the stern Catholic monarch, into whose domains we thus entered in the darkness of the night, to deliver up, as it were, to his guardianship an innocent little descendant of his race. It loomed out in the darkness, immense, mysterious, lonely. The snowy crowns of the Guadaramas were distinctly visible. The wind blew fiercely, and sounded like a sad and moaning requiem, proceeding from the everlasting hills. The stars shone out clearly and coldly, through the dark clouds that were blown across their silvery disks. The procession halted.

The Brigadier Purrind, chief of brigade; Moral, commander of the infantry; Velasquez de Velasco, commander of the artillery; and the constituent corporation, came out to meet and receive the body of the princess. The procession moved slowly towards the monastery, and drew up in front of the royal chapel. The two masters of the horse descended the coffin from the hearse, and delivered it to the lords of the royal household, who placed it upon a kind of *estrade,* prepared for its reception under the portico leading to the great entrance of the Spanish monarchs.

Here the scene was most striking; a long procession of chaplains and churchmen, headed by the abbot in his cope, the crucifix borne in front, advanced to meet the body.

Then the chaplain, *Prosecretario*, read in a loud and distinct voice an order from their majesties, transmitted to the abbot by the patriarch of the Indies, in which they communicated to him the death of her serene highness the Ynfanta, desiring that her royal body, now transported to the Escorial, should be deposited with the usual solemnities. The abbot, president of the royal chapel, then demanded of the Marquis de los Llanos whether he were charged to bring the royal body there, which he answered in the affirmative, at the same time delivering to the abbot the order which he had received from the *Mayordomo Mayor* to that effect.

Another schedule was then read by the *Archivero* (keeper of the records), in which King Philip IV had decided a controversy existing between the chapel of the royal palace at Madrid and that of the monastery of San Lorenzo. A new and solemn recognition of the body was then made, and being identified, the abbot, deacon, and subdeacon threw holy water on the corpse, and the solemn music of the church resounded through the lofty vaults: *Sit nomen Domine benedictum, Laudate pueri Dominum*, songs of praise and thanksgiving, suitable to the obsequies of the royal infant, who has exchanged her chance of an earthly crown for the certainty of one of eternal glory. Meanwhile it seemed as if all the winds of heaven were unchained that night, their hoarse voices howling round the massive building, blowing through the vaults, extinguishing the great torches, and moaning in tones that sounded like the wailing of infernal spirits, or of souls in agony.

The procession entered the church, and it required little imagination to believe the whole scene a vision of by-gone ages.

"A hut for myself, a palace for God," said the monarch who designed this glorious pile. I cannot pretend to describe it, for all was indistinct in gloom and grandeur. The blazing lights which yet but faintly illuminated the immense cathedral—the echo of the music, *Beati immaculati in via*—the abbot and priests—grandees and officers in uniform—all this preparation for receiving the remains of an infant who had scarcely opened her eyes on the light, but who was the descendant of a long line of princes—the immense magnitude of every thing in this gigantic temple, making the tallest men dwindle into pigmies by comparison—the whole produced an effect which no time can efface from my memory.

The procession proceeded, bearing the coffin, with all its rich adornings, and placed it upon a monument prepared for its reception in the centre of the church, upon the golden cushion, at the head of which was a royal crown; at each side numerous vases of flowers, and to the right and left eight tapers of white wax. On the high alter burned a huge bronze candelabra, destined exclusively for royal interments, with nine lighted torches. Though the whole edifice was illuminated, it still looked gloomy. When the prayers were concluded, the royal corps of monteros and the queen's guards received the body into their custody, and remained to keep watch over it during the night. I could not with propriety remain, as I would willingly have done, to examine the wonders of the church, so I took one glance at the little upturned waxen face of the Ynfanta, lying in her calm sleep, all unconscious of the royal honors paid her, left the guards to their cold and solemn nightwatch, and followed the procession into the palace.

I must confess that the sight of a spacious tapestried hall, well lighted, at the further end of which was a roaring fire of huge logs of wood, and of a long table covered with smoking dishes, brought me down to real life, and made me forget for a while every consideration but that of the intense cold and hunger from which I was suffering; feelings which had until then been kept in abeyance, probably from a philosophical conclusion that they could not be appeased.

The abbot, archbishop, lords of the bed-chamber, officers of the household, and other dignitaries, took their places with all due etiquette, and I found myself seated between two of my travelling companions, young Z. del V—— and F——, with a smoking turkey as a vis-à-vis. We did all justice to the feast, even while giving an occasional thought to the little princess with her monteros in the cold church. The repast was royal in its profusion, the guests quiet and decorous. The robes of the priests and the brilliant uniforms did not appear out of keeping with the ancient Flemish tapestries, marvellously preserved in their coloring. I felt as if we should hardly have been startled had Philip II with high ruff, black hat and plumes, glided in and assumed his chair of state at the head of the table.

It was late when the numerous party retired to the various apartments assigned to them. I was roused from a deep sleep by the increased fierceness of the wind, and by the tolling of the bells for the dead. The sun was already high in the heavens when all the persons composing the royal cortège were again assembled in the church of San Lorenzo, and together with the city corporation, had taken their seats on the long benches placed on either side of the monument. The Marquis de los Llanos, and the notary occupied two ancient velvet chairs at the head of the coffin—the monteros, royal guards and officers, stood in their respective places.

The snow had hardened in the night, and the sunbeams struggled through the lofty windows, the faint rays nearly extinguished by the blaze of the numerous tapers and torches. Even more wonderful the mighty temple appeared to me than it did on the preceding night. The great organ pealed forth a strain of solemn and triumphant psalmody, accompanying the voices of the choir. The pontifical mass *de los Angeles* was celebrated by the Archbishop of Seleucia, assisted by the royal chaplains. At its conclusion they left the high altar and sur-rounded the sepulchral monument, chanting the antiphon *Juvenes et Virgines*, followed by the psalm *Laudate pueri Dominum de Coelos*, during which the coffin was raised from its temporary resting-place by the four mayordomos, and car-ried to the entrance of the Pantheon, where it was received by the *Gentilhombres*, who carried it down to the second land-ing-place of the stair. There it was delivered to the monteros, and by them placed before the altar, on a tomb erected in the centre of the Pantheon.

Then the exterior was opened, and the Marquis de los Llanos, followed by the royal notary, advanced to identify the corps, declaring it to be that of her royal highness the Ynfanta of Spain, daughter of the illustrious sovereigns of Spain, Doña Ysabel Segunda and Don Francisco de Assis Maria. The same ceremony was performed by all the guards and noblemen, by the archbishop, chaplains, corporation, and in succession by all who were present. After which the Marquis de los Llanos asked aloud:

"Monteros of the royal chamber and guard, do you recog-nize in this corps that of her royal highness the Ynfanta of Spain, which was delivered to you by me in the royal palace of Madrid on the ninth day of this month?"

And the monteros replied, "Si Señor; this is the body of her royal highness the Ynfanta of Spain, which was delivered to us by your excellency, and as such we recognize it."

The same question was put by the notary, and the same an-swer given.

The exterior case of the coffin was then locked, and the key delivered by the Marquis de los Llanos to the abbot president of the royal chapel, with an order from their majesties that the royal corps should remain in the Pantheon, the iron door being locked until their majesties should dispose otherwise. The abbot received the key, and promised to obey faithfully the orders of their majesties. At the same moment a discharge of musketry was fired by the garrison. We reascended the gloomy staircase leading from the sepulchre. The iron doors were closed, and the little princess was left to moulder into dust amongst her royal ancestors. The absurd fancy that she must suffer from the coldness and gloom to which she was abandoned haunted me for hours afterward. . . .

As we drove off, I took one last look at the Escorial, now brilliantly illuminated by the morning sun! Alone in a desert, it can be compared with no surrounding object, unless with the lofty mountains behind it. The embodiment of a grand idea, a great and gloomy mind could alone have accomplished it. I promise myself to return hither in spring, yet it seems to me that winter is the most appropriate time for seeing the Escorial in all its stern gloom and grandeur.

On Wednesday last a diplomatic party was formed to visit Aranjuez, a place almost fabulously beautiful. As the Escorial is the grandest and most gloomy of royal residences, Aranjuez is the most enchanting—a very temple of pleasure. The one is well fitted to be the tomb of the Spanish monarchs; the other to be the theatre of their amusements. The railway, certainly, does not seem a poetical enough mode of approach to these gardens of Armida; but inasmuch as the carriages are comfortable, spacious, and well-arranged, and carry the traveller with the speed of thought over a dusty uninteresting road, they are not to be quarrelled with.

The day was warm, but not sultry; and from the moment of entering Aranjuez, we breathed an atmosphere of flowers. Situated on the left shores of the Tagus, the city itself contains upwards of five thousand inhabitants, though more than twenty thousand are said to be accommodated there in the season, that is, during the queen's visit, which is not expected to take place this year.

Formerly this royal retreat belonged to the knights of Santiago, and was the residence of the grand-masters of the order. Philip II was its first royal owner, and the construction of the palace was begun by his orders, under the direction of Juan de Herrera, a celebrated architect. It was continued during the reigns of Philip V and Ferdinand VI and concluded in that of Charles III. All these sovereigns contributed to the formation and beautifying of the gardens and fountains which embellish Aranjuez; but Charles IV it was who more especially adorned and extended the pleasure-grounds of this his favorite domain. The first sight of the beautiful valley in which Aranjuez lies, fertilized by the waters of the Tagus and Iarama, shows to the traveller like an oasis in the desert, especially as contrasted with the arid and stony country surrounding Madrid.

We took carriages in the village, for it is little more, in spite of its churches, military governor, hospital, theatre, *plaza de toros*, inns, cafés, and post-houses; and driving through the *Calle Larga*, or Long Street, shaded on either side with fine trees, entered the beautiful plaza de San Antonio, leaving on our right the palace with its parterres and waterfalls, and to the left the *Calle de la Reina* and the new garden of Ysabel Segunda; and following the advice of Count G——, who acted as our guide, directed our way to the gardens of the Principe.

In these beautiful gardens stands the pretty palace called the *Casa del Labrador*, the house of the workman, ironically, it is said, on account of the many rare and valuable objects which it contains. It was built by Charles IV, and looks like a pretty country-house, standing in the midst of groves and flower-gardens. It is full of curiosities and objects of art, all of Spanish workmanship. The rooms are long and low-roofed, some very small, but covered with paintings, chiefly by Luca Giordani.

The staircases are narrow, with gilt balustrades. In the first salon, is a long plateau of alabaster, covered with vases and statuettes of alabaster and porphyry; an ingenious clock, with a diamond star to mark the hours—beautiful candelabras, of which the mould was broken, that the form might not be repeated—marble pillars of different colors, &c. All is jasper and porphyry, and curious marbles and precious stones; a rare and costly bijou.

We made, however, rather a hurried inspection of the numerous apartments, and went out to walk in the gardens of the Principe, several miles in circumference, a labyrinth of the most brilliant and exquisite flowers of every color, shaded by the loftiest and noblest trees, brought from every quarter of the world, and flourishing in these favored regions as in their native soils. We particularly admired the gigantic poplars, and cedars which five men can scarcely span.

The fragrance of the flowers is wonderful, an essence of roses and jasmine. Notwithstanding their immense extent, these gardens are kept in perfect order. A strong dyke of masonwork defends them from the incursions of the Tagus; every species of fruit is cultivated within their precincts; clear tanks, shady islands, fountains of great architectural beauty, every where refresh the eye, and form a scene of constant and pleasing variety.

Towards mid-day the sun became oppressive, in spite of trees and fountains; and Mesdames —— proposed that we should return to our carriages, and drive to the palace in the *Jardin de la Ysla*. The Tagus, on whose banks this beautiful palace stands, was now a dark muddy color, but the waterfalls into which it forms in front of the palace, were clear as crystal. It is a charming residence; the rooms lofty and spacious—the views from the windows, one maze of groves and fountains, and flowers of the brightest colors. This extreme brightness of tint is remarkable, and was observed upon by all our party.

There is something tropical in the color. The roses are redder, the carnations a deeper crimson, the trees a more flashing green, than can be seen elsewhere.

The queen's sleeping apartments called forth general admiration, especially her dressing-room, fitted up with white Valencian silk, embroidered all over with bunches of pink roses. The carving of the bed, the elegance of the toilette-tables, were all commented on. Her Majesty's *Despacho*, where she receives her ministers, is a charming room, looking out upon the river; and the throne-room is a noble apartment. The furniture is entirely composed of dark ruby velvet and gold; chairs, sofas, curtains, &c. Fine paintings, as in the Casa del Labrador, adorn the roofs; chiefly by the indefatigable Luca Giordani. The chapel is handsome—the altar-piece a fine Annunciation by Bayen, a Spanish artist. "In the palaces of the Spanish monarchs," as Count A—— observed, "it is not so much the grandeur of the furniture or the size of the apartments that we admire; it is the intrinsic value and rarity of the objects which they contain; the fine paintings, the Flemish tapestries, the inlaid tables, the precious stones, so much that is rich and ancient and rare, lavished in every direction with an unsparing hand."

Here, however, one must always leave art for nature, though it would seem that both have striven together in amicable contest. But the "Garden of the Island" is the crowning charm of Aranjuez. The island is formed by the junction of the river with a canal. The fabled gardens of Armida, which inevitably present themselves to the imagination in wandering through this scene of beauty, cannot have had a fairer model than this, even in the mind of the poet.

The delicious shade of the lofty and spreading trees, impervious to the fiercest rays of the sun—the temples, fountains, and marble statues—the distant sound of the waterfall, the songs of myriads of birds, undisturbed inhabitants of these groves, the exquisite fragrance of the atmosphere,—every thing that can charm the senses is united here, to a degree that is almost overpowering. I wandered away from our party, who, tired of walking, had seated themselves in the temple beside the great fountain, agreeing to meet them at the house of S——a, where we were to adjourn before our departure.

Nothing could be more oppressive than the stillness. Not a sound but the murmuring water, and the songs of the birds. Turning the corner of a shady alley, I came upon so pretty a picture, that I would gladly have made a sketch of it. A beautiful boy of about four years old, brown, and with the eyes and hair of Murillo's children, was lying fast asleep with his head upon the knees of a grave little girl about three years older, seated upon the grass, by the margin of a dry stone fountain, and busily engaged in making up little bouquets of wild roses and corn-flowers. A man was mowing the grass at a little distance. Both children, though dark as gypsies, bare-legged and bare-footed, were eminently handsome, and had so noble an air, that one might have fancied them a couple of little Moorish captives, of the race of Boabdil.

The sun had set, and a soft breeze was rippling the waters of the Tagus, when I left these enchanted gardens, and made my way to the house of S——a, in time to partake of the refreshments which he had prepared for our party, whom I found seated before a feast of strawberries, purple grapes, and champagne—ices, and iced beverages of every description. It was dusk when we bid adieu to this paradise, and returned to the railroad and scenes of common life. I recommend all *nouveaux mariés* to take a house at Aranjuez in the month of May. The families from Madrid, however, who have country-seats there, complain of it as being extremely dull. Besides it is now decided that the queen will not visit Aranjuez this summer—a great disappointment to the residents. She intends going to La

Granja, the Spanish Versailles—and Count A—— has sent there to secure lodgings. Already the heat begins to be felt at Aranjuez; in a short time it will be sultry.

Although it is probable that a long residence there might cloy upon the senses, proving only that we are no longer fitted to pastoralize in Arcadia, I mark down this day in rose-color upon the tablets of my memory, as I do that spent in the Escorial in inky black; yet for a continuance, I should prefer to live in the gloomy precincts of the Escorial, but surrounded by mountains and with bracing air, rather than in this monotony of beauty and sweetness.

JOHN HAY

A Victorian Yankee Confronts Castile

A SELECTION FROM *Castilian Days*

*Born in Indiana in 1838 and educated at Brown, John Hay was
a writer, lawyer, businessman, and diplomat who capped a
successful career by serving as Secretary of State for Mc-
Kinley and Theodore Roosevelt.*

*Hay was clear-headed, cultivated, and assured; a substantial
American who believed in law and order at home and abroad.
Perhaps he was too assured to enjoy Spain, although he understood it remarkably well. Certainly he viewed that country
with considerable distaste during the year which he spent there*

as a young secretary in the U.S. legation. His impressions of his stay, published under the carefree title, Castilian Days, *are a cool, mature dissection of Spanish mores and monuments. Not that he saw only bad in Spain; Hay was no fool. But he was a first-class Anglophile and United States-phile, and it is fair to say that some of Hay's judgments on Spain and her history— on Philip II, for example—illustrate the Spanish philosopher Santayana's mot concerning "the infinitely closed mind of the nineteenth-century Masonic liberal." ("Thanks be to God," Hay wrote, "who has given us the victory, the English race is now incapable of making a new cathedral or a new king. Let us not in our safe egotism deny to others the possibility of like improvements.")*

In 1870 Madrid society had no more point, and probably less, than it had had in the time of Señora Calderón de la Barca in the 1850's. But the diplomatic whirl was not dull, for a time, for a young American, and while Hay had hard, and frequently merited, words to say against Spanish political and religious leaders and practices, he appreciated the character of Spaniards and of past Spanish architecture and painting. Tauromachy (bullfighting, that is) he allowed he did not comprehend, nor wish to, although one may detect faint signs in his writing that in his rejection of the corrida *he was struggling with his darker nature. But he was overwhelmed by the treasures of the Prado, and there is no more convincing statement of the glories heaped up in that building in Madrid than the tribute by the young man from Indiana.*

MADRID is a capital with malice aforethought. Usually the seat of government is established in some important town from the force of circumstances. Some cities have an attraction too powerful for the Court to resist. There is no capital of England possible but London. Paris is the heart of France. Rome is the predestined capital of Italy in spite of the wandering flirtations its varying governments in different centuries have carried on with Ravenna, or Naples, or Florence. You can imagine no Residenz for Austria but the Kaiserdstadt,—the gemüthliche Wien. But there are other capitals where men have arranged things and consequently bungled them. The great Czar Peter slapped his Imperial Court down on the marshy shore of the Neva, where he could look westward into civilization and watch with the jealous eye of an intelligent barbarian the doings of his betters. Washington is another specimen of the cold-blooded handiwork of the capital builders. We will think nothing less of the *clarum et venerabile nomen* of its founder if we admit he was human, and his building the seat of government nearer to Mount Vernon than Mount Washington sufficiently proves this. But Madrid more plainly than any other capital shows the traces of having been set down and properly brought up by the strong hand of a paternal government; and like children with whom the same regimen has been followed, it presents in its maturity a curious mixture of lawlessness and insipidity.

Its greatness was thrust upon it by Philip II. Some premonitory symptoms of the dangerous honor that awaited it had been seen in preceding reigns. Ferdinand and Isabella occasionally set up their pilgrim tabernacle on the declivity that overhangs the Manzanares. Charles V found the thin, fine air comforting to his gouty articulations. But Philip II made it his court. It seems hard to conceive how a king who had his choice of Lisbon, with its glorious harbor and unequalled communications; Seville, with its delicious climate and natural beauty; and Salamanca and Toledo, with their wealth of tradition, splendor of architecture, and renown of learning, should have chosen this barren mountain for his home, and the seat of his Empire. But when we know this monkish king we wonder no longer. He chose Madrid simply because it was cheerless and bare and of ophthalmic ugliness. The royal kill-joy delighted in having the dreariest capital on earth. After a while there seemed to him too much life and humanity about Madrid, and he built the Escorial, the grandest ideal of majesty and *ennui* that the world has ever seen. This vast mass of granite has somehow acted as an anchor that has held the capital fast moored at Madrid through all succeeding years.

It was a dreary and somewhat shabby court for many reigns. The great kings who started the Austrian dynasty were too busy in their world-conquest to pay much attention to beautifying Madrid, and their weak successors, sunk in ignoble pleasures, had not enough energy to indulge the royal folly of building. When the Bourbons came down from France there was a little flurry of construction under Philip V, but he never finished his palace in the Plaza del Oriente, and was soon absorbed in constructing his castle in cloud-land on the heights of La Granja. The only real ruler the Bourbons ever gave to Spain was Charles III, and to him Madrid owes all that it has of architecture and civic improvement. Seconded by his able and liberal minister, Count Aranda, who was educated abroad, and so free from the trammels of Spanish ignorance and superstition, he rapidly changed the ignoble town into something like a city. The greater portion of the public buildings date from this active beneficent reign. It was he who laid out the walks and promenades which give to Madrid almost its only outward attraction. The Picture Gallery, which is the shrine of all pilgrims of taste, was built by him for a Museum of Natural Science. In nearly all that a stranger cares to see, Madrid is not an older city than Boston.

There is consequently no glory of tradition here. There are no cathedrals. There are no ruins. There is none of that mysterious and haunting memory that peoples the air with spectres in quiet towns like Ravenna and Nuremberg. And there is little of that vast movement of humanity that possesses and bewilders you in San Francisco and New York. . . .

There is nothing indigenous in Madrid. There is no marked local color. It is a city of Castile, but not a Castilian city, like Toledo, which girds its graceful waist with the golden Tagus, or like Segovia, fastened to its rock in hopeless shipwreck.

But it is not for this reason destitute of an interest of its own. By reason of its exceptional history and character it is the best point in Spain to study Spanish life. It has no distinctive traits itself, but it is a patchwork of all Spain. Every province of the Peninsula sends a contingent to its population. The Gallicians hew its wood and draw its water; the Asturian women nurse its babies at their bosoms, and fill the promenades with their brilliant costumes; the Valentians carpet its halls and quench its thirst with orgeat of chufas; in every street you shall see the red bonnet and sandalled feet of the Catalan; in every *café*, the shaven face and red-tail chignon of the Majo of Andalusia. If it have no character of its own, it is a mirror where all the faces of the Peninsula may sometimes be seen. It is like the mockingbird of the West, that has no song, and yet makes the woods ring with every note they have ever heard.

Madrid is one of those cities where strangers fear the climate less than residents. Nothing is too bad for the Castilian to say of his native air. Before you have been a day in the city some kind soul will warn you against everything you have been in the habit of doing as leading to sudden and severe death in this subtle air. You will hear in a dozen different tones the favorite proverb which may be translated,—

> *The air of Madrid is as sharp as a knife,—*
> *It will spare a candle and blow out your life;*

141

and another where the truth, as in many Spanish proverbs, is sacrificed to the rhyme, saying that the climate is *tres meses invierno y nueve infierno,*—three months winter and nine months tophet. At the first coming of the winter frosts the genuine son of Madrid gets out his capa, the national full round cloak, and never leaves it off until late in the hot spring days. They have a way of throwing one corner over the left shoulder, so that a bright strip of gay lining falls outward and pleasantly relieves the sombre monotony of the streets. In this way the face is completely covered by the heavy woolen folds, only the eye being visible under the sombrero. The true Spaniard breathes no out-of-doors air all winter except through his cloak, and they stare at strangers who go about with uncovered faces enjoying the brisk air as if they were lunatics. But what makes the custom absurdly incongruous is that the women have no such terror of fresh air. While the hidalgo goes smothered in his wrappings his wife and daughter wear nothing on their necks and faces but their pretty complexions, and the gallant breeze, grateful for this generous confidence, repays them in roses. I have sometimes fancied that in this land of traditions this difference might have arisen in those days of adventure when the cavaliers had good reasons for keeping their faces concealed, while the señoras, we are bound to believe, have never done anything for which their own beauty was not the best excuse.

Nearly all there is of interest in Madrid consists in the faces and the life of its people. There is but one portion of the city which appeals to the tourist's ordinary set of emotions. This is the old Moors' quarter,—the intricate jumble of streets and places on the western edge of the town, overlooking the bankrupt river. Here is St. Andrew's, the parish church where Isabella the Catholic and her pious husband used to offer their stiff and dutiful prayers. Behind it a market-place of the most primitive kind runs precipitately down to the Street of Segovia, at such an angle that you wonder the turnips and carrots can ever be brought to keep their places on the rocky slope. If you will wander through the dark alleys and hilly streets of this quarter when twilight is softening the tall tenement-houses to a softer purpose, and the doorways are all full of gossiping groups, and here and there in the little courts you can hear the tinkling of a guitar and the drone of ballads, and see the idlers lounging by the fountains, and everywhere against the purple sky the crosses of old convents, while the evening air is musical with slow chimes from the full-arched belfries, it will not be hard to imagine you are in the Spain you have read and dreamed of. And, climbing out of this labyrinth of slums, you pass under the gloomy gates that lead to the Plaza Mayor. This once magnificent square is now as squalid and forsaken as the Place Royale of Paris, though it dates from a period comparatively recent. The mind so instinctively revolts at the contemplation of those orgies of priestly brutality which have made the very name of this place redolent with a fragrance of scorched Christians, that we naturally assign it an immemorial antiquity. But a glance at the booby face of Philip III on his round-bellied charger in the centre of the square will remind us that this place was built at the same time the Mayflower's passengers were laying the massive foundations of the great Republic. The Autos-da-Fe, the plays of Lope de Vega, and the bull-fights went on for many years with impartial frequency under the approving eyes of royalty, which occupied a convenient balcony in the Panaderia, that over-dressed building with the two extinguisher towers. Down to a period disgracefully near us those balconies were occupied by the dull-eyed, pendulous-lipped tyrants who have sat on the throne of St. Ferdinand, while there in the spacious court below the varied sports went on,—to-day a comedy of Master Lope, to-morrow the gentle and joyous slaying of bulls, and the next day, with greater pomp and ceremony, with banners hung

143

from the windows, and my Lord the King surrounded by his women and his courtiers in their bravest gear, and the august presence of the chief priests and their idol in the form of wine and wafers,—the judgment and fiery sentence of the thinking men of Spain. . . .

The movement of life and growth is bearing the population gradually away from that dark mediaeval Madrid of the Catholic kings through the Puerta del Sol to the airy heights beyond, and the new, fresh quarter built by the philosopher Bourbon Charles III is becoming the most important part of the city. I think we may be permitted to hope that the long reign of savage faith and repression is broken at last, and that this abused and suffering people is about to enter into its rightful inheritance of modern freedom and progress.

The Plaza de Toros stands just outside the monumental gate of the Alcalá. It is a low, squat, prison-like circus of stone, stuccoed and whitewashed, with no pretence or ornament of architectural effect. There is no nonsense whatever about it. It is built for the killing of bulls and for no other purpose. Around it, on a day of battle, you will find encamped great armies of the lower class of Madrileños, who being at financial ebb-tide, cannot pay to go in. But they come all the same, to be in the enchanted neighborhood, to hear the shouts and roars of the favored ones within, and to seize any possible occasion for getting in. Who knows? A caballero may come out and give them his check. An English lady may become disgusted and go home, taking away numerous lords whose places will be vacant. The sky may fall, and they may catch four reals' worth of larks. It is worth taking the chances.

One does not soon forget the first sight of the full coliseum. In the centre is the sanded arena, surrounded by a high barrier. Around this rises the graded succession of stone benches for the people; then numbered seats for the connoisseurs; and above a row of boxes extending around the circle. The building holds, when full, some fourteen thousand persons; and there is rarely any vacant space. For myself I can say that what I vainly strove to imagine in the coliseum at Rome, and in the more solemn solitude of the amphitheatres of Capua and Pompeii, came up before me with the vividness of life on entering the bull-ring of Madrid. This, and none other, was the classic arena. This was the crowd that sat expectant, under the blue sky, in the hot glare of the South, while the doomed captives of Dacia or the sectaries of Judea commended their souls to the gods of the Danube, or the Crucified of Galilee. Half the sand lay in the blinding sun. Half the seats were illuminated by the fierce light. The other half was in shadow, and the dark crescent crept slowly all the afternoon across the arena as the sun declined in the west.

It is hard to conceive a more brilliant scene. The women put on their gayest finery for this occasion. In the warm light, every bit of color flashes out, every combination falls naturally into its place. I am afraid the luxuriance of hues in the dress of the fair Iberians would be considered shocking in Broadway, but in the vast frame and broad light of the Plaza the effect was very brilliant. Thousands of party-colored paper fans are sold at the ring. The favorite colors are the national red and yellow, and the fluttering of these broad, bright disks of color is dazzlingly attractive. There is a gayety of conversation, a quick fire of repartee, shouts of recognition and salutation, which altogether make up a bewildering confusion.

The weary young water-men scream their snow-cold refreshment. The orange-men walk with their gold-freighted baskets along the barrier, and throw their oranges with the most marvellous skill and certainty to people in distant boxes or benches. They never miss their mark. They will throw over the heads of a thousand people a dozen oranges into the out-stretched hands of customers, so swiftly that it seems like one line of gold from the dealer to the buyer.

At length the blast of a trumpet announces the clearing of the ring. The idlers who have been lounging in the arena are swept out by the *alguaciles,* and the hum of conversation gives way to an expectant silence. When the last loafer has reluctantly retired, the great gate is thrown open, and the procession of the *toreros* enters. They advance in a glittering line: first the marshals of the day, then the picadors on horseback, then the matadors on foot surrounded each by his quadrille of *chulos.* They walk towards the box which holds the city fathers, under whose patronage the show is given, and formally salute the authority. This is all very classic, also, recalling the *Ave Caesar, morituri,* etc. of the gladiators. It lacks, however, the solemnity of the Roman salute, from those splendid fellows who would never all leave the arena alive. A bull-fighter is sometimes killed, it is true, but the percentage of deadly danger is scarcely enough to make a spectator's heart beat as the bedizened procession comes flashing by in the sun.

The municipal authority throws the bowing alguacil a key, which he catches in his hat, or is hissed if he misses it. With this he unlocks the door through which the bull is to enter, and then scampers off with undignified haste through the opposite entrance. There is a bugle flourish, the door flies open, and the bull rushes out, blind with the staring light, furious with rage, trembling in every limb. This is the most intense moment of the day. The glorious brute is the target of twelve thousand pairs of eyes. There is a silence as of death, while every one waits to see his first movement. He is doomed from the beginning; the curtain has risen on a three-act tragedy, which will surely end with his death, but the incidents which are to fill the interval are all unknown. The minds and eyes of all that vast assembly know nothing for the time but the movements of that brute. He stands for an instant recovering his senses. He has been shot suddenly out of the darkness into that dazzling light. He sees around him a sight such as he never confronted before,—a wall of living faces lit up by thousands of staring eyes. He does not dwell long upon this, however; in his pride and anger he sees a nearer enemy. The horsemen have taken position near the gate, where they sit motionless as burlesque statues, their long ashen spears, iron-tipped, in rest, their wretched nags standing blindfolded, with trembling knees, and necks like dromedaries, not dreaming of their near fate. The bull rushes, with a snort, at the nearest one. The picador holds firmly, planting his spear-point in the shoulder of the brute. Sometimes the bull flinches at this sharp and sudden punishment, and the picador, by a sudden turn to the left, gets away unhurt. Then there is applause for the torero and hisses for the bull. Some indignant amateurs go so far as to call him cow, and to inform him that he is the son of his mother. But oftener he rushes in, not caring for the spear, and with one toss of his sharp horns tumbles horse and rider in one heap against the barrier and upon the sand. The *capeadores*, the cloak-bearers, come fluttering around and divert the bull from his prostrate victims. The picador is lifted to his feet,—his iron armor not permitting him to rise without help,—and the horse is rapidly scanned to see if his wounds are immediately mortal. If not, the picador mounts again, and provokes the bull to another rush. A horse will usually endure two or three attacks before dying. Sometimes a single blow from in front pierces the heart, and the blood spouts forth in a cataract. In this case the picador hastily dismounts, and the bridle and saddle are stripped in an instant from the dying brute. If a bull is energetic and rapid in execution, he will clear the arena in a few moments. He rushes at one horse after another, tears them open with his terrible "spears" ("horns" is a word never used in the ring), and sends them madly galloping over the arena, trampling out their gushing bowels as they fly. The assistants watch their opportunity, from time to time, plug up their gaping rents with tow, and sew them roughly up for another sally. It is incredible to see what these poor creatures will endure,— carrying their riders at a lumbering gallop over the ring, when their thin sides seem empty of entrails. Sometimes the bull comes upon the dead body of a horse he has killed. The smell of blood and the unmoving helplessness of the victim excite him to the highest pitch. He gores and tramples the carcass, and tosses it in the air with evident enjoyment, until diverted by some living tormentor. . . .

The second act is the play of the *banderilleros*, the flag-men. They are beautifully dressed and superbly built fellows, principally from Andalusia, got up precisely like Figaro in the opera. Theirs is the most delicate and graceful operation of the bull-fight. They take a pair of barbed darts, with little banners fluttering at their ends, and provoke the bull to rush at them. At the instant he reaches them, when it seems nothing can save them, they step aside and plant the *banderillas* in the neck of the bull. If the bull has been cowardly and sluggish, and the spectators have called for "fire," darts are used filled with detonating powder at the base, which explodes in the flesh of the bull. He dances and skips like a kid or a colt in his agony, which is very diverting to the Spanish mind. A prettier conceit is that of confining small birds in paper cages, which come apart when the banderilla is planted, and set the little fluttering captives free.

Decking the bull with these torturing ornaments is the last stage in the apprenticeship of the chulo, before he rises to the dignity of the matador, or killer. The matadors themselves on special occasions think it no derogation from their dignity to act as banderilleros. But they usually accompany the act with some exaggeration of difficulty that reaps for them a harvest of applause. Frascuelo sits in a chair and plants the irritating bannerets. Lagartijo lays his handkerchief on the ground and stands upon it while he coifs the bull. A performance which never fails to bring down the house is for the torero to await the rush of the bull, and when the bellowing monster comes at him with winking eyes and lowered head, to put his slippered foot between the horns, and vault lightly over his back.

These chulos exhibit the most wonderful skill and address in evading the assault of the bull. They can almost always trick him by waving their cloaks a little out of the line of their flight. Sometimes, however, the bull runs straight at the man, disregarding the flag, and if the distance is great to the barrier the danger is imminent; for swift as these men are, the bulls are swifter. Once I saw the bull strike the torero at the instant he vaulted over the barrier. He fell sprawling some distance the other side, safe, but terribly bruised and stunned. As soon as he could collect himself he sprang into the arena again, looking very seedy; and the crowd roared, "Saved by a miracle." I could but think of Basilio, who, when the many cried, "A miracle," answered, "Industria! Industria!" But these bullfighters are all very pious, and glad to curry favor with the saints by attributing every success to their intervention. The famous matador, Paco Montes, fervently believed in an amulet he carried, and in the invocation of Our Lord of the True Cross. He called upon this special name in every tight place, and while other people talked of his luck he stoutly affirmed it was his faith that saved him; often he said he saw the veritable picture of the Passion coming down between him and the bull, in answer to his prayers. At every bull-ring there is a little chapel in the refreshment-room where these devout ruffians can toss off a prayer or two in the intervals of work. A priest is always on hand with a consecrated wafer, to visa the torero's passport who has to start suddenly for Paradise. It is not exactly regular, but the ring has built many churches and endowed many chapels, and must not be too rigidly regarded. In many places the chief boxes are reserved for the clergy, and prayers are hurried through an hour earlier on the day of combat.

The final act is the death of the bull. It must come at last. His exploits in the early part of his career afford to the amateur some indication of the manner in which he will meet his end. If he is a generous, courageous brute, with more heart than brains, he will die gallantly and be easily killed. But if he has shown reflection, forethought, and that saving quality of the oppressed, suspicion, the matador has a serious work before him. The bull is always regarded from this objective standpoint. The more power of reason the brute has, the worse opinion the Spaniard has of him. A stupid creature who rushes blindly on the sword of the matador is an animal after his own heart. But if there be one into whose brute brain some glimmer of the awful truth has come,—and this sometimes happens,— if he feels the solemn question at issue between him and his enemy, if he eyes the man and not the flag, if he refuses to be fooled by the waving lure, but keeps all his strength and all his faculties for his own defence, the soul of the Spaniard rises up in hate and loathing. He calls on the matador to kill him any way. If he will not rush at the flag, the crowd shouts for the demi-lune; and the noble brute is houghed from behind, and your soul grows sick with shame of human nature, at the hellish glee with which they watch him hobbling on his severed legs.

This seldom happens. The final act is usually an admirable study of coolness and skill against brute force. When the banderillas are all planted, and the bugles sound for the third time, the matador, the *espada*, the sword, steps forward with a modest consciousness of distinguished merit, and makes a brief speech to the corregidor, offering in honor of the good city of Madrid to kill the bull. He turns on his heel, throws his hat by a dexterous back-handed movement over the barrier, and advances, sword and cape in hand, to where his noble enemy awaits him. The bull appears to recognize a more serious foe than any he has encountered. He stops short and eyes the new-comer curiously. It is always an impressive picture: the tortured, maddened animal, whose thin flanks are palpitating with his hot breath, his coat one shining mass of blood from the darts and the spear-thrusts, his massive neck still decked as in mockery with the fluttering flags, his fine head and muzzle seeming sharpened by the hour's terrible experience, his formidable horns crimsoned with onset; in front of this fiery bulk of force and courage, the slight, sinewy frame of the killer, whose only reliance is on his coolness and his intellect. I never saw a matador come carelessly to his work. He is usually pale and alert. He studies the bull for a moment with all his eyes. He waves the blood-red *engaño*, or lure, before his face. If the bull rushes at it with his eyes shut the work is easy. He has only to select his own stroke and make it. But if the bull is jealous and sly, it requires the most careful management to kill him. The disposition of the bull is developed by a few rapid passes of the red flag. This must not be continued too long: the tension of the nerves of the auditory will not bear trifling. I remember one day the crowd was aroused to fury by a bugler from the adjoining barracks playing retreat at the moment of decision. All at once the matador seizes the favorable instant. He poised his sword as the bull rushes upon him. The point enters just between the left shoulder and the spine; the long blade glides in up to the hilt. The bull reels and staggers and dies.

Sometimes the matador severs the vertebrae. The effect is like magic. He lays the point of his sword between the bull's horns, as lightly as a lady who touches her cavalier with her fan, and he falls dead as a stone.

If the blow is a clean, well-delivered one, the enthusiasm of the people is unbounded. Their approval comes up in a thunderous shout of, "Well done! *Valiente! Viva!*" A brown shower of cigars rains on the sand. The victor gathers them up: they fill his hands, his pockets, his hat. He gives them to his friends, and the aromatic shower continues. Hundreds of hats are flung into the ring. He picks them up and shies them back to their shouting owners. Sometimes a dollar is mingled with the flying compliments; but the enthusiasm of the Spaniard rarely carries him so far as that. For ten minutes after a good *estocada*, the matador is the most popular man in Spain.

But the trumpets sound again, the door of the Toril flies open, another bull comes rushing out, and the present interest quenches the past. The play begins again, with its sameness of purpose and its infinite variety of incident.

As a general thing it is well to distrust a Spaniard's superlatives. He will tell you that his people are the most amiable in the world, but you will do well to carry your revolver into the interior. He will say there are no wines worth drinking but the Spanish, but you will scarcely forswear Clicquot and Yquem on the mere faith of his assertion. A distinguished general once gravely assured me that there was no literature in the world at all to be compared with the productions of the Castilian mind. All others, he said, were but pale imitations of Spanish masterwork. Now, though you may be shocked at learning such unfavorable facts of Shakespeare and Goethe and Hugo, you will hardly condemn them to an Auto da fé, on the testimony even of a grandee of Spain.

But when a Spaniard assures you that the picture gallery of Madrid is the finest in the world, you may believe him without reserve. He probably does not know what he is talking about. He may never have crossed the Pyrenees. He has no dream of the glories of Dresden, or Florence, or the Louvre. It is even possible that he has not seen the matchless collection he is boasting of. He crowns it with a sweeping superlative simply because it is Spanish. But the statement is nevertheless true.

The reason of this is found in that gigantic and overshadowing fact which seems to be an explanation of everything in Spain,—the power and the tyranny of the House of Austria. The period of the vast increase of Spanish dominion coincided with that of the meridian glory of Italian art. The conquest of Granada was finished as the divine child Raphael began to meddle with his father's brushes and pallets, and before his short life ended Charles, Burgess of Ghent, was Emperor and King. The dominions he governed and transmitted to his son embraced Spain, the Netherlands, Franche-Comté, the Milanese, Naples, and Sicily; that is to say, those regions where art in that age and the next attained its supreme development. He was also lord of the New World, whose inexhaustible mines poured into the lap of Europe a constant stream of gold. Hence came the riches and the leisure necessary to art.

Charles V, as well as his great contemporary and rival, Francis I, was a munificent protector of art. He brought from Italy and Antwerp some of the most perfect products of their immortal masters. He was the friend and patron of Titian, and when, weary of the world and its vanities, he retired to the lonely monastery of Yuste to spend in devout contemplation the evening of his days, the most precious solace of his solitude was that noble canvas of the great Venetian, where Charles and Philip are borne, in penitential guise and garb, on luminous clouds into the visible glory of the Most High.

These two great kings made a good use of their unbounded opportunities. Spain became illuminated with the glowing canvases of the incomparable Italians. The opening up of the New World beyond seas, the meteoric career of European and African conquest in which the Emperor had won so much land and glory, had given an awakening shock to the intelligent youth of Spain, and sent them forth in every avenue of enterprise. This jealously patriotic race, which had remained locked up by the mountains and the seas for centuries, started suddenly out, seeking adventures over the earth. The mind of Spain seemed suddenly to have brightened and developed like that of her great King, who, in his first tourney at Valladolid, wrote with proud sluggishness *Nondum*—not yet—on his maiden shield, and a few years later in his young maturity adopted the legend of arrogant hope and promise,—*Plus Ultra*. There were two emigrations of the young men of Spain, eastward and westward. The latter went for gold and material conquest into the American wilds; and the former, led by the sacred love of art, to that land of beauty and wonder, then, now, and always the spiritual shrine of all people,—Italy. . . .

There was no artist so great but he was honored by the commands of these lords of the two worlds. They thus formed in their various palaces, pleasure-houses, and cloisters a priceless collection of pictures produced in the dawn of the Spanish and the triumphant heyday of Italian genius. Their frivolous successors lost provinces and kingdoms, honor and prestige, but they never lost their royal prerogative nor their taste for the arts. They consoled themselves for the slings and arrows of outrageous fortune by the delights of sensual life, and imagined they preserved some distant likeness to their great forerunners by encouraging and protecting Velazquez and Lope de Vega and other intellectual giants of that decaying age. So while, as the result of a vicious system of kingly and spiritual thraldom, the intellect of Spain was forced away from its legitimate channels of thought and action, under the shadow of the royal prerogative, which survived the genuine power of the older kings, art flourished and bloomed, unsuspected and unpersecuted by the coward jealousy of courtier and monk.

The palace and the convent divided the product of those marvellous days. Amid all the poverty of the failing state, it was still the king and clergy who were best able to appropriate the works of genius. This may have contributed to the decay of art. The immortal canvases passed into oblivion in the *salons* of palaces and the cells of monasteries. Had they been scattered over the land and seen by the people they might have kept alive the spark that kindled their creators. But exclusiveness is inevitably followed by barrenness. When the great race of Spanish artists ended, these matchless works were kept in the safe obscurity of palaces and religious establishments. History was working in the interests of this Museum. The pictures were held by the clenched dead hand of the church and the throne. They could not be sold or distributed. They made the dark places luminous, patiently biding their time.

It was long enough coming, and it was a despicable hand that brought them into the light. Ferdinand VII thought his palace would look fresher if the walls were covered with French paper, and so packed all the pictures off to the empty building on the Prado, which his grandfather had built for a museum. As soon as the glorious collection was exposed to the gaze of the world, its incontestable merit was at once recognized. Especially were the works of Velazquez, hitherto almost an unknown name in Europe, admired and appreciated. Ferdinand, finding he had done a clever thing unawares, began to put on airs and *poser* for a patron of art. The gallery was still further immensely enriched on the exclaustration of the monasteries, by the hidden treasures of the Escorial, and other spoils of mortmain. And now, as a collection of masterpieces, it has no equal in the world.

A few figures will prove this. It contains more than two thousand pictures already catalogued,—all of them worth a place on the walls. Among these there are ten by Raphael, forty-three by Titian, thirty-four by Tintoret, twenty-five by Paul Veronese. Rubens has the enormous contingent of sixty-four. Of Teniers, whose works are sold for fabulous sums for the square inch, this extraordinary museum possesses no less than sixty finished pictures,—the Louvre considers itself rich with fourteen. So much for a few of the foreigners. Among the Spaniards the three greatest names could alone fill a gallery. There are sixty-five Velazquez, forty-six Murillos, and fifty-eight Riberas. Compare these figures with those of any other gallery in existence, and you will at once recognize the hopeless superiority of this collection. It is not only the greatest collection in the world, but the greatest than can ever be made until this is broken up. . . .

There is, in this glorious temple, enough to fill the least enthusiastic lover of art with delight and adoration for weeks and months together. If one knew he was to be blind in a year, like the young musician in Auerbach's exquisite romance, I know of no place in the world where he could garner up so precious a store of memories for the days of darkness, memories that would haunt the soul with so divine a light of consolation, as in that graceful Palace of the Prado.

ARCHER M. HUNTINGTON

The Emperor's Retreat

A SELECTION FROM
A Note-Book in Northern Spain

*Charles V, Sacred, Cesarean Majesty, Emperor of the Holy
Roman Empire and King of Spain, Duke-Count of Burgundy,
ruler of the Netherlands, Count of Flanders, King of Naples,
Duke of Milan, King of Aragón, of Castile, of León, Grand
Master of the Order of the Golden Fleece and of the Spanish
knightly orders of Santiago, Alcántara, and Calatrava, ruler of
the Indies, etc., in 1556 gave up his dominion over half the
world and retired to the monastery of Yuste, in the forested*

157

hills of Extremadura in the west of Spain. There he died two years later, no doubt recalling, in his last months, the time forty years earlier when he had first come to Spain, a pale, blond, Flemish-speaking boy of seventeen, disliked by his Spanish subjects and himself mistrustful of their hard land and proud ways.

But like the rest of us, Charles was conquered by Spain. He led it to its golden age, but at the age of fifty-six his burden became too heavy for him and he retreated to a most Spanish region to contemplate his eternal fate.

In the centuries after his death his monastery, in the Spanish way, was allowed to fall to ruin, a condition greatly aided by French soldiers, whose record of destruction of objects of Spanish culture is an unwritten chapter in the history of French culture. In recent years what could be restored of the monastery has been put back together, but it takes much imagination to see Yuste as it was when the most powerful man in the world paced its patios, prayed in the church, and fished in the shaded streams.

One man who could see deeply into the Spanish past, and who devoted his energy and wealth to its preservation, was Archer M. Huntington. An American of vast, inherited means, privately educated, Huntington's life was largely given up to the cultivation of Hispanic art and literature. He put millions of dollars into the creation of the Hispanic Society in New York City, whose building is a treasure house of Spanish sculpture, painting, and books.

Huntington knew Spain intimately at the turn of the century and wrote well about it. America—and Spain—are in his debt for preserving so much of the heritage that would otherwise have been lost, as was, nearly, the Emperor's retreat at Yuste.

FROM Madrid to Plasencia is never an inviting expedition, but the prospect of seeing Yuste was quite enough to ease somewhat the roughness of the journey, though it could not drown the incessant rattle of the ancient timbers of our railway compartment. Through a continued hail of cinders we had long vistas of bare, brown fields. Dust, dirt, fleas and fellow-passengers added to the general misery until, at last, we arrived at the station of Plasencia. The station—*only* the station! To the town we must take stage—six or seven miles.

More dust and fleas and fellow-passengers added to a weary rocking and bumping in the *berlina*, the right side window of which was broken and had been mended with brown paper, just enough to keep out fresh air, and let fine gray dust sift in. But we were resigned. My companion had sunk into silence and we sat staring out at intervals along the heaving, dusty mule-backs. At 4.35, we turned a bend and saw the town lying below us. As we came nearer, the walls could be made out and the whole took form as we passed the Jerte River.

Then, true to the time-honored custom of Spanish stagedrivers, we broke into a gallop, the inevitable method of entering a city after a long, weary journey. To be sure it deceived no one. No person believed for a moment that we had kept that merry pace through the long period of our martyrdom. No one dreamed that the *mayoral* was smoking any but his first cigar instead of the last of a series; no one who saw the *zagal* leaping to the ground at each few paces to goad the mules, pictured him thus nimbly careering from the first. All were perfectly aware that we had lagged and dragged and bumped and choked, and gone far beyond the merest joy of profanity on those miles of seething dust.

We stopped, got slowly down, and Athanasia met us. As soon as we saw her face we deserted our bags, and chanced their following us, that we might be led off at once by her. We loved her from the very first. We knew her to be our guardian angel. Through narrow streets we went under her protection, and into the Plaza Mayor, surrounded by fruit stalls and full of color and odors, some strange, others friends of long standing.

Fruit, fruit everywhere, but we could not stop. Out of the Plaza Mayor at the end by the Café, to the right and along the narrow streets, until hot, thirsty and grateful, we passed at last into the broad, covered court of the hotel of the Romero Brothers, the *Fonda del Oeste*.

The *Fonda del Oeste* is an old house preserved from antiquity, to be devoted to the purpose of an hotel. Up-stairs we wandered through dark, arched passages and at last found our small rooms. Our host we discovered when we went down, seated at a table afar off and we nodded to him but said nothing. We saw that he was old and had taken the place of Spanish age—silence and a corner. By and by his wife, the real host, appeared. Even she had reached an age when it is pleasanter to direct than to do. The real heart and soul of the whole place, we soon saw, was our guide from the station—the ever-present girl of all work—Athanasia. Industrious, excited, wonderful Athanasia. Shall I ever forget her! Her little india-rubber body went bobbing and bounding about unceasingly.

An ornamental daughter of the house, in black and surrounded by an atmosphere of dignity, heightened by a veil and much powder, sat in a central position of the hall and noticed us with some degree of kind condescension. We did not presume to address more than a dozen words to her, which she suffered herself to hear and acknowledge with monosyllables. Later she even smiled.

Outside we had discussions with the fruit women for melons and peanuts. A handful of the latter sold to me opened the sluices of inquiry.

"What do you call them?" she said. I told her.

"What a silly language," she laughed, turning her fat body half around towards a neighbor and kicking a hog which was rooting among her onions at the same moment.

"The hogs bother you?"

"Ah, yes. Customers who don't pay! There!" This was an accompaniment to a kick sent home. A violent squeal followed and he trotted off, nose and tail up, to his companions. The streets were full of these animals, and they would not move to let one pass. For is not this province the home of the Spanish hog? Here he is fattened and famous; from here he is sent out in the various forms by which he is best known after death. But of all is he fairest, best tasting and least like his living self as "*sweet hams*" of Estremadura.

As I write of the hogs of Estremadura I am reminded of the satire of the last few months expressing Spanish feeling against the United States and the amusement derived from the picturing of Uncle Sam and the hog. Scarcely an illustrated paper or a daily but had had its fling at so broad a mark. The hog has been represented as the chief domesticated animal of the North American people. He is pictured as riding-horse, beast of burden, household pet, guard, friend and food. It is said that he has supplanted the eagle on our currency, and that "*the hog*," valued at one hundred pigs, has become the standard of values.

At eight we dined with five other guests, and, while still at table, the muleteers, whom we had previously bespoken, arrived. They were a good-looking pair with great, gleaming teeth, shuffling feet, broad smiles and the dignity of good health. Discussion at once arose and every one joined. Were we to pay four or five dollars to be taken to Yuste? Two mules for two days, a man and thirty miles. Five dollars!

Everybody shouted in derision. We left it to our neighbors and it fell to four. There, however, it stuck. And after awhile, to ease the battle spirit which appeared on the point of rising, we accepted the twenty per cent discount and set time and details. As our guides departed, however, the landlady suddenly sprang to her feet. Her rasping voice rang out:

"Oh, what a set of fools!" she shouted. "Four dollars! And here was I holding up three fingers all the time. The thieves!" At intervals after that she would break out into muttered invectives against the muleteers, with upbraidings at our childish simplicity.

We were the last at table and received from each departing one a "*que aproveche*," the customary formula by which one wishes well to one's neighbor and to his digestion. And later, upstairs, as Athanasia handed each his glass of water, with its white *azucarillo* lying in the saucer beside it, she called to us to sleep well, her voice echoing along the turns and passage-ways of the old house.

As all had thought three too early a time for the start, we had agreed to four, and at that hour we heard the noise made by the approaching animals. We went down and found the great doors—a new pair, the pride of the owner who had discarded the ancient ones as not sufficiently effective—slowly giving back before the energetic pushes of Athanasia, disclosing dimly outside the splendor of our two beasts with their muleteers.

We had time to take a cup of smoking tea and, as dawn broke dimly, scrambled up on the backs of our animals. Our seats were not, however, of a kind which promised much comfort for the coming miles. They were the ordinary *albardas*, or pack-saddles, which have the faculty of straining the legs apart until they ache beyond endurance. The novice usually clings, I have noticed, with a grim tenacity to the first posi-

162

tion, until clinging is no longer necessary and the legs have assumed an icy fixedness.

We made our way very slowly along the narrow streets, the mules' feet slipping now and then over smooth, worn stones, and the scarcely distinguishable windows staring at us without expression. Grayness came in at the end of the streets as the faint dawn grew brighter, and we left the town and went down the hill and across the bridge, where low brush fires were sending up yellow flames to right and left. The rays of the sun shone faintly from behind the mountain and the valley was filled with a delicate blue haze. The wind came in little puffs, cool and refreshing, and brought with it the early morning sounds.

A woman in a red bodice and yellow skirt seemed to flare suddenly out of nowhere. On her head she was balancing a basket of melons. At her throat she wore a crucifix strung on a black velvet ribbon and I could see the little gleaming bit of silver rise and fall at each breath she drew.

"God be with you," she said, as she passed, in soft, serious tones.

Our dog appeared at this moment. He had found an old shoe which he carried in his mouth and worried at intervals. He was short, heavy and muscular, and his bark was like a sharp song of morning triumph echoing in the valley.

Now peasants passed us often, their patient little donkeys buried beneath great heaps of fruit and vegetables. The road was impassable for wheeled vehicles. Our animals picked their way among the rolling stones, now and then thrusting us against the branches of the scrub-oaks which grew irregularly between the great, uneven rocks. Only at long intervals was there a bit of cleared ground, a patch of peppers or corn, with melons trailing along the walls.

After a short halt the mules tossed their heads, rattling the hobbling chains about their necks, and we all mounted again. Our guides sent a long volley of invective in the direction of a dead cow at which a dozen red-necked vultures were feeding. The profanity was, however, in reality directed at our slow pace. At last, in the far distance, we sighted, between the oaks, the *Puerto* in the mountains by Pasaron, through which we must go to Yuste.

Across a little sandy pool at 8.10. The stream is called the Garganta de Gargüera and there is a bridge which no one takes.

At last we reached Tejeda. The main room of the *posada* has a brick floor and bright, whitewashed walls. On one side is arranged a good display of blue and white china, sieves of punched rawhides, and household articles hung on nails. All is refreshingly clean and free from evil smells.

As we sit here discussing the preliminaries of food and the possibility of a halt, the mules are led across the room and into the *cuadra*, or stable, a black depth behind, where are dimly visible and clearly audible hogs, chickens, goats, and other formless moving masses, too deep in the gloom for recognition. So is the mediaeval desire to have all one's wordly goods within one's walls preserved in these little places.

The landlady is a pleasant, toothless old soul, in a very short green-edged dress, and bare feet tucked into slippers. She and a man wearing a purple *faja* and leggings, on whose buttons is a portrait of the Pope, inquire about our trip, the man first carefully removing (one from under each arm) two dried codfish. There is much loud talking. In the *cuadra* the hogs come to the door and grunt; the chickens crow, until at last the barefooted landlady takes us into her own room, drives out her husband, who has the palsy, and fries us some eggs in oil. We sit down with our muleteer, who first pours red vinegar over his eggs and eats them between huge bites of cheese!

It was about ten when we started on, and we were soon out of sight of the little wayside *posada*. Partridges rose several times before us, doves flew past continually, and once we lost our way, but soon found it again.

"I know the way well enough," said my guide, "though it's twenty-three years since I went over it. Twenty-three years this coming March. I married from Pasaron and I used to come often enough, then." After this I felt confident of him.

The square tower of the church began to be very near. The little town lies in a break in the hills. We struggled up to it and entered the middle ages. Dark, over-hanging, narrow, filthy streets, filled with vile odors; half-naked children mingling with hogs, chickens and goats; women in brilliant colors, with bare feet; hags peering from grated windows; and now and then a sinister face at a half-open door. Strange cries, the tinkling of goat-bells, barking of dogs, gruntings, curses, all rising about us in a wild pandemonium.

We had to force our way through it all, now kicking the sullen, angry-eyed, half-savage dogs, now pushing between the great, gray backs of the monstrous hogs. At last we came to a fountain, at the head of the muddy street, over which was written a warning to the people not to defile the water by the washing of utensils therein.

From here we went upward along a street lined with huge wine-jars, the *amphora vinaria* of Rome, and a little farther, we passed the oven where they were baked. Then down through heavy chestnut groves into the open country once more, gaining two splendid views, between the ridges, of the low plain below, with the Sierras in the blue distance.

At a quarter to twelve we passed a cross by the roadside; an assassination had occurred there, and this had been set up to mark the point where the body had been found. I could not get the details of the story. The spot recalled Byron aptly enough:

And here and there, as up the crag you spring,
Mark many rude-carved crosses near the path;
Yet deem not these devotion's offering—
These are memorials frail of murderous wrath;
For wheresoe'er the shrieking victim hath
Poured forth his blood beneath the assassin's knife,
Some hand erects a cross of mouldering lath;
And grove and glen with thousand such are rife,
Throughout this purple land, where law secures not life.

Ferns began to cover the rough country, filling the spaces between the gray rocks and coloring the whole landscape curiously. Half an hour later we entered the *robledo* or oak forest of Jaráiz, and in a quarter of an hour had passed through it. At the edge my guide stopped and waited for me to come up. A broad valley opened before us to the left.

"Do you see that patch of trees over there across the valley under the mountain?" he said, sweeping his hand out in that direction.

"Yes."

"It is Yuste."

I forced my animal out of the road and upon a knoll, for a better view. The valley lay at my feet, gray, barren, forbidding. No forest was in sight save that from which we were just emerging, and the little clump of trees afar off, at the last home of the Emperor. The usual silence reigned; only above in the clear air a vulture wheeled suddenly and swept back into the forest from which he had come, curious, perhaps, at our sudden halt in a place where halting had for him but one significance.

The last house of Charles the Emperor. The spot with which the greatest name in the history of Spain is most intimately connected. The one spot on earth where the arbiter of the lives of a wonderful generation came as near as it is possible for such a man to approach the lowest of his subjects. An old, broken man, on whose mind was written the map of Europe and who had lived just long enough to see the danger signals in the north begin to shine. Low lights which, under his successor, were to flare along the whole horizon with a blaze which should draw out of Spain one vast stream of gold and men, poured in to quench it, and leave her sapped and exhausted after a desperate fight a century long.

"Are you through looking?" asked my guide at last.

We passed around a curve and into the town of Jaráiz. The sight of the place seemed to awaken in the mind of the muleteer some memories of the time twenty-three years past. He peered here and there curiously through the dirty streets and at doors and windows, as though he were living over some familiar scene. At last he stopped before a door and struck it several heavy blows. For a time all was silent. Then a window opened overhead and a woman's face appeared.

"Do you know where the wife of Silo lives?"

She shook her head and stood gazing after us, as we moved onward. A few steps farther another door seemed to strike his attention; he delivered a tremendous blow upon it. A man came out.

"Do you know where the wife of Silo lives?"

"The wife of Silo?"

"Yes."

He turned and raising his voice shouted down the streets:

"Pepe!" A head was thrust from a window afar off.

"Who is the wife of Silo?" More heads came to windows— lines of them were staring at us. The words were repeated over and over again. At last, far down the street, an old woman called in a treble:

"It is Bitorina Parejo he wants."

167

"Ah, yes, Bitorina Parejo!" said a dozen voices.

"Bitorina Parejo?" repeated the man who had called. "She lives there." And he pointed to a house.

"Let us go there," said the muleteer, "she is my sister."

Before I could express any surprise a little woman, past middle age, had let us in, and a family scene ensued. The two had not met in fourteen years!

I remained patiently standing on one side holding the *cabestro* of my mule until the Señora Bitorina deigned to notice me and listen to my plaint of hunger and fatigue. Then she was all attention. The small, nervous creature flew from her newly found brother to me like a highly excited little hen.

"What will the Señor have to eat?" She had said it three times before I could answer.

"What may we have?"

"Oh, anything—there is everything here!"

I told her I would take what she brought me, and gave my mule into the hands of her brother. We went up-stairs to the combined dining and bed-room which was just over the stable.

"It is warmer so," said Bitorina, in answer to my questions. "In winter it is good to have the beasts so close."

The apartment had two small alcoves filling one side. Adjoining it was the *taberna*, a longer and narrower room, the public drinking-place, run by the little woman.

At intervals men kept coming in and going to one of the alcoves. I inquired of the Señora Parejo if some one was ill. "Ah, yes, he will die, we think," she replied in a cheerful voice. "The doctor said so, and the fever is on him now these eight days."

I went over and looked in. The air was close and heavy, and by the half-light from the candle I could just see the outlines of the emaciated figure of a man. His face was hidden, but a thin hand and arm hung over the bedside. A man, a sympathetic friend, no doubt, was talking to him in a low voice.

I wondered how long, between friends and fever, he could last.

The other alcove bed, I saw, was vacant. I was tired, for the *albarda* had worn me nearly out, though I had changed my position continually.

Nothing could have seemed more tempting than the cool white of the bed after the laborious trip, and without a word to the Señora Parejo, I threw myself at full length upon it.

Scarcely had I done so when a shriek arose, and the little woman flew at me like a wild creature. She seized and dragged me off the bed with the strength of two men. I was too dazed to resist, but retreated before her.

"Oh, *Dios mío, Dios mío!*" she shrieked; "they are ruined—ruined!" She tore back the cover of the bed, and to my amazement disclosed row after row of—biscuits! Small, round biscuits! *They had been placed there to rise.* To rise! Down the centre of the rows my weight had flattened them beyond recognition; only at the farthest edge had a few escaped.

I apologized as best I could, but the harm was done. Still, the Señora Parejo bore no malice, and five minutes later she presented me with a sumptuous repast consisting of thirteen small pickled fish, fine white bread, goats'-milk cheese, wine or water unlimited, and the half of a watermelon, sandía, in the disposing of which my hostess joined me. We talked on amiably for some time, and I questioned her about the man who was ill. He was of the village and unmarried. The doctor, she said, was a most wonderful man. I made no comment, but my expression may have betrayed a doubt.

"Oh, but you don't know—you don't know! Why, he has cured me twice." I congratulated her.

"Yes, I was mad—quite mad. It came from a blow on the head. See here, you can feel it." Sure enough, when I put my finger on the place she indicated, I felt the spot yield. The woman's skull had been fractured!

"How long ago was it?"

"Two years."

"And you have done nothing for it?"

"Nothing! Did I not say the doctor had saved me twice. What with poultices and hot bandages and the cutting of the hair, I have had enough done. But, sometimes, even now, it bothers me a little and I have had a headache these three weeks. Though not when I wear this." And she held up a small brass image of the Virgin.

It is probable that this woman died or, perhaps, became insane. The operation which was evidently needed for relieving the pressure on the brain had, doubtless, never occurred to her doctor, or if it had he was evidently afraid to risk trephining. The treatment she had received told its own tale.

We left town followed by children and descended into the valley, where, after a good deal of bare road, we crossed a stone bridge and began to climb the low central ridge which divides it.

"You should have turned to the left a good way back," said a boy who was eating figs by the roadside, in answer to our question. "But go on now up through the *barranca*, and then keep to the right by the cross."

We soon discovered the *barranca* and climbed up through it. The way was difficult, nothing more than the bed of a mountain torrent which had cut deep into the soil between the rocks, leaving great masses of fantastically worn and tottering clay and gravel, ready to fall at the slightest jar.

This passed, we found ourselves on a long slope stretching down to the edge of the woods of Yuste, which we reached and skirted at a stumbling gait, making a long swing to the left. Then we found the cross, and, after it, the entrance.

At the latter, after a refreshing ride through the cool woods, we came upon a group of women washing under the great walnut-tree, where the Emperor used to pass when he came down from the square brick building above, by the inclined pathway on massive arches.

The present owner of Yuste is the Marquis of Mirabel, who keeps an overseer on the grounds. I followed the latter carefully over the place, through desolate halls and bare, dark rooms. By a low door we entered the Chapel—bare and chilling like the rest. A stray beam of sunlight fell on the floor near a line of graves, at the foot of a raised tiled portico where stood the altar. Opposite the low door beneath which the Emperor's head had so often bowed in passing, in a niche to the left and perhaps fifteen feet above the blue-tilted altar base, may still be seen the coffin in which the body lay while at Yuste. There is an inscription below:

> *Within this box of chestnut-*
> *wood was deposited, during*
> *the four years that*
> *it remained in this con-*
> *vent, the body of our Lord*
> *the Emperor and King Charles*
> *the First of Spain and*
> *Fifth of Germany, of un-*
> *dying memory.*

The sunbeam faded away while I read, and we left the dreary chapel and continued our walk.

Outside it was little less dreary. Among the grapes and fig trees the hogs were hard at work, and a calf started up from one of the crumbling arches of what had once been the favorite walk of Charles. The path is still clearly marked, but time will finish what it has begun. At its end lies the open forest. I turned back and found the famous "fish-pond," now almost dry. Ripe oranges hung over the wall and a few of the golden balls had fallen into the green stagnant pool and were floating there, flamingly suggestive of decay. I tried one, but, as was fitting, it was bitter.

W. SOMERSET MAUGHAM

Food for Thought

A SELECTION FROM *Don Fernando*

Long ago, before this century had begun, yet after he had become a doctor, Somerset Maugham went on the first of many trips to Spain—more precisely, to Andalucía. On horseback he rode the southern countryside and learned to know the white villages—Carmona, Écija, Luisiana—as well as he knew the white, winding streets of Sevilla. He got the Mediterranean, and some of Africa, in his blood.

Maugham saw other parts of Spain, and wrote about it all with perception, cool and ironic, yet with more love showing through his sophistication than he has displayed for any other land and people.

In this selection he discusses Spanish food at various places and levels of cuisine. In the decades since his grim experiences in walled Ávila, restaurants in Spain have improved greatly. A few of them rank nearly with the best in Europe, and certainly, in situation, antiquity, and hospitality, some are among the most interesting in the world.

But there is, for the generality, always olive oil, excellent in itself, but often bad in the quantities and odd situations in which it turns up, and there is an appalling monotony about watery chicken soup, veal, and the eternal flán, or custard, which will remind any foreigner that even at the more prosperous dietary levels Spain is a poor land—one wonders, indeed, on seeing the greater part of the country, how any food is produced out of such barren earth—and, furthermore, that Spaniards really don't give a damn about good eating.

ÁVILA is a city in which it should be pleasant to linger. There is nothing much to do there and little to see. The walls, greatly restored, are like the walls of an old city in a book of hours. The neat, round towers placed at regular intervals look like the trim curls of a seventeenth century peruke. The cathedral with its fortress-like air has not much to offer you but an effect of sombreness, and its Gothic porches and windows are not so good as many you have seen elsewhere. Besides, now we are all a little bored with Gothic architecture. But the houses of the old *hidalgos* have still kept something of their grave stateliness; those grand escutcheons over the doorways are impressive. A silent city. There are many streets in which you may stand for an hour without seeing a passer-by. The men of Avila are soberly dressed and the women wear deep mourning. The air even in summer has a certain sharpness; in spring and autumn the wind blows bitter, and in winter the cold is severe. It is Castile with its reserve, its taciturnity and its ceremonial stiffness. But the hotel is one of the worst in Spain. The rooms are bare and comfortless, it is none too clean and it smells; the food, served in a grim, large dining-room in which there is a harsh blaze of electric light, is frightful; one uneatable dish follows another, thrown at you by a slovenly waiter with dirty hands, on cold plates, and the cellar can provide hardly any of the wines the list offers.

I can eat almost anything, if not with pleasure, without distaste, and a bad dinner does nothing to disturb my serenity. I can say with truth that I have a soul above food, but alas, though my spirit is strong my flesh is weak, and a poor meal, which I have devoured without complaint, will make me as sick as a dog for a week. That body which Fray Roldan spoke of as the *asinillo*, the little donkey, will let my dancing spirit take no liberties with it. On one occasion in Avila, having at last fallen asleep after tossing from side to side on my hard bed for hours, I was awakened by the crowing of a cock, and a few minutes later I heard the sudden hubbub of a bell. It was quite startling in that deep night. It occurred to me that they must be ringing for early mass. I got up, slipped a pair of trousers over my pyjamas and put on a great-coat; the night-porter opened the door for me and I walked across the street. The cathedral was in darkness but for one chapel in which burned an electric light. A sacristan, muffled up in a cloak, with a grey woolen scarf over his mouth and nose, was lighting candles. I saw the backs of three women in black kneeling before the altar. A peasant-woman, with a basket on her arm and a handkerchief over her head, came along just before the priest. He seemed to be in a hurry, a fat little man with grey hair and an earthy face, he walked so quickly that the acolyte behind him was almost running. As he uttered the first words of the mass, gabbling unintelligibly in a low voice,

174

a man stepped out of the darkness. I glanced at him with surprise. I had not thought that anyone was there but those four women. He was a tall, thin man, with a voluminous cloak draped round him; he had flashing eyes under bushy eyebrows, a big hooked nose and an immense head of long, curling, grey hair; his face was harsh and rugged. So might have looked one of the old *conquistadores*. He did not kneel. He stood motionless, his mouth tight-closed, with his strange eyes fixed on the altar. I wondered what he did there. It was bitterly cold. I felt very sick. I went back to the hotel and they gave me goat's milk with my coffee and rancid butter with my bread. It was too much.

You must not be blamed then if in Avila you say that it is impossible to get a decent meal in Spain. But it is an error. You can eat very well in Spain, only you must know where to go and how to set about it. In the first place you must decide how to make your meal of a single dish and it may be that this is a very wise thing. For thus you do not overeat. However good one dish is you can only eat as much as will satisfy your hunger.

The Spaniards are coarse, but sparing eaters. They do not seem to mind if their food is bad and ill-cooked, they will eat fish that is far from fresh, and *bollito* and *garbanzos*, boiled beef and chick-peas, monotonous fare, day after day without disgust. They have always been frugal. Indeed one of the great virtues of the Spanish soldier was that he could march and fight on so little food that you would have thought it hardly enough to keep body and soul together. The traveller, you read in the picaresque novels, was content to make a meal off a hunk of bread and an onion. On the other hand it must be admitted that when it came to a feast their capacity was enormous. When Sempronio and Parmeno wanted to offer their two girl friends and the old bawd Celestina a supper they sent along (for five persons) a ham, six pairs of young chickens and some pigeons, Murviedo wine and white bread. When I first went to Spain it was difficult, except in one or two hotels in Madrid, Barcelona and Seville where they made a poor imitation of French rolls, to get any bread except a sort of double roll of a doughy white substance unappetising to look at, tasteless to eat and heavy on the stomach. Now you can get French bread in any town of consequence, but it is neither crisp nor savoury. If you want good bread you must go to some of the mountain villages in the north, where, if you are lucky enough to get there just when it comes from the baker's, you may eat a loaf of rye bread, beautiful in colour and sweet-smelling, with a crust that crumbles in the mouth deliciously. With this and some butter—almost unobtainable in Spain thirty years ago, but now to be found everywhere—a few olives, anchovies and a goat cheese you can make a repast fit for a king.

Of course no one who has any sense will eat the *table d'hôte* meals provided in hotels. They are long and bad after the French style in the first-class hotels; they are long and no worse after the Spanish style in the second-class. Their monotony is deplorable. In both you will get the same insipid clear soup; and you will seldom see any fish but the coarse, tough, savourless *merluza*. Hake! You can bake it, boil it, stew it, fry it, grill it; you can tickle it up with worcester sauce, you can drench it in tomato ketchup, you can souse it in oil and vinegar, you can dabble it in mayonnaise, *Bearnaise*, *Hollandaise, sauce tartare;* it remains savourless, coarse and tough.

But even in the hotels, in those not quite of the first class that is, if they are not very busy and you will talk it over in a friendly way with the head waiter or the cook, you can often get very good things to eat. Thus at Alicante, one of those agreeable towns in which there is nothing whatever to see, to which I went in the dead season, I got an *arroz à la Valenciana* which was perfect. I drank the local wine with it, a pale wine, very palatable, with a faint flavour of muscatel. I forgot to say that you will never like Spanish fare unless you can stomach food cooked in oil; if you insist that everything you eat should be cooked in butter then you must expect nothing from Spain but the gratifications of the spirit; the table can have no pleasures to offer you.

Arroz à la Valenciana is the local dish of Valencia and I dare say it was invented in that dull and noisy city. When Ruy Dias de Bivar conquered Valencia he proceeded according to the poem as follows:

With my Cid to the Alcazar went straight his wife and
  daughters.
Once there he led them to the highest point of all,
Where did fair eyes look on all sides around.
At their feet they behold the city, Valencia where it lies,
And yonder on the other side within their view is the sea.

I like to think that then he took them by the hand and led them to where was waiting for them a goodly dish of *arroz à la Valenciana*. I wish that Professor Peers, who spent some months there, I believe, had for a little while diverted his erudite studies on El Cid Campeador (an engaging ruffian) to look into the origins of this tasty dish. I should like to know whether it was the discovery of a Moor of genius, or whether it invented itself by accident, simultaneously, in the kitchens of a hundred Moorish housewives. Though it is called after Valencia it is eaten all along the coast from Barcelona to Malaga. In Andalusia it is called *paella*. It is never bad and sometimes of an excellence that surpasses belief. Rice is of course its foundation, saffron and red peppers give it a Spanish tang; it has chicken in it, clams, mussels, prawns and I know not what. It takes a long time to make and is a great deal of trouble. It is worth the time and worth the trouble. But the best *arroz* I ever ate was at Tarragona.

Tarragona has a cathedral that is grey and austere, very plain, with immense, severe pillars; it is like a fortress; a place of worship for headstrong, violent and cruel men. The night falls early within its walls and then the columns in the aisles seem to squat down on themselves and darkness shrouds the Gothic arches. It terrifies you. It is like a dungeon. I was there last on a Monday in Holy week and from the pulpit a preacher was delivering a Lenten sermon. Two or three naked electric globes threw a cold light that cut the outline of the columns against the darkness as though with scissors. It only just fell upon the crowd, mostly women, who sat, between the chancel and the choir, huddled together as though they cowered in fear of a foe that besieged the city. With violent gestures, in a loud, scolding voice, the preacher poured forth with extreme rapidity a torrent of denunciation. Each angry, florid phrase was like a blow and one blow followed another with vicious insistence. From the farthest end of the majestic church, winding about the columns and curling round the groining of the arches, down the great austere nave and along the dungeon-like aisles, that rasping, shrewish voice pursued you.

But a devout admirer had entertained the preacher at luncheon that day in the hotel in which I was staying. It was quite a party. There were the host's grey-haired and corpulent wife, his two sons with their wives, or his two daughters with their husbands (I could only guess), and eight or nine children of various ages, whom I tried to sort out. The preacher tucked in to the *arroz* like one o'clock. It comforted me at that moment to remember this. It was a bad, bad world, but a merciful providence had allowed occasional alleviations to the miserable lot of man, and among these must undoubtedly be placed *arroz à la Valenciana* as we had both eaten it that noon at Tarragona.

In almost every town in Spain you can find a restaurant in which you can eat well enough to satisfy an exigent taste. In Madrid you can find half a dozen. But there is one that should be known to all travellers. It is in the Plaza de los Herradores. It is bare and comfortless; you sit on a hard chair; the linen is coarse and the light is harsh. But you do not care, for your mouth waters with pleasant anticipation: you are going to eat sucking-pig. Four or five of them lie on a dish in the window, with cut throats, and they look so like new-born babies that it gives you quite a turn. But you must avert your mind resolutely from this notion. They are killed at three weeks old. It is impossible to describe how good they are, how tender, how succulent, how juicy, and what spiritual ecstasy there is in the crackling: just as there is nothing really to say about a symphony, you must listen to it; so there is nothing to be said about a sucking-pig, you must eat it.

For a reason that I have never been able to discover you eat much better in the north of a country than in the south. The English cherish the ingenuous notion that you can eat well anywhere in France. It is not true. They think that you can go to no restaurant in France, to no hotel, in which you cannot get a good omelette. It is not true. You cannot eat well south of Vienne. And in Andalusia you eat romantically rather than to the satisfaction of your palate. My thoughts wander back to a tavern in Seville, just off the Sierpes, where the *manzanilla* was good and the inn-keeper got his hams from Estremadura. You used to go there late at night, after the *zarzuela* at the theatre was over, and order yourself half a portion of smoked ham and a dish of black, juicy olives. A boy would cut across the street and bring you from the cook-shop a plate of fried fish. You sat in a little cubicle, on a wooden bench, with a companion (for who can eat alone?)

and in the next cubicle, if you were in luck, there would be a little party, one of the men with a guitar, and after a long introductory twanging a woman broke into the melancholy, Moorish wail of a *seguidilla*.

The Spanish are fond of sea-food. The itinerant salesmen with their baskets of shrimps, huge prawns, clams, and sea-urchins do a great trade as they wander from tavern to tavern. The fish in the fried fish shops is very fresh and provided of course that you do not mind its being cooked in oil, exceedingly good. But if you want to eat fish you must really go to Vigo. When, notwithstanding all I have written, I am inclined with melancholy to agree with those who say that you cannot eat well in Spain, I think of Vigo and tell myself that this is nonsense. Vigo is one of the few ports in Europe where you can get fish. Boulogne is another. There are none in England. I have never eaten a better luncheon in my life than I ate at Vigo. There was every variety of fish as hors d'oeuvre, clams, prawns, mussels, anchovies and a dozen more, a shrimp omelette, and then a delicious fried fish that you knew had come out of the sea that very morning, kid, very tender and good, and two or three dishes to follow. But these, my hunger satisfied, I left untouched. It was a wonderful meal.

WILLIAM DEAN HOWELLS

Sevilla

A SELECTION FROM *Familiar Spanish Travels*

*There may be a village in Spain where one would wish to live
for a month or for a lifetime: near Calella de Palafrugell on the
Costa Brava, or on the Levante, the southeast coast, or among
the valleys and mountains of Granada; perhaps in Navarra,
where the setting sun strikes the Pyrenees. But if you are obliged to choose a Spanish city in which to live—make no
error: choose Sevilla.*

*Is it too hot there in summer? (No need to speak of the
perfection of fall and spring.) Not in the protection of the
narrow, canvas-covered lane-street, Sierpes, where one may
sit in front of a casino (no gambling; just a club), and watch
a world go by, over a manzanilla. Is it too cold in winter?
Never, under the sun shining in the Plaza de Doña Elvira,*

where the wrought-iron grills and lampposts cast black shadows, and the flowers in the window boxes against the pure white walls bloom forever.

Sevilla today is not changed from the city of fifty or one hundred years ago, at least in important external appearances, to American and English eyes.

William Dean Howells, in his boyhood in the 1850's, created images of Spain out of books of literature and history which he found in his town in the Ohio Valley. He loved Spain, but the affair was conducted by proxy, for although he lived in Europe for many years, chiefly as a United States consular official in Italy, Howells did not visit Spain until the end of his life.

His book about that experience, Familiar Spanish Travels, *is sometimes painfully Victorian in style and judgment; for example, the author implies, or makes explicit, his Anglo-American curse of excessive cleanliness and punctuality. But his wisdom, showing in an acute perception of alien reality, and his long love for Spain combine to make his book about that difficult land one of the few written by another American generation and still worth reading.*

In this selection, William Dean Howells, in 1911 at the age of seventy-four, tells of his journey south from Córdoba to Sevilla, and describes some of the qualities of that city which he found most interesting, as they remain today: the willing, if intrusive service; the impassioned noise generated in the streets; and the cathedral.

WE were running at once over a gentle ground-swell which rose and sank in larger billows now and then, and the yellow

Guadalquivir followed us all the way, in a valley that sometimes widened to the blue mountains always walling the horizon. We had first entered Andalusia after dark, and the scene
had now a novelty little staled by the distant view of the
afternoon before. The olive orchards then seen afar were
intimately realized more and more in their amazing extent.
None of the trees looked so old, so world-old, as certain
trees in the careless olive groves of Italy. They were regu-
larly planted, and most were in a vigorous middle life; where
they were old they were closely pollarded; and there were
young trees, apparently newly set out; there were holes in-
definitely waiting for others. These were often, throughout
Andalusia, covered to their first fork with cones of earth; and
we remained in the dramatic superstition that this was to protect them against the omnivorous hunger of the goats, till we
were told that it was to save their roots from being loosened
by the wind. The orchards filled the level foregrounds and
the hilly backgrounds to the vanishing-points of the mountainous perspectives; but when I say this I mean the reader to
allow for wide expanses of pasturage, where lordly bulls were
hoarding themselves for the feasts throughout Spain which
the bulls of Andalusia are happy beyond others in supplying.
With their devoted families they paraded the meadows, black
against the green, or stood in sharp arrest, the most characteristic accent of the scene. In the farther rather than the
nearer distance there were towns, very white, very African,
keeping jealously away from the stations, as the custom of
most towns is in Spain, beyond the wheatlands which dis-
puted the landscape with the olive orchards. . . .

I could not honestly say that the stations or the people
about them were more interesting than in La Mancha. But
at one place, where some gentlemen in linen jackets dismounted with their guns, a group of men with dogs leashed
in pairs and saddle-horses behind them, took me with the

sense of something peculiarly native where everything was so native. They were slim, narrow-hipped young fellows, tight-jerkined, loose-trousered, with a sort of divided apron of leather facing the leg and coming to the ankle; and all were of a most masterly Velasquez coloring and drawing. As they stood smoking motionless, letting the smoke drift from their nostrils, they seemed somehow of the same make with the slouching hounds, and they leaned forward together, giving the hunters no visible or audible greeting, but questioning their will with one quality of gaze. The hunters moved toward them, but not as if they belonged together, or expected any sort of demonstration from the men, dogs, and horses that were of course there to meet them. As long as our train paused, no electrifying spark kindled them to a show of emotion; but it would have been interesting to see what happened after we left them behind; they could not have kept their attitude of mutual indifference much longer. These peasants, like the Spaniards everywhere, were of an intelligent and sagacious look; they only wanted a chance, one must think, to be a leading race. They have sometimes an anxiety of appeal in their apathy, as if they would like to know more than they do.

. . . At Seville . . . a walrus-mustached old porter, who looked like an old American car-driver of the bearded eighteen-sixties, eased us—not very swiftly, but softly—through the local customs, and then we drove neither so swiftly nor so softly to the hotel, where we had decided we would have rooms on the *patio*. We had still to learn that if there is a *patio* in a Spanish hotel you cannot have rooms in it, because they are either in repair or they are occupied. In the present case they were occupied; but we could have rooms over the street, which were the same as in the *patio*, and which were perfectly quiet, as we could perceive from the trolley-cars grinding and squealing under their windows. The manager (if that was the quality of the patient and amiable old official who received us) seemed surprised to see the cars there, perhaps because they were so inaudible; but he said we could have rooms in the annex, fronting on the adjoining plaza and siding on an inoffensive avenue where there were absolutely no cars. The interior, climbing to a lofty roof by a succession of galleries, was hushed by four silent señoras, all in black, and seated in mute ceremony around a table in chairs from which their little feet scarcely touched the marble pavement. Their quiet confirmed the manager's assurance of a pervading tranquility, and though the only bath in the annex was confessedly on the ground floor, and we were to be two floors above, the affair was very simple: the chambermaid would always show us where the bath was.

With misgivings, lost in a sense of our helplessness, we tried to think that the avenue under us was then quieting down with the waning day; and certainly it was not so noisy as the plaza, which resounded with the whips and quips of the cabmen, and gave no signs of quiescence. Otherwise the annex was very pleasant, and we took the rooms shown us, hoping the best and fearing the worst. Our fears were wiser than our hopes, but we did not know this, and we went as gaily as we could for tea in the *patio* of our hotel, where a fountain typically trickled amidst its water-plants and a noiseless Englishman at his separate table almost restored our lost faith in a world not wholly racket. A young Spaniard and two young Spanish girls helped out the illusion with their gentle movements and their muted gutturals, and we looked forward to dinner with fond expectation. To tell the truth, the dinner, when we came back to it, was not very good, or at least not very winning, and the next night it was no better, though the head waiter had then made us so much favor with himself as to promise us a side-table for the rest of our stay. He was a very friendly head waiter, and the dining-room was a long glare of the encaustic tiling which all Seville seems lined with, and of every Moorish motive in the decoration. Besides, there was a young Scotch girl, very interestingly pale and delicate of face, at one of the tables, and at another a Spanish girl with the most wonderful fire-red hair, and there were several miracles of the beautiful obesity which abounds in Spain.

When we returned to the annex it did seem, for the short time we kept our windows shut, that the manager had spoken true, and we promised ourselves a tranquil night, which, after our two nights in Cordova, we needed if we did not merit. But we had counted without the spread of popular education in Spain. Under our windows, just across the way, there proved to be a school of the "Royal Society of Friends of their Country," as the Spanish inscription in its front proclaimed; and at dusk its pupils, children and young people of both sexes, began clamoring for knowledge at its doors. About ten o'clock they burst from them again with joyous exultation in their acquirements; then, shortly after, every manner of vehicle began to pass, especially heavy market wagons overladen and drawn by horses swarming with bells. Their succession left scarcely a moment of the night unstunned; but if ever a moment seemed to be escaping, there was a maniacal bell in a church near by that clashed out: "Hello! Here's a bit of silence; let's knock it on the head!"

We went promptly the next day to the gentle old manager and told him that he had been deceived in thinking he had given us rooms on a quiet street, and appealed to his invention for something, for anything, different. His invention had probably never been put to such stress before, and he showed us an excess of impossible apartments, which we subjected to a consideration worthy of the greatest promise in them. Our search ended in a suite of rooms on the top floor, where we could have the range of a flat roof outside if we wanted; but as the private family living next door kept hens, led by a lordly turkey, on their roof, we were sorrowfully forced to forego our peculiar advantage. Peculiar we then thought it, though we learned afterward that poultry-farming was not uncommon on the flat roofs of Seville, and there is now no telling how we might have prospered if we had taken those rooms and stocked our roof with Plymouth Rocks and Wyandottes. At the moment, however, we thought it would not do, and we could only offer our excuses to the manager, whose resources we had now exhausted, but not whose patience, and we parted with expressions of mutual esteem and regret.

Our own grief was sincere in leaving behind us the enthusiastic chambermaid of the annex who had greeted us with glad service, and was so hopeful that when she said our doors should be made to latch and lock in the morning, it was as if they latched and locked already. Her zeal made the hot water she brought for the baths really hot, *"Caliente, caliente,"* and her voice would have quieted the street under our windows if music could have soothed it. At a friendly word she grew trustful, and told us how it was hard, hard for poor people in Seville; how she had three dollars a month and her husband four; and how they had to toil for it. When we could not help telling her, cruelly enough, what they singly and jointly earn in New York, she praised rather than coveted the happier chance impossible to them. They would like to go, but they could not go! She was gay with it all, and after we had left the hotel and come back for the shawl which had been forgotten, she ran for it, shouting with laughter, as if we must see it the great joke she did; and she took the reward offered with the self-respect never wanting to the Spanish poor. . . .

When we definitely turned our backs on the potential poultry-farm offered us at our hotel, we found ourselves in as good housing at another, overlooking the length and

breadth of the stately Plaza San Fernando, with its parallelo-
gram of tall palms, under a full moon swimming in a cloudless
heaven by night and by day. By day, of course, we did not see
it, but the sun was visibly there, rather blazing hot, even in
mid-October, and showing more distinctly than the moon the
beautiful tower of the Giralda from the waist up, and the
shoulder of the great cathedral, besides features of other noble,
though less noble, edifices. Our plaza was so full of romantic
suggestion that I am rather glad now I had no association with
it. I am sure I could not have borne at the time to know, as I
have only now learned by recurring to my Baedeker, that in
the old Franciscan cloister once there had stood the equestrian
statue of the Comendador who dismounts and comes unbidden
to the supper of Don Giovanni in the opera. That was a statue
which, seen in my far youth, haunted my nightmares for
many a year, and I am sure it would have kept me from sleep
in the conditions, now so perfect, of our new housing if I had
known about it.

The plaza is named, of course, for King Fernando, who
took Seville from the Moors six hundred years ago, and was
canonized for his conquests and his virtues. But I must not
enter so rashly upon the history of Seville, or forget the
arrears of personal impression which I have to bring up. The
very drive from the station was full of impressions, from the
narrow and crooked streets, the houses of yellow, blue, and
pink stucco, the flowered and fountained *patios* glimpsed
passingly, the half-lengths of church-towers, and the fleeting
façades of convents and palaces, all lovely in the mild afternoon light. These impressions soon became confluent, so that
without the constant witness of our notebooks I should now
find it impossible to separate them. If they could be imparted
to the reader in their complexity, that would doubtless be the
ideal, though he would not believe that their confused
pattern was a true reflex of Seville; so I recur to the record,

which says that the morning after our arrival we hurried to see the great and beautiful cathedral. It had failed, in our approach the afternoon before, to fulfill the promise of one of our half-dozen guide-books (I forget which one) that it would seem to gather Seville about it as a hen gathers her chickens, but its vastness grew upon us with every moment of our more intimate acquaintance. Our acquaintance quickly ripened into the affectionate friendship which became a tender regret when we looked our last upon it; and vast as it was, it was never too large for our embrace. I doubt if there was a moment in our fortnight's devotion when we thought the doughty canons, its brave-spoken founders, "mad to have undertaken it," as they said they expected people to think, or any moment when we will not revere them for imagining a temple at once so beautiful and so big.

Our first visit was redeemed from the commonplace of our duty-round of the side-chapels by two things which I can remember without the help of my notes. One, and the great one, was Murillo's "Vision of St. Anthony," in which the painter has most surpassed himself, and which not to have seen, Gautier says, is not to have known the painter. It is so glorious a masterpiece, with the Child joyously running down from the clustering angels toward the kneeling saint in the nearest corner of the foreground, that it was distinctly a moment before I realized that the saint had once been cut out of his corner and sent into an incredible exile in America, and then munificently restored to it, though the seam in the canvas only too literally attested the incident. I could not well say how this fact then enhanced the interest of the painting, and then how it ceased from the consciousness, which it must always recur to with any remembrance of it. If one could envy wealth its chance of doing a deed of absolute good, here was the occasion, and I used it. I did envy the mind, along with the money, to do that great thing. Another great thing which still more swelled my American heart and made it glow with patriotic pride was the monument to Columbus, which our suffering his dust to be translated from Havana has made possible in Seville. There may be other noble results of our war on Spain for the suzerainty of Cuba and the conquest of Puerto Rico and the Philippines, but there is none which matches in moral beauty the chance it won us for this Grand Consent. I suppose those effigies of the four Spanish realms of Castile, Leon, Aragon and Navarre, which bear the coffin of the discoverer in stateliest processional on their shoulders, may be censured for being too boldly superb, too almost swagger, but I will not be the one to censure them. They are painted the color of life, and they advance colossally, royal-robed and mail-clad, as if marching to some proud music, and would tread you down if you did not stand aside. It is perhaps not art, but it is magnificent; nothing less stupendously Spanish would have sufficed; and I felt that the magnanimity which had yielded Spain this swelling opportunity had made America her equal in it.

We went to the cathedral the first morning after our arrival in Seville, because we did not know how soon we might go away, and then we went every morning or every afternoon of our fortnight there. Habitually we entered by that Gate of Pardon which in former times had opened the sanctuary to any wickedness short of heresy; but, as our need of refuge was not pressing, we wearied of the Gate of Pardon, with its beautiful Saracenic arch converted to Christianity by the Renaissance bas-relief obliterating the texts from the Koran. We tried to form the habit of going in by other gates, but the Gate of Pardon finally prevailed; there was always a gantlet of cabmen to be run beside it, which brought our sins home to us. It led into the badly paved Court of Oranges, where the trees seem planted haphazard and where there used to be fountains. Gate and court are remnants of the mosque, patterned upon that of Cordova by one of the proud Moorish kings of Seville, and burned by the Normans when they took and sacked his city. His mosque had displaced the early Christian basilica of San Vicente, which the still earlier temple of Venus Salambo had become. Then, after the mosque was rebuilt, the good San Fernando in his turn equipped it with a Gothic choir and chapels and turned it into the cathedral, which was worn out with pious uses when the present edifice was founded, in their *folie des grandeurs*, by those glorious madmen in the first year of the fifteenth century.

Little of this learning troubled me in my visits to the cathedral, or even the fact that, next to St. Peter's, it was the largest church in the world. It was sufficient to itself by mere force of architectural presence, without the help of incidents or measurements. It was a city in itself, with a community of priests and sacristans dwelling in it, and a floating population of sightseers and worshipers always passing through it. The first morning we had submitted to make the round of the chapels, patiently paying to have each of them unlocked and wearily wondering at their wonders, but only sympathizing really with the stern cleric who showed the ceremonial vestments and jewels of the cathedral, and whose bitter face expressed, or seemed to express, abhorrence of our whole trivial tourist tribe. After that morning we took our curiosity into our own keeping and looked at nothing that did not interest us, and we were interested most in those fellow-beings who kept coming and going all day long.

Chiefly, of course, they were women. In Catholic countries women have either more sins to be forgiven than the men, or else they are sorrier for them; and here, whether there was service or not, they were dropped everywhere in veiled and motionless prayer. In Seville the law of the mantilla is rigorously enforced. If a woman drives, she must wear a hat; but if she walks, she must wear a mantilla under pain of being pointed at by the finger of scorn. If she is a young girl she may wear colors with it (a cheerful blue seems the favorite), but by far the greater number came to the cathedral in complete black. Those somber figures which clustered before chapel, or singly dotted the pavement everywhere, flitted in and out like shadows in the perpetual twilight. For far the greater number, their coming to the church was almost their sole escape into the world. They sometimes met friends, and after a moment, or an hour, of prayer they could cheer their hearts with neighborly gossip. But for the greater part they appeared and disappeared silently and swiftly, and left the spectator to helpless conjecture of their history. Many of them would have first met their husbands in the cathedral when they prayed, or when they began to look around to see who was looking at them. It might have been their trysting-place, safeguarding them in their lovers' meetings, and after marriage it had become their social world, then their husbands left them for the clubs or the cafés. They could not go at night, of course, except to some special function, but they could come by day as often as they liked. I do not suppose that the worshipers I saw habitually united love or friendship with their devotions in the cathedral, but some certainly joined business with devotion; at a high function one day an American girl felt herself sharply nudged in the side, and when she turned she found the palm of her kneeling neighbor stretched toward her. They must all have had their parish churches besides the cathedral, and a devotee might make the day a social whirl by visiting one shrine after another. But I do not think that many do. The Spanish women are a domestic genus, and are expected to keep at home by the men who expect to keep abroad.

I do not know just how it is in the parish churches; they must each have its special rite, which draws and holds the frequenter; but the cathedral constantly offers a drama of irresistible appeal. We non-Catholics can feel this even at the distance to which our Protestantism has remanded us, and at your first visit to the Seville cathedral during mass you cannot help a moment of recreant regret when you wish that a part in the mystery enacting was your birthright. The esthetic emotion is not denied you; the organ-tide that floods the place bears you on it, too; the priests perform their rites before the altar for you; they come and go, they bow and kneel, for you; the censer swings and smokes for you; the little wicked-eyed choir-boys and mischievous-looking acolytes suppress their natures in your behalf as much as if you were a believer, or perhaps more. The whole unstinted hospitality of the service is there for you, as well as for the children of the house, and the heart must be rude and the soul ungrateful that would refuse it. For my part, I accepted it as far as I knew how, and when I left the worshipers on their knees and went tiptoeing from picture to picture and chapel to chapel, it was with shame for the unscrupulous sacristan showing me about, and I felt that he, if not I, ought to be put out and not allowed back till the function was over. I call him sacristan at a venture; but there were several kinds of guides in the cathedral, some in the livery of the place and some in civil dress, willing to supplement our hotel interpreter, or lying in wait for us when we came alone. I wish now I had taken them all, but at the time they tired me, and I denied them.

Though not a day passed but we saw it, I am not able to say what the cathedral was like. The choir was planted in the heart of it, as it might be a celestial refuge in that forest of mighty pillars, as great in girth as the giant redwoods of California, and climbing to a Gothic firmament horizoned round as with sunset light from near a hundred painted windows. The chapels on each side, the most beautiful in Spain, abound in riches of art and pious memorials, with chief among them the Royal Chapel, in the prow, as it were, of the ship which the cathedral has been likened to, keeping the bones not only of the sainted hero, King Fernando, but also, among others, the bones of Peter the Cruel, and of his unwedded love, Maria de Padilla, far too good for Peter in life, if not quite worthy of San Fernando in death. You can see the saint's body on certain dates four times a year, when, as your Baedeker will tell you, "the troops of the garrison march past and lower their colors" outside the cathedral. We were there on none of these dates, and, far more regrettably, not on the day of Corpus Christi, when those boys whose effigies in sculptured and painted wood we had seen in the museum at Valladolid pace in their mystic dance before the people at the opposite portal of the cathedral. But I appoint any reader, so minded, to go and witness the rite some springtime for me.

GERTRUDE BONE

Saint James of the Field of Stars

A SELECTION FROM *Days in Old Spain*

Only Jerusalem and Rome were greater Christian shrines in medieval times than Santiago de Compostela. In that city of remote northwestern Spain grew devotion to the saint who had brought Christianity across the long Mediterranean and over the harsh peninsula, and there in his honor a mighty church was erected. To the shrine pilgrims came by the thousands, from the British isles and Germany and farther still, crossing the Pyrenees, trudging toward their goal in Galicia. Pilgrims still come, many out of religious devotion; others, pilgrims of art; many, the modern pilgrims of restless curiosity—tourists.

Santiago, the city, has other medieval wonders in addition to the great church. The Hostal de los Reyes Católicos, for example, is a Renaissance palace of admirable proportions and decoration, built by Isabella as a resting place for the pilgrims.

The city is utterly Spanish, and yet it is Galician first, in tone more somber, stonier, than other parts of Spain, even Toledo; and mist and rain are frequent softeners of the appearance of the rugged stonework, but also give a chill which turns the thoughts of all but the most devout to summer lands.

Lady Gertrude Bone's book, Days in Old Spain, *an account of her visit there in 1925, is charmingly illustrated by her husband, Sir Muirhead Bone. It is a lovely book in content and form and further evidence of the affection of the English and the Scots for alien and entrancing Spain.*

ATLANTIC weather with its prevalent moisture visits these hills of Galicia. Clouds and energetic skies are everywhere among the beauties of Spanish landscape, for the sky, even in Southern Spain, is not always of unclouded blue, and in the neighbourhood of any of the Sierras their chief company is the heavens in majesty. In Galicia it seems as though the exhalations which rise amid the hills take with them also something of their colour. Mobile, gathering, dispersing, the ethereal hills are built anew every day above long valleys like the beds of lakes drained of everything save the light.

Deep, heath-coloured country and granite mountains guard the hills of Compostela with its shrine and church of Santiago

(St. James) the Apostle, a place of pilgrimage, an ascent, with bronze bells telling the hours of centuries and of history. As the sunlight and bright wind open distances on the surrounding hills, roads are visible on their slopes converging from all sides to the hill of Santiago, beautiful for situation. White glimpses faint in summer heat, paths broken by declivities to reappear higher among the heather, one has only to enter Compostela from any road over the hills to see how often the towers of her cathedral appear through openings across the valleys long before the streets of the town give their certainty to the way-farer.

Compostela, with its guard of hills, once the most famous shrine in Europe, with roads trodden to it from every quarter by the feet of pilgrims, was once further gathered up into walls on its own eminence like a fortress. To-day it remains compact, its centre heavily magnificent, its streets arcaded with strong granite porticos, its domestic architecture unpretentious, here and there the sombre mass of a religious house shuttered and blind, with valerian and borage growing on its walls as on a forsaken grave, taking emotion from the volume of sunlight which envelops its immobility with shadows. Below the hill on every side are villages attached to Compostela by the wavering thread of a rivulet. Where water is abundant and fluent one expects animation about its confluences, and shadowed by little granite calvaries the washerwomen kneel and wash.

In the poorer part of the town modest streets of houses with cockle-shells carved about the doors announce the ancient inns for pilgrims, and Isabella's guest-house and sanctuary the royalty of demeanour of that high-spirited lady towards the wayfaring Catholic. For although three active streams of life flow through Compostela—the youth of the University, the peasants surging up to the marketplace, and the activities of the cathedral—it is still the hospitality and interest of the shrine of Santiago which dominates them all. Legends stand like sentinels about the militant apostle. Fire-balloons float over the hills which proclaim the arrival of a group of pilgrims at his doors. One can tell the moment at which a pilgrimage mounts the great stair beneath the Porch of Glory by the explosion of bombs. Women working in the fields outside the town straighten themselves, and look up. The road watchman sitting in his stone hut and the shepherd on the hillside turn towards the breaking of flames in the sky. It is both announcement and fulfilment.

> *"How should I your true love know*
> *From another one?"*
> *"By his cockle hat and staff,*
> *And his sandal shoon."*

I never had a mind to go on a pilgrimage except to the days of my youth that I might know whether the years condemn false hopes or low fears, and only a few times in Europe have I met genuine wayfaring pilgrims, each time very old people, regarded with an indulgent smile by the officials from whom they asked their way, as people given to occupations a little behind the times. But the Tower of London once made a steady revenue from the tax of sixpence imposed on every English pilgrim who wore the cockle-shell badge for a pilgrimage to St. James overseas. Ophelia knew it. Helena's disguise was the palmer's habit for Saint Jacques le Grand. The Wife of Bath had added a pilgrimage to Saint Jaime in Galice to her record; and the polyglot hymn of the early pilgrimages shows the popularity of St. James's shrine in the Low Countries:

> *"Herru Sanctiagu*
> *Got Sanctiagu*
> *eullreja*
> *esus eja*
> *Deus adjuva nos."*

198

It is from the point of view of the town which receives the pilgrims that one has watched them come up to the shrine of the Apostle for many past months. For though the great pilgrimage ways of Europe are travelled no longer and St. James is now a Spanish saint, since the station is a long way off, the town of Compostela on a hill, and the diligences stop outside, there is still the illusion as the processions of pilgrims come to the Pórtico de la Gloria that they have come on foot; and though the pilgrimages have more the air of a Sunday-school outing than a spiritual effort, they are still interesting, the ceremonies dignified and adequate, the hospitality of the town attractive. Isabella's handsome idea of a guest-house for pilgrims, with its beautiful Plateresque balcony and interior chapel and courtyards, witnesses to the difficulty of housing the multitudes who travelled over the pilgrimage roads to Compostela. So many came that the inns of the town could not suffice for accommodation and the pilgrims often slept in the cathedral itself. Probably indeed, the origin of the giant censer, *el botafumeiro,* was hygienic, for braziers of incense are said to have burned all night in the cathedral in medieval times, and an ancient cross upon the parapet of the church is shown as the place where the pilgrims washed and hung their travel-worn clothes to dry, change of clothing being provided by the archbishop.

No one washes clothes there now or hangs them on the cross. If the pilgrims are country folks come in by the early morning diligences you will meet the women thronging the shops where the coloured silk squares are sold with which they cover their heads, and the men in the smithies leaving their sickles and knives to be sharpened, or waiting round the menders of umbrellas or farm implements who sit in the markets. This until the time for the cathedral dignitaries to receive the pilgrimage. Then the pilgrims assemble in the Plaza and ascend the stairs to the Porch of Glory. Banners are carried and sometimes the saint of the village, and often the Galician pilgrimage comes with the *gaiteros* (pipers) playing them in. The houses of the town hang festival cloths of red and yellow on the balconies, and the pilgrim song is played by the town band. Fireworks and bombs and balloons announce the arrival of the procession at the cathedral doors.

Within, there is the welcome by the canons, mass, and a sermon from the Archbishop, a visit to the shrine of the Apostle and the censing of the whole congregation by the botafumeiro. This heavy silver censer (six feet high as it swings) is carried like the grapes of Eschol on a staff borne on the shoulders of two men. It is attached to a rope and pulley pendent from the central dome, the pilgrims throng to the transepts across the entire breadth of which it swings, the dignitaries emerge with an extraordinary effect of colour from the Coro, and having paced the ambulatory halt in the transept. Two very primitive bassoons and some horns begin the wailing, lulling, swaying melody of the pilgrims' hymn, and seven men raise and swing the botafumeiro. The arc of silver (with its smoke circling about it like swarming bees) cuts the gloom of the vaulting from transept to transept. It is a strange scene in the dim church—the upturned faces of the pilgrims; the boys holding the tall candles in silver candlesticks; the smoke and fragrance of the censer filling the dome; the brave Titian reds and gold and purple of the ecclesiastics making credible at last the sombre and elaborate gilding of altar and sanctuary; the image of Santiago in his cape of jewelled gold, motionless in the tabernacle, and the reedy ancient cradle-song of the botafumeiro finding its way through centuries to the echo and gloom of the aisles.

From the dominance of Compostela as a place of pilgrimage it became greatly prosperous in commerce, being one of the first towns of Northern Spain to acquire independence as a township. Its bishop Gelmírez maintained a private navy: and the history of the building of its cathedral—with the central motive of interest in the shrine—is the record of the rising or passing of architectural styles, proportioned to the ambitious of churchmen and the prosperities of trade. This beautiful Romanesque cathedral is one of the disguised Gothic churches of Spain; so re-made and re-decorated as to its outer walls after Churriguera that one seems to have wandered through another door and mistaken the church when the antique and undisturbed Romanesque interior finally receives one. Something of the unfamiliarity of impression (to English eyes) left by a Spanish cathedral of familiar architectural invention, comes from an unaccustomed lighting (the desire, it may be, to preserve the luxury of quiet for the eye from the volume of sunlight out of doors). There is no clerestory. The light flows through the aisles on the level of the lower windows, except where the flood descends from the dome above the Coro. So that the dimness of the nave becomes part of the architectural intention, as it were, and darkness deepens to a colour. Something, too, a little ancient and immobile clings to the arrangement of a Spanish cathedral attached still, one imagines, to some monastic idea. The central position of the Coro seems to shoulder the congregation outside, and the nave appears a little purposeless. Yet there are times (one such being that of the National Offering) when the very emptiness of the nave gives moment to the grouping of ecclesiastics before its altar. Some effect from very long ago seems to be "staged," as it were, from an older Spain than the present, from ceremonials very established and unchanged, from something even deeper still, it may be, the desire to leave them unchanged.

"Now tell me," said a Spanish architect, "would you *like* a Spanish cathedral to be like an English or a French one?

Oh yes! I know that to come into one of our cathedrals gives a French architect the vertigo! But would you like Santiago to be so cold, so empty?"

It is on the day of the Ofrenda Nacional that I am in accord with the feelings of the Spaniard.

From the time when it seemed as though Spain must make visible the wealth of the Indies, those gilded sanctuaries, now so deep and sombre in tone, stole within the severe Gothic shell. When empty of ceremony the pillars and angels and clouds have the effect of an over-elaboration of preposterous glories. But the deep glow from the ornate gilding takes its relation fitly enough when the tapers are lit and the purple and ruby and gold vestments group and pass and shimmer and live before the altar, as a rich shrine for a very splendid pomp. Nothing less magnificently glowing could support the weight of colour which fills the sanctuary on the day of the National Offering and the Feast of the Apostle.

When Sancho Panza tempts Don Quixote to abandon knight-errantry and become a saint, since even kings visit the shrines of saints and he never heard of any august person taking much notice of a knight-errant, he might well have had Santiago in his mind. During Apostle's Week (the offering is made on St. James's Day) pilgrims surge up from the country literally in thousands, singing as they approach. Highly placed officers of the Spanish army collect in the town. Ecclesiastics gather daily. Every day another coloured uniform or cloak is added to the brightness of the streets. Festival hangings shine in the cathedral: the silver altar is uncovered; candles fill dark recesses with their mystical flowering. Through the whole town a deeper colour, a quicker life, passes like a wind, to culminate in the ceremony and magnificence of the Apostle's Day.

One day, at sundown, a line of cavalry officers covered with dust ride up the arcaded streets, each with drawn sword or

Torija (Guadalajara) Castillo

The Costa Brava

Basque Girls

The Alhambra

The Escorial

The Palace,
Aranjuez

The Royal Palace, Madrid

Yuste

The Walls of Ávila

Santiago de Compostela

The Cathedral of Toledo

Loyalists on the Aragón Front

Civil Guard

Flamenco

Feria in Sevilla

Sherry Bodega

Palma de Mallorca

Belmonte

the banner of St. James in his hand (the hilt of the banner stuck in his boot), and dismounting at the cathedral steps kneel and kiss the hand of the Archbishop and place their banners before the altar. For Santiago, the caballero and militant saint of legend, gives his name to the chief military religious Order of Spain, and it is the privilege of the Knights of Santiago to accompany the National Offering to his shrine. Again the quality of some unaltering and very ancient outlook seems to stir the surface, some deeply homogeneous quality of the Spanish mentality—ecclesiastics, people, soldiers, in equal parts of the ceremony.

Fairs of horses and cattle are taking place in the town, pageants are making ready for the streets, fireworks for the evening. Within the cathedral the transepts grow dim, as colour slowly amasses within the shining sanctuary. Fifteen bishops in purple and gold vestments, with gold and silver mitres, and with their attendant canons, set themselves within the chancel; while the Knights of Santiago, robed in the white cloak and red cross of their Order, await the arrival of the Infante with the King's offering at the Porch of Glory. He comes as a pilgrim up the pilgrims' stairway and is conducted by his companions in the Order to the sacristy to be robed. The Mass advances to the Gloria—the botafumeiro swings above the heads of a vast congregation, its little reedy cradle-song on the horns sounding with a naïve familiarity like a child's voice singing a hymn at a coronation; the moment for the offering arrives.

Though the Spaniard may at times pay the penalty of those who go their own way through the changes of history, there are moments when he is justified—of effect at any rate. Titian and Veronese come nearest to the suggestion of glowing colour now moving in ceremonial. The red-gold sanctuary with the silver altar and the archaic figure of the Apostle in his jewelled cape of gold; the light of tapers absorbed, as it were, rather than reflected in the gilding; fifteen gold-mitred and vested bishops seated on either side of the altar, servitors with tall silver croziers and candlesticks, are all grouped and motionless, and between the choir and the sanctuary there advance two by two the Knights of Santiago, each now with his long white velvet train fastened to his shoulders. The Infante kneels with the offering, and each knight receives a posy presented on the enormous silver cockle-shell salver which carries the vestments of the Archbishop. The dignitaries leave the altar, their sudden emergence into the crowded aisles so vivid that the colours seem to live of themselves in the gloom, and passing down to the sunshine of the Western Door descend the pilgrims' stair. And now, there is still another ceremony to add to those of the Apostle's Day. For in the outer wall of the cathedral lodge eight giants invisible for all the rest of the year (large wicker frames for bodies, papier mâché for their eighteenth-century heads). On the day of the Apostle's vigil they come out of their cupboard, dance round the Plaza three times, and then, accompanied by dwarfs and two pipers in yellow, promenade the streets of the town. And on the Apostle's Day? The gorgeous stream of dignitaries has passed out into the sunlight of the Plaza—authority, as it were, has looked the other way; and again the giants emerge, this time into the cathedral, with their two pipers in yellow, piping boldly through the aisles. The sanctuary is empty. The tapers are still lighted before the image of the Apostle. No living person is there. The two smaller giants enter the sanctuary (the six tall ones standing to attention outside), dance solemnly on the empty carpet before the Apostle, and then all retreat, and, making the ambulatory of the whole cathedral, go back into their cupboards until the Apostle's Day of the succeeding year. It is like an imagination of Hans Andersen: the fantasies after the pageant, the strange image and the lit candles in the deserted sanctuary, the giants popping in as soon as authority smiles and looks the other way, dancing their top-heavy minuet on the empty carpet and clapping back into their cupboards when the candles are put out.

GEORGIANA GODDARD KING

Toledo

A SELECTION FROM *Heart of Spain*

(edited by Agnes Mongan)

Toledo, gray and granite, is the heart of historic Spain. The city existed before the Romans came to the peninsula; it was the center of Visigothic Christendom, as it is today the see of the Catholic primate of Spain; artists in stone and metal and oils spread its fame through the Western world.

Georgiana Goddard King, a teacher at Bryn Mawr during the early decades of this century, added to a profound knowledge of Spanish art and literature an evocative prose style.

WE had been traveling for hours through a country filled with an immense energy—with the energy of silence. The enormous plain stretches out to the blue horizon's bound; it is brown as dust, it is grey and ashen, but with the changing hours the colors change. It is mauve and it is réséda, it is sage green and periwinkle blue; and set in the midst thereof, and fair as a star sapphire, and so old that age is nonexistent, is the city. Time has no power upon her beauty, which was ordained before time was. The twilight of the ages is luminous upon her; she broods, aloof and fair, a place of enchantments. As Spain has no dew, so Spain has no dreams, but she has magic, and some of it is black magic; as Siena is a city of dreams, so Toledo is a city of enchantments, legendary and magical.

This is the city, says a great master of living thought in Spain, which offers most completely and characteristically, in its entirety, all that has been of civilization and soil genuinely Spanish, the intensest, most brilliant and suggestive summing up of Spanish history. Toledo expresses perfectly the interpenetration of the two capital elements of the national culture, which are the Christian and the Semite, Gothic and Celtiberian intermingling with Hebraic and Arab. This is the note of Spain, the typical quality in literature as in the other arts. No other city in Spain has such a series of monuments so splendid. To the situation inconceivably picturesque—a harsh and lofty rock of granite, straitly girt around by the profound gulf of the Tagus—is added the spectacle of uncounted civilizations superimposing and coexisting, in churches and convents innumerable, dwellings Gothic or Mudéjar or plateresque; narrow lofty Moorish alleys; a picture, in sum, still breathing, still untouched, of a town where every stone is a voice to cry to the spirit.

The outlying landscape sums up and concentrates the characteristics of the lofty plains of Castile: on one hand the vast, unpeopled, and arid stretch where steppe alternates with red ploughland, and the delicate modeling of the ancient *cerro* beyond, ashen grey; the river quietly ploughing a long crooked furrow bordered with gardens and avenues; elsewhere the abrupt and hard *sierra* with its loving rock, its evergreen oaks, its thyme and rosemary, its honey-growing gardens and fruit trees on the sunny slopes, and the Tagus, when it reaches this, breaks through in a foam-lined gorge.

The history is as long as the memory of man. Celtiberian graves exist in the hillsides, and Roman stonework in the river bottom and on the steep crest. There is a legend that the Jews of Toledo were consulted, at the time of the trial of Christ, and they recommended that He should be released, as He seemed an innocent person and one whose ideas were commendable, but events moved fast and their letter came too late. The Visigoths who took over the dominion from Rome in the fifth century, when antiquity was dying, made this their chief seat, capital of their fantastically named kings, Recared and Chindaswinth and the rest; in Toledo soil were found the votive crowns called the Treasure of Guarrazar, set with pale sapphires and tinkling with gold pendants, and Madrid keeps, along with the crowns, a fibula, an eagle of strange barbaric work, inlaid with bright gems, like those preserved in the museums at Budapest and Leningrad which were dug up in grave mounds along the Cimmerian Bosphorus. The last of the Gothic kings, D. Roderick, was to end his days in exile among the ruins of his land, not perhaps because he loved the frail beauty of La Cava but because he penetrated into the enchanted Cave of Hercules, and, desiring to know certainly of the future, incontinent brought it about.

When the Moors reached Toledo they stayed there, and in a sense they are not yet gone. Arabic inscriptions are built into the walls, and carved on timbers older than the Reconquest; delicate work of molded plaster adorns arch heads and ceilings that graced a conqueror's dwelling. The restless interlacing brickwork marks Christian building executed by Moorish slaves. When with the Cid's help Alfonso VI retook Toledo, and gained thereby his title in history—*el que ganó Toledo*—he left his building, apparently, in these Mudéjar hands. The great Romanesque of the eleventh and twelfth century is the one style wanting in the city. The mosque that he had promised to respect, though the Queen and the Archbishop had brought his pledge to naught, still imposed its form on the cathedral that was begun only under S. Ferdinand, and in the Mudéjar style the triforium windows were traced, the towers of parish churches erected, and the synagogues built which are called now *El Tránsito* and S. María la Blanca. Private houses and convent parlors carry the same manner into the fifteenth century. It mingles with the early Gothic in the cathedral, and in S. John of the Kings with the late-Gothic style called Isabellan, which offers such close parallels to the English Tudor. The rich plateresque, which is a genre essentially Spanish, may be found in perfection at the hospital of Santa Cruz. Master Enrique Egas, who built this for the great cardinal of Spain, Mendoza, and another in the same style for the Catholic kings at Santiago in Galicia, lived to see the Cardinal's tomb in the cathedral erected in a pure Italian style; and he was hardly dead before, in a new Italian vein, another hospital had been begun, dedicated to the Baptist, which Greco was to complete and adorn. The same noble, classical air which marks Greco's hospital church and the altars therein that enframe his paintings is so plainly manifest at S. Domingo and the Town Hall that these pass for inventions, if not of himself, then of his son George; and though from the oratory of S. José the paintings have been sold, yet the building remains to testify still to the master's mind. The

Jesuit church of St. John, at the top of the town, has its own nobility of a rather massive and organic baroque, and the three main doors of the cathedral are overlaid with a late imitation of Gothic devised in the same epoch. And everywhere behind the house-fronts, chapels, patios, secluded chambers may be divined, which were erected, furnished, and occupied in one or another of these long ages of the past.

Spain is full of cities thousands of years old, choked up with immense convents and great houses of ancient families. Here in Toledo the span of the years is widest, and the types of art most various: the goldsmith's work, and that in iron and bronze, the wood sculpture, often polychrome and gilded, the *artesonado* ceilings. Textiles and embroideries, though abundant throughout the town, are richest in the treasuries of the cathedral. The tiles of the south of Spain and the east coast, and the lovely ceramic of Talavera de la Reina, abound likewise throughout the city, often in pieces veritably ancient, and again in good copies, very pleasant to possess.

The cathedral is reared in the very heart of the town, so that the shortest way from anywhere to anywhere else lies under the wide span of its brooding vaulted aisles, and between the carved altarpiece and the carved choir stalls: this is a place for all hours of summer and winter—all days, from Candlemas to Christmas. Never twice alike is the Office, with its customs and ceremonies of very ancient use, saved by a hard struggle after the Council of Trent; nowhere else in Spain is the Mass so venerable, so sumptuous, so sacred with its observances of an immemorial past, and its memories of things old, far-off, and forgotten. When we went up into Las Claverías, the dwellings, above the cloister, of the cathedral dependents, and came back again to sit as we were wont, under the lofty crossing, for the evening Office, we knew that the cathedral was an abiding place of the spirit, that we too, like the sacristan and beadles, were domiciled there.

After the warmed and golden dusk of the fragrant Office we paused an instant before Nuestra Señora del Sagrario, where she glitters in her sanctuary among the innumerable lights. Then we went out into the grey cold of winter twilight. Always we were going about in the streets, the countless streets, devious, labyrinthine.

Somewhere between the grey palaces, in one of the innumerable decaying churches, is hidden the tomb of Garcilaso de la Vega. I recall our making a pious pilgrimage thereto, though I cannot recall now where it lies forgotten, and they say his ashes were lost long ago; but he was a gracious poet and a goodly knight, another Sidney, dying like him by the wanton stroke of fate, in the full flight of exquisite Italianate poetry.

The Renaissance in Toledo lasted long, like the light on August lawns; the longer because on the Tagus the Court was no more situate. The city was still, however, a capital, and enjoyed the early drama, and learning of the ripest humanistic sort, and gatherings of poets and scholars for pleasant talk among the gardens across the river, the so-called *cigarrales*. Thither came Greco, for among the poet-haunted trees his friends were wont to walk. He built Buena Vista, the country seat of the archbishop Sandoval y Rojas, a palace embowered in olives and myrtles above the Tagus gorge, and shared the cultured talk on long perfumed summer nights, when the constellation that swung across the arc of sky had paled in white dawn before any sought his bed. There Sandoval had consciously re-evoked the Medicean gardens, and the company was at least as learned and as witty as that in Italy, though it is our misfortune that we know them less well.

Where the brown Tagus has cut down through the purple shale there is not a blade of green to be seen; the *cigarrales*, where you walk on the heights over against the city, are set out with silvery agave tipping the red earth banks or planted with olive orchards blue as smoke where you look across their tops to the ancient city. At the weirs the river shows its teeth, and sends up irregularly a faint rustling noise, lost when a mule shakes his bells on the Puente de S. Martín, and from high among the rocks still you may hear his driver, "Arré, burro!" At the sanctuary of Our Lady of the Valley, terraced out where two gorges are cloven down toward the stream-side, a little bell clatters and whimpers below your feet; it is sunset there above the darkening waters, though across on its citadel height the Alcázar shines bright as marble and the cathedral spire is filmy and fair, and the grave male towers of brickwork, S. Tomás and S. Román, and S. Andrés, and the twin towers of the Baptist, are ruddy till long after the bell has ceased. Then the Toledo of Greco is seen in lilac-blue; like an enchanted city it hangs its towers against a sky as pale as glass, and darkness comes up cold out of the river gorges, and the sound of the waters is constant. Flocks go by on the road with a hurried tinkle and a muddled patter. Walking is easy on that lonely road, in the clear dark, where Ángel Guerra passed so many times; but the descent is long to the bridge where about the piers the foam-flecks swirl white and lisp; and the climb is even longer by narrow winding streets where the third turn to the right and then two to the left may signify the way home, but anything else means getting lost completely.

We watched the figures passing in the narrow streets, ways strait and steep as the path to heaven, that now drop to the river's edge and a ferry, and anon climb to S. Román and the city reservoir on the highest hilltop, where, laying an ear to the ancient stones and listening to the strange murmuring noise always changing and never silent, one might wonder if it were the entrance to the fabled Cave of Hercules. The narrow streets are like corridors of a convent, so deserted and so hushed; and between the ancient houses still move the gaunt Castilians in *alpargatas*, on soundless feet. Emerging in an open square, or on a lofty terrace, under the bright fierce caress of the heat, reason half swoons, and the vision is dazzled with evocations of time long past.

Everywhere about Toledo the air is astir with wizardy and fragrant with memory, and tales are told like fairy tales, of great riches and great wrongs, and magic hangs about the place. What we call El Tránsito was once a synagogue built for loyal subjects by King Peter [1] and Queen Blanche and the treasurer Samuel Levi, and hard by stands the house that once was the latter's palace, called now the House of Greco. On a bench in the sun we re-read the story, how in one day God's judgment fell on him and he died by the king's order, he and all his kin anywhere in the realm, and the king's new treasurer, Martín Yáñez, standing in those vaults where we ourselves had stood, cried out that one-quarter of the riches therein amassed would have saved his stubborn life. The tale is probably not true: there is reason to believe that the Ghetto palace housed its magnificence unpillaged for nine years after the alleged murder of Samuel Levi, while just across the street the congregation worshipped unharmed, till their benefactor died quietly and was buried decently. The life will have been very splendid in the rich Jew's palace, with vases of gold and platters of silver, with its hangings of Persian and Egyptian textiles, cloth of gold and cloth of sendal, samite and cramoisy; with its trusty dark-skinned menservants and maidservants, its philosophic monotheism, its secluded luxury, its privacy unspied upon. Time went on, and in the same house, it is said, thereafter, lived D. Enrique de Villena, a great lord, a king's grandson and of reigning princes the cousin and the uncle,

---

[1] Peter I of Castile, called the Cruel, or the Just, 1334–1369.

a profound humanist, the Master of Calatrava, yet a shadowed and tragical figure. Men have always looked at him askance. As Samuel Levi owned too much, so he knew too much.

He had studied, they said, with Merlin in Rome: he had made a compact with the devil and got hardly out of it, escaped, indeed, but with the loss of his shadow; he was associated somehow with a brass head like Friar Bacon's and a magical mirror that showed what was happening at a distance. Friar Bacon kept such another at Oxford. After he died, his entire library was burned, and the loss to learning was irreparable. It is said that in these well-built brick vaults which Romans laid perhaps and where the king's treasurer had laid up for himself treasure under earth, the Marquis held meetings with others of his art, with witches and wizards such as that D. Illán to whom came a Dean of Santiago desiring to be initiated in necromacy, and in the end had not even a taste of partridges for his supper. There beneath the palace, it seems, the company were wont to brew enchantments, and to practise such black art as that of having oneself cut up and securely bottled away to emerge whole and young again when the whirligig of time has brought about his revenges. Indeed, according to some he bottled himself, and though Quevedo dreamed of uncorking that vial, perhaps he still awaits a joyful re-emergence.

The popular imagination has always loved the site, and mumbled stories in the dark to credulous ears for centuries. It has seen as in an enchanted mirror the gaunt old Cretan El Greco with his large-eyed shrinking daughter-in-law and behind them the Master of Calatrava who had sold his shadow, lonely among his undecipherable tomes; and vaguely glowing in the background the oriental splendor in the old Jew's house, the Arab slave girls dancing, the yellow-hatted merchants conspiring; below whom, in the cellar, are blazing by their own radiance carbuncle and diamond, male sapphires, balas rubies, Indian emeralds, piled-up church plate, custodials and candlesticks, pyxes and paxes and chalices, crammed to the thrice-barred door, wedges of gold, bars of fine silver, piles of agate and sardonyx, columns of jasper, heaps of pearls. But at the last, old townsfolk say, a later master burnt the palace, wall and rooftree, because his house was defiled by lodging a great traitor. At the emperor's command he had entertained the constable of Bourbon. All these, interwoven, like figures moving in a dream, still pass and repass and shift their personality but hardly change their aspect.

Airs of enchantment still hang about the house, in truth, while Theotocopuli inhabits there, and, if not a savor of magic, yet a sense of the untoward. Men whisper and draw back as the occupant passes by. Was he married ever? they ask. Whence comes that gallant youth? Whose is that lovely woman's face that canvases repeat; was it ever seen at a *reja*, or as the iron-studded door swung open?

Greco was a complete humanist. He kept, moreover, a kind of lonely state in his crumbling palace; he had musicians to play to him at dinner. Leonardo, as we remember, commanded music while he painted, sweet-breathing flutes and viols filling the chambered air in the pauses of discourse. The Toledan master, who knew Leonardo's text, may have adapted thence the idea. Whether he brought his way of life from Italy or the East, we may be sure he kept good company or none. We know that he read much, not only as a gentleman should, but profoundly in the mystical vein, for he left a choice library of Greek and Italian books. A young Spanish scholar has lately discovered the inventory of the painter's effects, taken after his death; to read it is like standing in his studio in the dusty sunlight, when the master has just stepped out. I know no document so poignant, so evocative of the past. The dead comes back, and for an hour we are in his company.

Greco, when he first lived in these quarters, had just finished the great painting in a chapel of S. Tomé that depicts the

Burial of the Count of Orgaz. With the calm distinction of the heads and the brocades, with the lucent power of the vast and heaving composition in the *Gloria* overhead, an art has culminated. Depth beyond depth in the clouds the witnesses are assembled, light above light the splendor mounts in waves.

Life does not stop at culmination, however, and as the animal spirits are burned out of the blood the soul burns clearer and intenser. When he returned to this dwelling again, counting then not far from sixty years, his art had grown so strange a thing that men took fright before it. They disowned for human those gigantic apparitions, with their little heads and their monstrous shoulders, their enormous arms and thighs that swerved in the standing as though fierce blasts blew on them. Nor are the faces reassuring, ghost-seers' all. That silent company assembled in the studio for the notary to take his inventory were, if he had looked, more spectral than any Villena entertained.

The strange and difficult beauty of El Greco's latest period, in its cold passion, its ambiguous and mysterious color which he had brought with him from Crete, its shifting pattern and thrice-implicate design, anticipates indeed our ultimate modernity. Yet he is the most Spanish of painters. As when we walk upon the heights across the Tagus, in the winter afternoon or before the summer sunrise, and looking across at the city behold the forms indued with the strange colors of Greco's painting, cold green, metallic blue, and yellow like sulphur or like the lightning, so in his pictures we taste the distilled spirit of Spain, and read the secrets of the Spanish soul. These figures are not human, but they are miraculous, seraphic or apocalyptic. Out of a world of elemental spirits or of pure intelligences were they evoked. Lights burn upon the canvas of balefire and *ignis fatuus*, of stormy sunsets rifted over tumbling seas, of northern lights upon unmeasured snows, pale Pentecostal flares and comets' fiery hair. Only nowhere are seen the

fires of hell. If ominous lights hang over the small picture of
Toledo, it is only the breaking of the Judgment Day. The
perturbed spirits with whom Domenico Theotocopuli holds
converse might well be those, the sorry tribe, who made no
choice when Lucifer arrayed all heaven, and are now reborn
on earth to make the great election, troubled indeed, but with
ultimate confidence in God's mercy.

GEORGE ORWELL

War, 1937

A SELECTION FROM *Homage to Catalonia*

The Spanish Civil War (1936–1939) is often described as the rehearsal for World War II. This is true, no doubt, as a quick journalistic statement, but the phrase brings to mind an image of easy theatricals which does no justice to the terror of either war. The Spanish Civil War was, in fact, the first twentieth-century war—the first conflict in which twentieth-century weapons, military, political, and psychological, were used in prolonged combat. Pre-eminently the war was fought over ideas; here Spain fulfilled tragically her role as a land of paradoxes. How did it happen that a "backward" country which the rest of the world had almost forgotten became the stage for a military-ideological struggle marked by events such as the first saturation air bombing of a town, by the development of the Fifth Column, by the clash of men from almost all the nations of the Western world, who used such dread means that they, with disease, caused the death of one million people?

That question has not yet been well met, but it is a mistake to assume that the answer is to be found in a facile interpretation of the war as a struggle between Right and Left, much less as a battle of Good with Evil. The outsider (that is, any person not a Spaniard) forgets that the war was a Spanish *war, in its beginning and in its end, and that it was, therefore, deeply rooted in the complex depths of Spain's history and in the spirits of her men and women. It was a war which destroyed the few illusions which history had left to some Spaniards, especially illusions about the possibility of establishing stable political democracy. But the war was a more profound disillusionment for the foreigner who was touched by it: it stripped him of his image of the brave new world. The Civil War in Spain ended the Enlightenment.*

George Orwell was among the disillusioned. He was an English left-Socialist (whose true name was Eric Blair) who went to Spain to fight for the Republic in the early months of the conflict. There he joined the P.O.U.M., the military organization of the Spanish anti-Stalin Marxists. He fought on the Aragón front in the first winter, and in the spring of 1937 he received a nearly mortal throat wound. But it was not the wound which forced him back to England; it was the maelstrom of political cynicism and betrayal which swept the Left, in which he had believed, into the same pit with the Right, which he had always thought he hated.

Orwell possessed unusual courage, honesty, and common sense. These qualities were his real weapons against the Spanish madness. Because he had these gifts to a high degree—and the gift of a lucid prose style—he was able to write Homage *to Catalonia in 1937, while the war gathered fury and his contemporaries became savagely dogmatic about events of which they had little knowledge. Disillusioned, yet never ceasing to believe in freedom, Orwell gave us his low-key description of twentieth-century war, with its medieval, Spanish overtones, which did much to make him, as his countryman, V. S. Pritchett, has written, "the conscience of his generation."*

BARBASTRO, though a long way from the front line, looked bleak and chipped. Swarms of militiamen in shabby uniforms wandered up and down the streets, trying to keep warm. On a ruinous wall I came upon a poster dating from the previous year and announcing that "six handsome bulls" would be killed in the arena on such and such a date. How forlorn its faded colours looked! Where were the handsome bulls and the handsome bullfighters now? It appeared that even in Barcelona there were hardly any bullfights nowadays; for some reason all the best matadors were Fascists.

They sent my company by lorry to Sietamo, then westward to Alcubierre, which was just behind the line fronting Zaragoza. Sietamo had been fought over three times before the Anarchists finally took it in October, and parts of it were smashed to pieces by shell-fire and most of the houses pockmarked by rifle-bullets. We were 1,500 feet above sea-level now. It was beastly cold, with dense mists that came swirling up from nowhere. Between Sietamo and Alcubierre the lorry-driver lost his way (this was one of the regular features of the war) and we were wandering for hours in the mist. It was late at night when we reached Alcubierre. Somebody shepherded us through morasses of mud into a mule-stable where we dug

ourselves down into the chaff and promptly fell asleep. Chaff
is not bad to sleep in when it is clean, not so good as hay but
better than straw. It was only in the morning light that I discovered that the chaff was full of breadcrusts, torn news-
papers, bones, dead rats, and jagged milk tins.

We were near the front line now, near enough to smell
the characteristic smell of war—in my experience a smell
of excrement and decaying food. Alcubierre had never been
shelled and was in a better state than most of the villages
immediately behind the line. Yet I believe that even in peace-
time you could not travel in that part of Spain without being
struck by the peculiar squalid misery of the Aragonese villages. They are built like fortresses, a mass of mean little
houses of mud and stone huddling round the church, and even
in spring you see hardly a flower anywhere; the houses have
no gardens, only back-yards where ragged fowls skate over
the beds of mule dung. It was vile weather, with alternate
mist and rain. The narrow earth roads had been churned
into a sea of mud, in places two feet deep, through which the
lorries struggled with racing wheels and the peasants led their
clumsy carts which were pulled by strings of mules, sometimes
as many as six in a string, always pulling tandem. The constant
come-and-go of troops had reduced the village to a state of
unspeakable filth. It did not possess and never had possessed
such a thing as a lavatory or a drain of any kind, and there
was not a square yard anywhere where you could tread without watching your step. The church had long been used as a
latrine; so had all the fields for a quarter of a mile around. I
never think of my first two months at war without thinking of
wintry stubble fields whose edges are crusted with dung.

Two days passed and no rifles were issued to us. When
you had been to the Comite de Guerra and inspected the row
of holes in the wall—holes made by rifle-volleys, various
Fascists having been executed there—you had seen all the

sights that Alcubierre contained. Up in the front line things were obviously quiet; very few wounded were coming in. The chief excitement was the arrival of Fascist deserters, who were brought under guard from the front line. Many of the troops opposite us on this part of the line were not Fascists at all, merely wretched conscripts who had been doing their military service at the time when the war broke out and were only too anxious to escape. Occasionally small batches of them took the risk of slipping across to our lines. No doubt more would have done so if their relatives had not been in Fascist territory. These deserters were the first "real" Fascists I had ever seen. It struck me that they were indistinguishable from ourselves, except that they wore khaki overalls. They were always ravenously hungry when they arrived—natural enough after a day or two of dodging about in no man's land, but it was always triumphantly pointed to as a proof that the Fascist troops were starving. I watched one of them being fed in a peasant's house. It was somehow rather a pitiful sight. A tall boy of twenty, deeply windburnt, with his clothes in rags, crouched over the fire shovelling a pannikinful of stew into himself at desperate speed; and all the while his eyes flitted nervously round the ring of militiamen who stood watching him. I think he still half-believed that we were blood-thirsty "Reds" and were going to shoot him as soon as he had finished his meal; the armed man who guarded him kept stroking his shoulder and making reassuring noises. On one memorable day fifteen deserters arrived in a single batch. They were led through the village in triumph with a man riding in front of them on a white horse. I managed to take a rather blurry photograph which was stolen from me later.

On our third morning in Alcubierre the rifles arrived. A sergeant with a coarse dark-yellow face was handing them out in the mule-stable. I got a shock of dismay when I saw the thing they gave me. It was a German Mauser dated 1896—

more than forty years old! It was rusty, the bolt was stiff, the wooden barrel-guard was split; one glance down the muzzle showed that it was corroded and past praying for. Most of the rifles were equally bad, some of them even worse, and no attempt was made to give the best weapons to the men who knew how to use them. The best rifle of the lot, only ten years old, was given to a half-witted little beast of fifteen, known to everyone as the *maricon* (Nancy-boy). The sergeant gave us five minutes' "instruction," which consisted in explaining how you loaded a rifle and how you took the bolt to pieces. Many of the militiamen had never had a gun in their hands before, and very few, I imagine, knew what the sights were for. Cartridges were handed out, fifty to a man, and then the ranks were formed and we strapped our kits on our backs and set out for the front line, about three miles away.

The *centuria,* eighty men and several dogs, wound raggedly up the road. Every militia column had at least one dog attached to it as a mascot. One wretched brute that marched with us had had P.O.U.M. branded on it in hugh letters and slunk along as though conscious that there was something wrong with its appearance. At the head of the column, beside the red flag, Georges Kopp, the stout Belgian commandante, was riding a black horse; a little way ahead a youth from the brigand-like militia cavalry pranced to and fro, galloping up every piece of rising ground and posing himself in picturesque attitudes at the summit. The splendid horses of the Spanish cavalry had been captured in large numbers during the revolution and handed over to the militia, who, of course, were busy riding them to death.

The road wound between yellow infertile fields, untouched since last year's harvest. Ahead of us was the low sierra that lies between Alcubierre and Zaragoza. We were getting near the front line now, near the bombs, the machine-guns and the mud. In secret I was frightened. I knew the line was quiet at present, but unlike most of the men about me I was old enough to remember the Great War, though not old enough to have fought in it. War, to me, meant roaring projectiles and skipping shards of steel; above all it meant mud, lice, hunger, and cold. It is curious, but I dreaded the cold much more than I dreaded the enemy. The thought of it had been haunting me all the time I was in Barcelona; I had even lain awake at nights thinking of the cold in the trenches, the stand-to's in the grisly dawns, the long hours on sentry-go with a frosted rifle, the icy mud that would slop over my boot-tops. I admit, too, that I felt a kind of horror as I looked at the people I was marching among. You cannot possibly conceive what a rabble we looked. We straggled along with far less cohesion than a flock of sheep; before we had gone two miles the rear of the column was out of sight. And quite half of the so-called men were children—but I mean literally children, of sixteen years old at the very most. Yet they were all happy and excited at the prospect of getting to the front at last. As we neared the line the boys round the red flag in front began to utter shouts of "Visca P.O.U.M.!" "Fascistas-maricones!" and so forth—shouts which were meant to be war-like and menacing, but which, from those childish throats, sounded as pathetic as the cries of kittens. It seemed dreadful that the defenders of the Republic should be this mob of ragged children carrying worn-out rifles which they did not know how to use. I remember wondering what would happen if a Fascist aeroplane passed our way—whether the airman would even bother to dive down and give us a burst from his machine gun. Surely even from the air he could see that we were not real soldiers?

As the road struck into the sierra we branched off to the right and climbed a narrow mule-track that wound round the mountain-side. The hills in that part of Spain are of a queer formation, horseshoe-shaped with flattish tops and very steep sides running down into immense ravines. On the higher slopes nothing grows except stunted shrubs and heath, with the white bones of the limestone sticking out everywhere. The front line here was not a continuous line of trenches, which would have been impossible in such mountainous country; it was simply a chain of fortified posts, always known as "positions," perched on each hill-top. In the distance you could see our "position" at the crown of the horseshoe; a ragged barricade of sand-bags, a red flag fluttering, the smoke of dug-out fires. A little nearer, and you could smell a sickening sweetish stink that lived in my nostrils for weeks afterwards. Into the cleft immediately behind the position all the refuse of months had been tipped—a deep festering bed of breadcrusts, excrement, and rusty tins.

The company we were relieving were getting their kits together. They had been three months in the line; their uniforms were caked with mud, their boots falling to pieces, their faces mostly bearded. The captain commanding the position, Levinski by name, but known to everyone as Benjamin, and by birth a Polish Jew, but speaking French as his native language, crawled out of his dug-out and greeted us. He was a short youth of about twenty-five, with stiff black hair and a pale eager face which at this period of the war was always very dirty. A few stray bullets were cracking high overhead. The position was a semi-circular enclosure about fifty yards across, with a parapet that was partly sand-bags and partly lumps of limestone. There were thirty or forty dug-outs running into the groung like ratholes. Williams, myself, and Williams's Spanish brother-in-law made a swift dive for the nearest unoccupied dug-out that looked habitable. Somewhere in front an occasional rifle banged, making queer rolling echoes among the stony hills. We had just dumped our kits and were crawling out of the dug-out when there was another bang and one of the children of our company rushed back from the parapet with his face pouring blood. He had fired his rifle and had somehow managed to blow out the bolt; his scalp was torn to ribbons by the splinters of the burst cartridge-case. It was our first casualty, and, characteristically, self-inflicted.

In the afternoon we did our first guard and Benjamin showed us round the position. In front of the parapet there ran a system of narrow trenches hewn out of the rock, with extremely primitive loopholes made of piles of limestone. There were twelve sentries, placed at various points in the trench and behind the inner parapet. In front of the trench was the barbed wire, and then the hillside slid down into a seemingly bottomless ravine; opposite were naked hills, in places mere cliffs of rock, all grey and wintry, with no life anywhere, not even a bird. I peered cautiously through a loophole, trying to find the Fascist trench.

"Where are the enemy?"

Benjamin waved his hand expansively. "Over zere." (Benjamin spoke English—terrible English.)

"But *where?*"

According to my ideas of trench warfare the Fascists would be fifty or a hundred yards away. I could see nothing—seemingly their trenches were very well concealed. Then with a shock of dismay I saw where Benjamin was pointing; on the opposite hill-top, beyond the ravine, seven hundred metres away at the very least, the tiny outline of a parapet and a red-and-yellow flag—the Fascist position. I was indescribably disappointed. We were nowhere near them! At that range our rifles were completely useless. But at that moment there was a shout of excitement. Two Fascists, greyish figurines in the distance, were scrambling up the naked hill-side opposite. Benjamin grabbed the nearest man's rifle, took aim, and pulled the trigger. Click! A dud cartridge; I thought it a bad omen.

The new sentries were no sooner in the trench than they

began firing a terrific fusillade at nothing in particular. I could see the Fascists, tiny as ants, dodging to and fro behind their parapet, and sometimes a black dot which was a head would pause for a moment, impudently exposed. It was obviously no use firing. But presently the sentry on my left, leaving his post in the typical Spanish fashion, sidled up to me and began urging me to fire. I tried to explain that at that range and with these rifles you could not hit a man except by accident. But he was only a child, and he kept motioning with his rifle towards one of the dots, grinning as eagerly as a dog that expects a pebble to be thrown. Finally I put my sights up to seven hundred and let fly. The dot disappeared. I hope it went near enough to make him jump. It was the first time in my life that I had fired a gun at a human being.

Now that I had seen the front I was profoundly disgusted. They called this war! And we were hardly even in touch with the enemy! I made no attempt to keep my head below the level of the trench. A little while later, however, a bullet shot past my ear with a vicious crack and banged into the parados behind. Alas! I ducked. All my life I had sworn that I would not duck the first time a bullet passed over me; but the movement appears to be instinctive, and almost everybody does it at least once.

In trench warfare five things are important: firewood, food, tobacco, candles and the enemy. In winter on the Zaragoza front they were important in that order, with the enemy a bad last. Except at night, when a surprise-attack was always conceivable, nobody bothered about the enemy. They were simply remote black insects whom one occasionally saw hopping to and fro. The real preoccupation of both armies was trying to keep warm.

I ought to say in passing that all the time I was in Spain I saw very little fighting. I was on the Aragon front from January to May, and between January and late March little or nothing happened on that front, except at Teruel. In March there was heavy fighting round Huesca, but I personally played only a minor part in it. Later, in June, there was the disastrous attack on Huesca in which several thousand men were killed in a single day, but I had been wounded and disabled before that happened. The things that one normally thinks of as the horrors of war seldom happen to me. No aeroplane ever dropped a bomb anywhere near me, I do not think a shell ever exploded within fifty yards of me, and I was only in hand-to-hand fighting once (once is once too often, I may say). Of course I was often under heavy machine-gun fire, but usually at longish ranges. Even at Huesca you were generally safe enough if you took reasonable precautions.

Up here, in the hills round Zaragoza, it was simply the mingled boredom and discomfort of stationary warfare. A life as uneventful as a city clerk's, and almost as regular. Sentry-go, patrols, digging; digging, patrols, sentry-go. On every hill-top, Fascist or Loyalist, a knot of ragged, dirty men shivering round their flag and trying to keep warm. And all day and night the meaningless bullets wandering across the empty valleys and only by some rare improbable chance getting home on a human body.

Often I used to gaze round the wintry landscape and marvel at the futility of it all. The inconclusiveness of such a kind of war! Earlier, about October, there had been savage fighting for all these hills; then, because the lack of men and arms, especially artillery, made any large-scale operation impossible, each army had dug itself in and settled down on the hill-tops it had won. Over to our right there was a small outpost, also P.O.U.M., and on the spur to our left, at seven o'clock of us, a P.S.U.C. position faced a taller spur with several small Fascist posts dotted on its peaks. The so-called line zigzagged to and fro in a pattern that would have been quite unintelligible

228

if every position had not flown a flag. The P.O.U.M. and
P.S.U.C. flags were red, those of the Anarchists red and black;
the Fascists generally flew the monarchist flag (red-yellow-
red), but occasionally they flew the flag of the Republic (red-
yellow-purple). The scenery was stupendous, if you could forget that every mountain-top was occupied by troops and was
therefore littered with the cans and crusted with dung. To the
right of us the sierra bent south-eastwards and made way for
the wide, veined valley that stretched across to Huesca. In the
middle of the plain a few tiny cubes sprawled like a throw of
dice; this was the town of Robres, which was in Loyalist possession. Often in the mornings the valley was hidden under seas
of clouds, out of which the hills rose flat blue, giving the landscape a strange resemblance to a photographic negative. Beyond Huesca there were more hills of the same formation as
our own, streaked with a pattern of snow which altered day
by day. In the far distance the monstrous peaks of the Pyrenees, where the snow never melts, seemed to float upon nothing. Even down in the plain everything looked dead and bare.
The hills opposite us were grey and wrinkled like the skins of
elephants. Almost always the sky was empty of birds. I do not
think I have ever seen a country where there were so few
birds. The only birds one saw at any time were a kind of mag-
pie, and the coveys of partridges that startled one at night with
their sudden whirring, and, very rarely, the flights of eagles
that drifted slowly over, generally followed by rifle-shots
which they did not deign to notice.

At night and in misty weather patrols were sent out in the
valley between ourselves and the Fascists. The job was not
popular, it was too cold and too easy to get lost, and I soon
found that I could get leave to go out on patrol as often as I
wished. In the huge jagged ravines there were no paths or
tracks of any kind; you could only find your way about by
making successive journeys and noting fresh landmarks each

time. As the bullet flies the nearest Fascist post was seven hundred metres from our own, but it was a mile and a half by the only practicable route. It was rather fun wandering about the dark valleys with the stray bullets flying high overhead like redshanks whistling. Better than nighttime were the heavy mists, which often lasted all day and which had a habit of clinging round the hill-tops and leaving the valleys clear. When you were anywhere near the Fascist lines you had to creep at a snail's pace; it was very difficult to move quietly on those hillsides, among the crackling shrubs and tinkling limestones. It was only at the third or fourth attempt that I managed to find my way to the Fascist lines. The mist was very thick, and I crept up to the barbed wire to listen. I could hear the Fascists talking and singing inside. Then to my alarm I heard several of them coming down the hill towards me. I cowered behind a bush that suddenly seemed very small, and tried to cock my rifle without noise. However, they branched off and did not come within sight of me. Behind the bush where I was hiding I came upon various relics of the earlier fighting—a pile of empty cartridge-cases, a leather cap with a bullet-hole in it, and a red flag, obviously one of our own. I took it back to the position, where it was unsentimentally torn up for cleaning rags.

I had been made a corporal, or *cabo*, as it was called, as soon as we reached the front, and was in command of a guard of twelve men. It was no sinecure, especially at first. The *centuria* was an untrained mob composed mostly of boys in their teens. Here and there in the militia you came across children as young as eleven or twelve, usually refugees from Fascist territory who had been enlisted as militiamen as the easiest way of providing for them. As a rule they were employed on light work in the rear, but sometimes they managed to worm their way to the front line, where they were a public menace. I remember one little brute throwing a hand-grenade into the

dug-out fire "for a joke." At Monte Pocero I do not think
there was anyone younger than fifteen, but the average age
must have been well under twenty. Boys of this age ought
never to be used in the front line, because they cannot stand
the lack of sleep which is inseparable from trench warfare. At
the beginning it was almost impossible to keep our position
properly guarded at night. The wretched children of my
section could only be roused by dragging them out of their
dug-outs feet foremost, and as soon as your back was turned
they left their posts and slipped into shelter; or they would
even, in spite of the frightful cold, lean up against the wall of
the trench and fall fast asleep. Luckily the enemy was very
unenterprising. There were nights when it seemed to me that
our position could be stormed by twenty Boy Scouts armed
with air-guns, or twenty Girl Guides armed with battledores,
for that matter.

At this time and until much later the Catalan militias were
still on the same basis as they had been at the beginning of the
war. In the early days of Franco's revolt the militias had been
hurriedly raised by the various trade unions and political parties; each was essentially a political organization, owing allegiance to its party as much as to the central Government.
When the Popular Army, which was a "non-political" army
organized on more or less ordinary lines, was raised at the beginning of 1937, the party militias were theoretically incorpo-
rated in it. But for a long time the only changes that occurred
were on paper; the new Popular Army troops did not reach
the Aragon front in any numbers till June, and until that time
the militia-system remained unchanged. The essential point of
the system was social equality between officers and men.
Everyone from general to private drew the same pay, ate the
same food, wore the same clothes, and mingled on terms of
complete equality. If you wanted to slap the general commanding the division on the back and ask him for a cigarette,

you could do so, and no one thought it curious. In theory at any rate each militia was a democracy and not a hierarchy. It was understood that orders had to be obeyed, but it was also understood that when you gave an order, you gave it as comrade to comrade and not as superior to inferior. There were officers and N.C.O.'s, but there was no military rank in the ordinary sense; no titles, no badges, no heel-clicking and saluting. They had attempted to produce within the militias a sort of temporary working model of the classless society. Of course there was not perfect equality, but there was a nearer approach to it than I had ever seen or than I would have thought conceivable in time of war.

But I admit that at first sight the state of affairs at the front horrified me. How on earth could the war be won by an army of this type? It was what everyone was saying at the time, and though it was true it was also unreasonable. For in the circumstances the militia could not have been much better than they were. A modern mechanized army does not spring up out of the ground, and if the Government had waited until it had trained troops at its disposal, Franco would never have been resisted. Later it became the fashion to decry the militias, and therefore to pretend that the faults which were due to lack of training and weapons were the result of the equalitarian system. Actually, a newly raised draft of militia was an undisciplined mob not because the officers called the privates "Comrade" but because raw troops are *always* an undisciplined mob. In practice the democratic "revolutionary" type of discipline is more reliable than might be expected. In a workers' army discipline is theoretically voluntary. It is based on class-loyalty, whereas the discipline of a bourgeois conscript army is based ultimately on fear. (The Popular Army that replaced the militias was midway between the two types.) In the militias the bullying and abuse that go on in an ordinary army would never have been tolerated for a moment. The normal military punishments existed, but they were only invoked for very serious offences. When a man refused to obey an order you did not immediately get him punished; you first appealed to him in the name of comradeship. Cynical people with no experience of handling men will say instantly that this would never "work," but as a matter of fact it does "work" in the long run. The discipline of even the worst drafts of militia visibly improved as time went on. In January the job of keeping a dozen raw recruits up to the mark almost turned my hair grey. In May for a short while I was acting-lieutenant in command of about thirty men, English and Spanish. We had all been under fire for months, and I never had the slightest difficulty in getting an order obeyed or in getting men to volunteer for a dangerous job. "Revolutionary" discipline depends on political consciousness—on an understanding of *why* orders must be obeyed; it takes time to diffuse this, but it also takes time to drill a man into an automaton on the barrack-square. The journalists who sneered at the militia-system seldom remembered that the militias had to hold the line while the Popular Army was training in the rear. And it is a tribute to the strength of "revolutionary" discipline that the militias stayed in the field at all. For until about June 1937 there was nothing to keep them there, except class loyalty. Individual deserters could be shot—were shot, occasionally—but if a thousand men had decided to walk out of the line together there was no force to stop them. A conscript army in the same circumstances—with its battle-police removed—would have melted away. Yet the militias held the line, though God knows they won very few victories, and even individual desertions were not common. In four or five months in the P.O.U.M. militia, I only heard of four men deserting, and two of those were fairly certainly spies who had enlisted to obtain information. At the beginning the apparent chaos, the general lack of training, the fact that you often had to argue for five minutes before you could get an order obeyed, appalled and infuriated me. I had British Army ideas, and certainly the Spanish militias were very unlike the British Army. But considering the circumstances they were better troops than one had any right to expect.

Meanwhile, firewood—always firewood. Throughout that period there is probably no entry in my diary that does not mention firewood, or rather the lack of it. We were between two and three thousand feet above sea-level, it was mid-winter and the cold was unspeakable. The temperature was not exceptionally low, on many nights it did not even freeze, and the wintry sun often shone for an hour in the middle of the day; but even if it was not really cold, I assure you that it seemed so. Sometimes there were shrieking winds that tore your cap off and twisted your hair in all directions, sometimes there were mists that poured into the trench like a liquid and seemed to penetrate your bones; frequently it rained, and even a quarter of an hour's rain was enough to make conditions intolerable. The thin skin of earth over the limestone turned promptly into a slippery grease, and as you were always walking on a slope it was impossible to keep your footing. On dark nights I have often fallen half a dozen times in twenty yards; and this was dangerous, because it means that the lock of one's rifle became jammed with mud. For days together clothes, boots, blankets, and rifles were more or less coated with mud. I had brought as many thick clothes as I could carry, but many of the men were terribly underclad. For the whole garrison, about a hundred men, there were only twelve great-coats, which had to be handed from sentry to sentry, and most of the men had only one blanket. One icy night I made a list in my diary of the clothes I was wearing. It is of some interest in showing the amount of clothes the human body can carry. I was wearing a thick vest and pants, a flannel shirt, two pull-overs, a woollen jacket, a pigskin jacket, corduroy breeches, puttees, thick socks, boots, a stout trench-coat, a muffler, lined leather gloves, and a woollen cap. Nevertheless, I was shivering like a jelly. But I admit I am unusually sensitive to cold.

Firewood was the one thing that really mattered. The point about the firewood was that there was practically no firewood to be had. Our miserable mountain had not even at its best much vegetation, and for months it had been ranged over by freezing militiamen, with the result that everything thicker than one's finger had long since been burnt. When we were not eating, sleeping, on guard or on fatigue-duty we were in the valley behind the position, scrounging for fuel. All my memories of that time are memories of scrambling up and down the almost perpendicular slopes, over the jagged limestone that knocked one's boots to pieces, pouncing eagerly on tiny twigs of wood. Three people searching for a couple of hours could collect enough fuel to keep the dug-out fire alight for about an hour. The eagerness of our search for firewood turned us all into botanists. We classified according to their burning qualities every plant that grew on the mountain-side; the various heaths and grasses that were good to start a fire with but burnt out in a few minutes, the wild rosemary and the tiny whin bushes that would burn when the fire was well alight, the stunted oak tree, smaller than a gooseberry bush, that was practically unburnable. There was a kind of dried-up reed that was very good for starting fires with, but these grew only on the hill-top to the left of the position, and you had to go under fire to get them. If the Fascist machine-gunners saw you they gave you a drum of ammunition all to yourself. Generally their aim was high and the bullets sang overhead like birds, but sometimes they cracked and chipped the limestone uncomfortably close, whereupon you flung yourself on your face. You went on gathering reeds, however; nothing mattered in comparison with firewood.

Beside the cold the other discomforts seemed petty. Of

course all of us were permanently dirty. Our water, like our food, came on mule-back from Alcubierre, and each man's share worked out at about a quart a day. It was beastly water, hardly more transparent than milk. Theoretically it was for drinking only, but I always stole a pannikinful for washing in the mornings. I used to wash one day and shave the next; there was never enough water for both. The position stank abominably, and outside the little enclosure of the barricade there was excrement everywhere. Some of the militiamen habitually defecated in the trench, a disgusting thing when one had to walk round it in the darkness. But the dirt never worried me. Dirt is a thing people make too much fuss about. It is astonishing how quickly you get used to doing without a handkerchief and to eating out of the tin pannikin in which you also wash. Nor was sleeping in one's clothes any hardship after a day or two. It was of course impossible to take one's clothes and especially one's boots off at night; one had to be ready to turn out instantly in case of an attack. In eighty nights I only took my clothes off three times, though I did occasionally manage to get them off in the daytime. It was too cold for lice as yet, but rats and mice abounded. It is often said that you don't find rats and mice in the same place, but you do when there is enough food for them.

In other ways we were not badly off. The food was good enough and there was plenty of wine. Cigarettes were still being issued at the rate of a packet a day, matches were issued every other day, and there was even an issue of candles. They were very thin candles, like those on a Christmas cake, and were popularly supposed to have been looted from churches. Every dug-out was issued daily with three inches of candles, which would burn for about twenty minutes. At that time it was still possible to buy candles, and I had brought several pounds of them with me. Later on the famine of matches and candles made life a misery. You do not realize the importance of these things until you lack them. In a night-alarm, for instance, when everyone in the dug-out is scrambling for his rifle and treading on everybody else's face, being able to strike a light may make the difference between life and death. Every militiaman possessed a tinder-lighter and several yards of yellow wick. Next to his rifle it was his most important possession. The tinder-lighters had the great advantage that they could be struck in a wind, but they would only smoulder, so that they were no use for lighting a fire. When the match famine was at its worst our only way of producing a flame was to pull the bullet out of a cartridge and touch the cordite off with a tinder-lighter.

It was an extraordinary life that we were living—an extraordinary way to be at war, if you could call it war. The whole militia chafed against the inaction and clamoured constantly to know why we were not allowed to attack. But it was perfectly obvious that there would be no battle for a long while yet, unless the enemy started it. Georges Kopp, on his periodical tours of inspection, was quite frank with us. "This is not a war," he used to say, "it is a comic opera with an occasional death." As a matter of fact the stagnation on the Aragon front had political causes of which I knew nothing at that time; but the purely military difficulties—quite apart from the lack of reserves of men—were obvious to anybody.

To begin with, there was the nature of the country. The front line, ours and the Fascists', lay in positions of immense natural strength, which as a rule could only be approached from one side. Provided a few trenches had been dug, such places cannot be taken by infantry, except in overwhelming numbers. In our own position or most of those round us a dozen men with two machine-guns could have held off a battalion. Perched on the hill-tops as we were, we should have made lovely marks for artillery; but there was no artillery. Sometimes I used to gaze round the landscape and long—oh, how passionately!—for a couple of batteries of guns. One could have destroyed positions one after another as easily as smashing nuts with a hammer. But on our side the guns simply did not exist. The Facists did occasionally manage to bring a gun or two from Zaragoza and fire a very few shells, so few that they never even found the range and the shells plunged harmlessly into the empty ravines. Against machine-guns and without artillery there are only three things you can do: dig yourself in at a safe distance—four hundred yards, say—advance across the open and be massacred, or make small-scale night attacks that will not alter the general situation. Practically the alternatives are stagnation or suicide.

And beyond this there was the complete lack of war materials of every description. It needs an effort to realize how badly the militias were armed at this time. Any public school O.T.C. in England is far more like a modern army than we were. The badness of our weapons was so astonishing that it is worth recording in detail.

For this sector of the front the entire artillery consisted of four trench-mortars with *fifteen rounds* for each gun. Of course they were far too precious to be fired and the mortars were kept in Alcubierre. There were machine-guns at the rate of approximately one to fifty men; they were oldish guns, but fairly accurate up to three or four hundred yards. Beyond this we had only rifles, and the majority of the rifles were scrap-iron. There were three types of rifles in use. The first was the long Mauser. These were seldom less than twenty years old, their sights were about as much use as a broken speedometer, and in most of them the rifling was hopelessly corroded; about one rifle in ten was not bad, however. Then there was the short Mauser, or *mousqueton*, really a cavalry weapon. These were more popular than the others because they were lighter to carry and less nuisance in a trench, also because they were comparatively new and looked efficient. Actually they were almost useless. They were made out of reassembled parts, no bolt belonged to its rifle, and three-quarters of them could be counted on to jam after five shots. There were also a few Winchester rifles. These were nice to shoot with, but they were wildly inaccurate, and as their cartridges had no clips they could only be fired one shot at a time. Ammunition was so scarce that each man entering the line was only issued with fifty rounds, and most of it was exceedingly bad. The Spanish-made cartridges were all refills and would jam even the best rifles. The Mexican cartridges were better and were therefore reserved for the machine-guns. Best of all was the German-made ammunition, but as this came only from prisoners and deserters there was not much of it. I always kept a clip of German or Mexican ammunition in my pocket for use in an emergency. But in practice when the emergency came I seldom fired my rifle; I was too frightened of the beastly thing jamming and too anxious to reserve at any rate one round that would go off.

We had no tin hats, no bayonets, hardly any revolvers or pistols, and not more than one bomb between five or ten men. The bomb in use at this time was a frightful object known as the "F.A.I. bomb," it having been produced by the Anarchists in the early days of the war. It was on the principle of a Mills bomb, but the lever was held down not by a pin but a piece of tape. You broke the tape and then got rid of the bomb with the utmost possible speed. It was said of these bombs that they were "impartial"; they killed the man they were thrown at and the man who threw them. There were several other types, even more primitive but probably a little less dangerous—to the thrower, I mean. It was not till late March that I saw a bomb worth throwing.

And apart from weapons there was a shortage of all the minor necessities of war. We had no maps or charts, for instance. Spain has never been fully surveyed, and the only detailed maps of this area were the old military ones, which were almost all in the possession of the Fascists. We had no range-finders, no telescopes, no periscopes, no field-glasses except a few privately-owned pairs, no flares or Very lights, no wire-cutters, no armourers' tools, hardly even any cleaning materials. The Spaniards seemed never to have heard of a pull-through and looked on in surprise when I constructed one. When you wanted your rifle cleaned you took it to the sergeant, who possessed a long brass ramrod which was invariably bent and therefore scratched the rifling. There was not even any gun oil. You greased your rifle with olive oil, when you could get hold of it; at different times I have greased mine with vaseline, with cold cream, and even with bacon-fat. Moreover, there were no lanterns or electric torches—at this time there was not, I believe, such a thing as an electric torch throughout the whole of our sector of the front, and you could not buy one nearer than Barcelona, and only with difficulty even there.

As time went on, and the desultory rifle-fire rattled among the hills, I began to wonder with increasing scepticism whether anything would ever happen to bring a bit of life, or rather a bit of death, into this cock-eyed war. It was pneumonia that we were fighting against, nor against men. When the trenches are more than five hundred yards apart no one gets hit except by accident. Of course there were casualties, but the majority of them were self-inflicted. If I remember rightly, the first five men I saw wounded in Spain were all wounded by our own weapons—I don't mean intentionally, but owing to accident or carelessness. Our worn-out rifles were a danger in themselves. Some of them had a nasty trick of going off if the butt was tapped on the ground; I saw a man shoot himself through the hand owing to this. And in the darkness the raw recruits were always firing at one another. One evening when it was barely even dusk a sentry let fly at me from a distance of twenty yards; but he missed me by a yard—goodness knows how many times the Spanish standard of marksmanship has saved my life. Another time I had gone out on patrol in the mist and had carefully warned the guard commander beforehand. But in coming back I stumbled against a bush, the startled sentry called out that the Fascists were coming, and I had the pleasure of hearing the guard commander order everyone to open rapid fire in my direction. Of course I lay down and the bullets went harmlessly over me. Nothing will convince a Spaniard, at least a young Spaniard, that fire-arms are dangerous. Once, rather later than this, I was photographing some machine-gunners with their gun, which was pointed directly towards me.

"Don't fire," I said half-jokingly as I focused the camera.

"Oh, no, we won't fire."

The next moment there was a frightful roar and a stream of bullets tore past my face so close that my cheek was stung by grains of cordite. It was unintentional, but the machine-gunners considered it a great joke. Yet only a few days earlier they had seen a mule-driver accidentally shot by a political delegate who was playing the fool with an automatic pistol and had put five bullets in the mule-driver's lungs.

The difficult passwords which the army was using at this time were a minor source of danger. They were those tiresome double passwords in which one word has to be answered by another. Usually they were of an elevating and revolutionary nature, such as *Cultura—progreso*, or *Seremos—invencibles*, and it was often impossible to get illiterate sentries to remember these highfalutin words. One night, I remember, the password was *Cataluña—eroica*, and a moon-faced peasant lad named Jaime Domenech approached me, greatly puzzled, and asked me to explain.

"Eroica—what does eroica mean?"

I told him that it meant the same as valiente. A little while later he was stumbling up the trench in the darkness, and the sentry challenged him:

"Alto! Cataluña!"

"Valiente!" yelled Jaime, certain that he was saying the right thing.

Bang!

However, the sentry missed him. In this war everyone always did miss everyone else, when it was humanly possible.

GERALD BRENAN

Search for
a Dead Poet

A SELECTION FROM *The Face of Spain*

*Gerald Brenan may know Spain better, or at least more inti-
mately (which comes to more than the same thing), than any
other British or American author. Certainly he has lived long
there and written much about the people, their politics, and
their literature.*

*A Protestant-Irish-Englishman who grew up in South Af-
rica, India, and England, Brenan went to Spain from service in
World War I, bought a house in a remote southern village, and
lived there five years. He returned to England but came again*

to Spain in 1930 and bought a house for his wife and himself near Málaga. From this house he was driven out by the Civil War; he did not return until 1949. The Face of Spain describes his homecoming and his travels of that year in a country staggering under the heritage of the Civil War and the World War.

Federico García Lorca was a poet. He was not a political man; that is, he was not active in politics. But many of his poems cut like keen knives into the Spanish body, and the bitter beauty of his songs made him, for some, worse than a political opponent—a revolutionary. Yet, when he was shot in 1936, at the age of thirty-seven, it was because of a personal grudge which the Civil War shrouded in the anonymity of many murders, official and unofficial.

Once, the reticent Brenan wrote of himself, "I am an individualist and value liberty above everything else." That statement explains his love of Spain and his search for the burial place of García Lorca.

OUR next destination was Granada. Instead of taking the usual bus or train, we decided to travel by the more direct but slower route through Alhama. This meant starting off in the little train we had taken before to Torre del Mar. So, after an early lunch, we found ourselves rattling along once more beside the sea that glittered in the sunlight like a net of fishes. Black boats of the fishermen, white lateen sails and, when one stood on the platform at the end of the carriage, the peculiar salty smell of this sea which is so different to that of the Atlantic with its tides and wrack.

After Vélez the train began to climb on a cogged rail. All afternoon it wound among red earthy hills covered with vineyards, then descended at a breakneck speed, then climbed again towards the Bocada or pass. Night fell. When we reached the summit, which is also the terminus, it was quite dark and we packed into the small bus that was to take us twenty miles on to Alhama.

It was ten o'clock when we arrived and very cold. We found our way to the posada, a clean whitewashed building which had a fire of oak logs burning under a great hooded chimney and a row of copper pots on a shelf above. Muleteers were lying asleep on the floor, rolled in their blankets. A meal was served and a lieutenant of the Civil Guard sat down with us. He was a Navarrese, precise and natty, with a sharp, schoolmaster's voice and long white well-manicured fingers.

"The times are bad," he said. "We are living among people any one of whom may have murdered our father or our brother, and yet we have to treat them as if they were our friends."

"And they," I answered, "as if you were theirs."

We went out to get a drink. The air of the street was bitterly cold and the stars overhead shook and glittered. From some way off came the sound of rushing water.

In the café sat the usual crowd of bored yokels: they stared at us in their blank Iberian way while we sipped our cognac; then we went home to bed.

At dawn we dragged ourselves up. A pale rosy light was showing over the mountains and, going out to get some coffee, we saw the long summit of the Sierra de Tejada, apparently just above the town, covered with a deep blanket of snow. Below the square lay a deep gorge, at the bottom of which we could see and hear the river.

The castle of Alhama was once the key to Granada. Its capture in 1482 from the Moors was a famous feat, celebrated in a ballad which Byron has translated. It still stands, a square building with high, red, turreted walls; to-day it is used as a granary.

245

As we drank our coffee, the market was opening. Groups of dark-clothed countrymen stood about in caps and berets and women wearing black handkerchiefs on their heads. Although we had only come a few miles from the coast, we were in a new world, austere, harsh and puritanical. Even the language was different. For girl they said *mozuela* (maid) instead of *chica*, and the accent struck an answering chord in me, for it was that in which I had first learned Spanish.

At eight the bus appeared and we set off. Bare, bone-coloured hills, tinged with rose—thin young corn in places—no leaves or flowers. In the valleys a few poplar trees: every village smoking like bonfire as the women lit their hearths with lavender or gorse. All the time we were descending. Soon we came to orchards bright with peach and apricot blossom, passed a cave village, passed low hills that looked like trains of pack animals, then another village destroyed by earthquake. Suddenly a great sight. Hanging in the air as if it were a cloud stood the Sierra Nevada, and below its smooth slopes of snow lay the green and brown plain of the Vega. Between them we could see Granada.

It was fifteen years since I had been in this town and more since I had lived here. I expected to find many changes. But in external appearances there were few. A new modernistic building put up here, a shop gone there and of course the usual decrease in the number of cafés and increase in the number of banks. But the change of atmosphere was striking. Granada had always been a sober town, austere and conventional as a provincial capital in Castile, though tempered by a certain Andalusian refinement, but now it seemed to me that it was more than austere—it was sad. The faces of the passers-by were long and gloomy, the shops were empty and the popular quarters had lost their animation. The Plaza Bibarrambla, once so gay and lively with its stalls of sweets, roasted chestnuts and flour fritters, was dead and lifeless.

Yet the signs of great poverty, which had made such a painful impression in Cordova and Malaga, were lacking. People seemed to eat, even if they did not eat much: the irrigated Vega gave regular employment. But the result was not contentment. There was a suppressed anger and tension I had not seen anywhere else on my journey: the working men held their heads high and spoke with unconcealed bitterness, while even the beggars were disdainful, asked as if from right and pocketed the alms they got without thanks. I was told that the *fiestas*, once the delight of the city, had fallen off and that Corpus, with its famous processions, was observed without enthusiasm. And the police were everywhere.

The confectioners had been forbidden to make pastries and so were in a bad humour.

"There's no understanding our shortages," said one of them. "Last year there was a terrific crop of olives, yet this year oil is short. Two years ago there was a phenomenal wheat crop, yet the ration remained as before. The fact is that these gentry take our food and sell it abroad. This is a country of *pillos, muchos pillos*, rogues, many rogues. *Si señor.*"

To change the subject I praised the large new blocks of flats at controlled rents that had been put up on the edge of the city.

"But their rents are a thousand pesetas a month. Who can afford that? *No señor.* These flats are for the police and the Black Marketeers."

And two middle-class people who had come in to buy chocolate nodded their heads in approval.

Walking down the Gran Vía, we came to a new building of palatial size. It was a branch of the Banco de España. These new banks, put up on the proceeds of inflation, are to the present regime what the great cathedrals were to the Middle Ages. They symbolise the ruling passion. Close by stands the ugly church of the Sacred Heart. As we passed it, a noisy crowd of several hundred young men was pouring out of it: they had been taking an Easter course of the Exercise of St. Ignatius. There is a curious connection between sweets and piety in Spain and every confectioner's shop has a notice enjoining young and old, masters and servants, to take them. Then in the church porch, beside the usual list of films that may safely and without risk to morals be seen, we observed a notice of the services to be held in honour of *Nuestro Señor de la Misericordia,* Our Lord of Pity, which are organized by a confraternity known as the Confraternity of Silence. I could not help thinking that the name of this confraternity had been well chosen, for when in 1936 *Acción Católica* was hunting down and killing the Liberals and freemasons, the voice of pity was not heard. One is told—and not only by people on the Left—that during the first months of the Civil War between twenty and thirty thousand persons were shot in this town in cold blood. What reliance can be placed on such figures I do not know, but it seems to be the general opinion that in Granada the number of executions was higher in proportion to the population than anywhere else. It is significant that the patroness of the city, *Nuestra Señora de las Angustias,* Our Lady of Agonies, is represented by the figure of a weeping woman holding the head of the dead Christ on her lap. In this city of blood and massacre she might stand for any woman of the working classes.

On the morning following our arrival we set off for a walk in the old Moorish quarter known as the Albaicín. Steep cobbled lanes, white houses rising above one another, terraced gardens. A stream of women and children moving up and down, but few men. A feeling of tension. After we had climbed a certain distance, we caught on our right the sound of dogs barking and the harsh jangling of a guitar: they came from the gipsy quarter with its whitewashed caves and grey-green cactus. Then we reached a little square with a crenellated gate and trees and in a few minutes were out above the houses on the open hillside.

How touching, in some way I cannot describe, are these *terrains vagues* of old cities, where the last houses meet and mingle with the countryside! Here was a wall of dried mud, an agave plant and a leafless fig tree which, clumsy and babyish, groped in the air with its blunt fingers. An old woman carried a pitcher, a man was relieving himself, while far below lay the flat green plain, stretching away to its rim of mountains. From it there rose the crowing of cocks—faint, shrill and charged with distance and memory—into a grey sky that spread over everything.

Yes, this was the Albaicín as it used to be—yet why did it seem so changed, so different? As I sat listening to the cock-crows, the answer came to me. This was a city that had killed its poet. And all at once the idea entered my mind that I would visit, if I could find it, García Lorca's grave and lay a wreath of flowers upon it.

Next morning we set out to climb the hill of the Alhambra. The sun was shining and a dry wind raised the dust in eddies. As we passed the English pension, the intense pale blue of the sky, seen against the brown tops of the elm wood, gave me a thrill of excitement. This blue of Granada skies is to other blues what the colour of fresh blood is to other reds and if one calls Spain, as well one may, the country of bloodshed, its pure sky blue, like that of the Virgin's dress in a Fra Angelico picture, seems to be pitying that bloodshed.

We took the road that runs past the cypress avenue of the Generalife. Up this road, morning after morning, the lorries packed with prisoners had passed. The foreign visitors in the Washington Irving Hotel had listened to them changing gear and pulled the blankets over their heads when the shots rang out. After that the nightingales, noisy as frogs, had resumed their chug chugging.

Crowning the hill in front of us stood the high white walls of the cemetery, where for generations all the *hijos de Granada* have been buried. As we came up to it we could see that a new enclosure, several acres in extent, had been added. We entered and began to wander among the graves. Soon, in the newest and poorest part, where the sun glared down and the wind blew the loose earth into eddies, we came on a man driving a small donkey.

"We are looking for a grave," I began, and explained the circumstances.

"Well," he said, "you will have to enquire at the office. The names of all those who were shot at the cemetery are recorded there."

"Really," I exclaimed, for I was surprised that they had taken the trouble to do this.

"Oh yes," he said. "Those who were shot here were shot by order of the military authorities and so all the formalities were observed. By every grave a label was put up with the name of its owner upon it and when three or four were buried together in the same grave, well, three or four names were written down."

"Were you here then?"

"Not me. I spent the war fighting on the Red side. When it finished and I'd done my term in the labour camps, I got this job."

Leaving his donkey, which was carrying a pannier of earth, he accompanied us back to the office. There a little old man, shabby and frail, came scraping up to us. On his nose, which was very thin, he wore a pair of steel-rimmed spectacles and on his head an official peaked cap which was too large for him. He listened to my enquiries with an air of reserve and obsequiousness, but the whole cast of his face expressed fear and sadness. At any moment, it seemed, these might descend in a landslide and bury him.

Whom did I say I was looking for? Federico García Lorca? Ah yes, he remembered the name, for we were not the first persons to have enquired about him. Only last year some foreigners—Argentines, he thought—had driven up to the gate with a wreath of flowers. But he had been unable to satisfy them. Señor García Lorca's remains had been dug up after the regulation five years in the earth because no one had paid the requisite fee for their removal to a permanent resting place. They were now in the bone pit.

"Could we see it?"

"Certainly. There is no objection."

And he handed to the man who accompanied us a large key. Then, with the same sad, deferential manner with which he had addressed us, he turned to bow to a funeral party which had just arrived.

Jangling key and talking breezily of the secrets of his trade —how long, for example, it took corpses to decay in the local earth—the grave digger led the way across the dusty, sundrenched hill-side, pitted with humble graves. Then he stopped before a small enclosure surrounded by a high wall.

"Here we are," he said, unlocking a door. "This is the ossuary."

A curious sweetish smell met us as we entered and a disagreeable, uneasy feeling of isolation and silence. Like the silence at a dinner party when someone has committed a grave *faux pas*. Pulling ourselves together, we saw that we were in a sort of open court scattered with torn and blackened fragments of clothing. It was as though a rag fair had been held here a dozen years ago or a collection of gipsy caravans made it their camping ground. But, quickly, our eyes were drawn from these sordid remains to a pit which lay in the centre of the enclosure. It was some thirty feet square, to all appearance deep, and filled to within a half a dozen feet of the surface with skulls and bones. Among these lay a few parched and shrunken bodies, lying in distraught postures as though they had come flying down through the air, and wrapped in mouldering cerements.

"Here you have what was once the flower of Granada," said the man. "Look well and you'll see the bullet holes."

And in fact nearly every skull was shattered.

But what was that? Stretched across the rubble of bones, in an attitude of rigid attention, was a complete and well preserved corps, dressed in a green and black braided uniform. Its face, a little greenish too with dark markings, as though the flesh were trying to take on the colour of the uniform, had the severe, self-concentrated look of a man who is engaged on some important task.

"Ah, that one!" exclaimed the grave digger. "He's a fine bird. A colonel, if you please, of the Civil Guard, He's been lying for fifty years or so in one of the upper niches and that's why he's so well mummified. Even his complexion is as fresh as though he had just been laid out. We took him up the other day because his family have stopped paying the rent, and here he is."

A colonel of the police guarding the bones of the Reds whom his successors had shot! Could Goya have thought of a better subject?

"And how many would you say are buried in this pit?" I asked.

"Well, the list of those officially shot shows some eight thousand names. All but a few of them are here. Then there's a thousand or so more who had the originality to die natural deaths. *Vamos*, say nine or ten thousand. And all good friends, good company."

"Why do you say that?"

"Well, why not? They're all there together."

He laughed as he locked the door and, passing once more the donkey, still patiently waiting with its load of soil, we went back to the cemetery entrance.

"Can you point out to me," I asked, "where the executions took place?"

"I'll take you there," he said, pocketing my tip. "Then you won't lose yourselves."

"But what if that gets you into trouble?"

"No, why should it? They were officially shot, weren't they? By order of the military authorities. *Puñeta*, a great act of justice!"

And he led us out through the iron gates to the wall that bounds the lower side of the cemetery. The bullet marks were still there, and a few dried stains of blood. They had been bundled out of the lorries and machine-gunned in groups with the rope manacles still on them. Only the city councillors had been granted the privilege of lighting cigarettes and so showing the traditional contempt and defiance. There they had stood, looking at a red ploughed field planted with olive trees and sloping up to the gradually brightening sky. After that—nothing.

We set off back to the town. Just beyond the Washington Irving Hotel, at the entrance to the wooded region of the Alhambra, lies the drive to the Carmen de los Mártires. Here St. John of the Cross had written his mystical works and M. Meersmans, a Belgian mine owner and prospector, had entertained his friends with bad dinners served on gold plate. A new, monstrous building had now shoved itself up, inscribed with the initials of the *F.E.T. de la Jons*, otherwise known as the Falange. Painted on the wall beside it was their symbol, a hand clutching a dagger dyed in red.

The more I thought over the results of this expedition, the less satisfied I was with them. The old man at the office had been elusive. The grave digger's emphasis on official executions seemed to suggest that there had been others which could not be so classified. I decided to return to the cemetery that afternoon and to demand to see the list of those executed. If Lorca was really buried there, surely his name would be on it?

At four o'clock therefore we were back again. This time we made our way into that part of the cemetery where the middle classes are buried, either in niches round the patio walls or in more expensive marble tombs under the cypress trees. Here we started a conversation with two grave diggers, one of whom, the older and more talkative, had been present when the military rising began, and asked them to show us where those executed in 1936 had been re-buried.

"You've come straight to the spot," replied the elder. "The most celebrated ones are all here."

And he led us to the grave of Montesinos, the Socialist mayor who had been Lorca's brother-in-law, and then to those of the city councillors and their officials, all of whom, with two exceptions, had been put to death. Next came the graves of various doctors, including that of a famous specialist in children's diseases. I knew his story: a much loved man, he had been shot, not on political grounds, but as a freemason. Every group that supported the rising had had the right to proscribe its particular enemies and the Church—or, to be more exact, Catholic Action—had put on its list the masons and the Protestants.

Our guides, who took a professional interest in showing us the sights, now led us to a different part of the cemetery, where, among other things, we saw the corner where the postmen were interred: they had been shot, it appeared, because their jobs were wanted by other people. After this came what was evidently regarded as the high-light. In the Civil Section, where non-Catholics and prisoners who refused confession were buried, stood the tomb of the Protestant pastor, whose crime was that he had kept a free school for poor children in the Cuesta Gomeres. Poor man, he had been well liked by the foreign residents, including those who were Catholics, but even a British Consul's friendship could not save him.

I observed that these tombstones all had the same formula

254

for the epitaph, saying *ceased to exist* instead of *died* and at the end *Your mother (sister, daughters) will not forget you.* It would no doubt have been unwise to mention the unforgetfulness of brothers, sons or fathers.

"All this is very interesting," I said at length, "but the person I am looking for is not here. Perhaps you can tell me where he is buried. He is called Federico García Lorca."

"That is a famous name," said the elder of the grave diggers. "There is much talk about him."

"He is famous all the world over," I replied. "His poems are read from Buenos Aires to New York and London. Some of them have been translated into English."

"There you are," exclaimed the grave digger to his companion. "These foreigners know more about us than we know about ourselves. I tell you, there's as much knowledge in one of their little fingers as there is in the whole of our bodies. Compared to them we're nothing."

"That's it," agreed his friend solemnly. "Just savages."

"You don't understand me," I said. "This man whose grave I am looking for was a friend of mine. When many years ago I lived in Granada, I used to know him."

"Ah, that makes a difference. Still I must tell you that you've come to the wrong place. He is not here."

"I have been told that he was. Anyhow I want to see the lists."

"They are at the office. But I warn you that his name is not on them. I have been through them all many times."

"What are they like?"

"Well, there is just a list of names with a number after each. When the name was not known, as often happened, there was written *varón* or *hembra*, 'man' or 'woman.' "

"Perhaps he was one of those unknowns."

"No, he was not. I tell you he is buried somewhere else. . . . At Víznar."

"Víznar?"

"Yes, in the trenches in the *barranco*. They shot him there."

"How do you know?"

"How is anything known? These things come out." And he refused to say any more about it.

In the office I found the old caretaker alone, entering something with a scratchy pen in a ledger. I told him that I was not satisfied that García Lorca's remains were in the bone pit and asked to see the books in which the names of those shot had been recorded.

"I cannot show them without permission," he said, glancing up at me sharply. "You must go to the military authorities."

"At least tell me if my friend's name is on the lists."

He looked at me through his glasses in his half-frightened, half-appealing way.

"No, señor, it is not. The person you are enquiring about was not buried here."

"Then he was buried somewhere else?"

"Evidently."

"At Víznar?"

His eyes met mine for a moment in an uncertain glance. Then without a word he gave a slight inclination with that perpetually deferential body of his and turned away. I could see his thin bent back and the scuff of grey hair that ran down his neck under his dirty collar as he scratched with his pen on the pages of the ledger. We went out.

The next two days were spent in making further enquiries. I had once known many people in Granada and though some of these were dead or absent, there were others who were ready to tell me what they could. One family in particular, who had had every opportunity for knowing what was going on, were most helpful. On calling on them I found that the horrors that had occurred when the military rising broke out thirteen years ago were as present to their minds as though they had happened yesterday. They described the nightly roaring of the lorries up the road to the cemetery, then the rattle of the volleys! Every morning the wives and mothers of the people who had been arrested would climb the hill to search for the bodies of their men folk. There they lay in heaps as they had fallen, till later in the day squads of Falangists would set about burying them. Since the labour of interring so many bodies was considerable, they were bundled into shallow cavities from which their feet and hands often stuck out. An English friend of mine who, at some risk to himself, visited the place a number of times, told me that he saw the bodies of boys and girls still in their teens. "But were they political?" Who could say? In the hysterical atmosphere of those days, anyone even remotely connected with the Left might find himself arrested and then, unless some person with influence put in a word for him, he would automatically be shot because the prisons had to be emptied to make room for fresh arrivals. The Spaniards' innate love of destruction, their obsession with death, their tendency to fanaticism found full vent in these orgiastic scenes because there was no civil or religious authority, no moral force or inhibition, that could restrain them. Were not the Bishops, who alone could have put on the brake, as deeply committed as anyone else? The only pronouncement they made was no one should be killed without the opportunity for confession.

How catching the hysteria was may be seen from the fact that an ordinary English girl, whose parents were living in Granada, donned the uniform of the Falange, stuck a revolver in her belt and boasted that, like other Spanish *señoritas*, she had taken part in executions and shot men with her own hand. Later, when the European war broke out, she returned to England and joined an ambulance unit.

Whenever I enquired about García Lorca I heard, if any place was mentioned at all, the word Víznar. Víznar is a small village lying a few miles away in the hills and its *barranco* or ravine was one of the Falangist burial grounds. Such secret caches lie all over the country. But no one that I met had visited the site and the story of Lorca's death there was just hearsay. Further acquaintance, however, with the grave diggers showed me that they belonged to a sort of freemasonry concerned with the things of the dead and that they had access to information that was not available to other people. Also they were without prejudices: their interest in these matters was professional. This inclined me to believe that, when they said that García Lorca was buried at Víznar, they had good reasons for thinking so.

There was however a story current all over Spain about his death that seemed at first sight to point to a different conclusion. To explain this, I must recapitulate a little. Lorca arrived in Granada a day or two before the military rising broke out and, on the first news of this, took refuge in the house of a friend and fellow poet, Luis Rosales, close to the Cathedral. The fact that Rosales' brother, who also lived there, was a leading Falangist appeared to offer complete protection, yet a couple of days later, during the temporary absence of his hosts, a car manned by gunmen drew up at the door and carried him away. None of his friends ever saw him again.

For twelve years the Spanish censorship kept his name and his books under an almost complete ban. Then in December 1948 José María Pemán, the leading publicist and author laureate of the regime, wrote an article in *A.B.C.* castigating his murder by unknown persons as a crime against the nation. The reason for this change in the official attitude seems to have been that Lorca's many admirers in the Argentine had created a prejudice against the Franco regime which was affecting the commercial negotiations then going on with that country. The blame had therefore to be shifted from the leaders of the military rising to certain irresponsible and criminal persons. But

what persons? Only two authorized parties or groups of opinion existed in Spain—the Falange and the Clericals. They were
on bad terms and it at once became the business of each to fix
the blame on the other.

The first open blow in this controversy had already been
struck by the Falangist ex-minister, Serrano Suñer. In December 1947 he gave an interview to a Mexican journalist, Alfonso Junco, in which he asserted that the man who had given
the order to kill Lorca was the Catholic Conservative deputy
to the Cortes, Ramón Ruíz Alonso. Such an accusation could
not of course be published in the Spanish press, but it conveyed
accurately enough what the Falangists were saying. They
were organizing a whispering campaign to claim the poet for
their friend and lay the blame for his death on the Clericals.

The story, as it is usually told, is as follows. A day or two
after the beginning of the rising a rumour reached Granada
that the playwright Benavente, who is still alive and well and
writing as much as ever, had been shot in Madrid by the Reds.
The Catholic deputy, Ruíz Alonso, was sitting in a café with
his friends. "Well, if they have killed Benavente," he exclaimed, "we have García Lorca. Why doesn't someone go out
and fix him?" And so, like Fitz Urse obeying Henry II's command to kill Becket, a couple of men got up and went out.

Now there is nothing inherently improbable in such a story:
indeed, if there were not some truth in it, it would hardly be
repeated so openly. García Lorca had scandalised the narrow
minded and provincial citizens of his town in the same way
that Picasso scandalises many people to-day. But there is more
to be said about the motives for his assassination than that.
Lorca was not only a poet; he was also the brother-in-law of
the Socialist mayor of Granada, Montesinos, and the intimate
friend and collaborator of Fernando de los Ríos, the leading
Socialist intellectual in the city and the man most hated by
every section of the Nationalists. Thousands were shot for less

reason than this and, though Lorca had influential friends on the Right, he must have had even more enemies, not only among the Conservatives but in the ranks of the Falange. And who, one may ask, would have dared to take him from the house of a Falangist such as Rosales, unless he had the connivance and protection of other Falangists?

To understand the matter better, we have to throw our minds back to the confusion and horror of those weeks. The Falange was a loose, amorphous body organized like the Anarchists in small secret cells. The Youth Organization of the Catholic Party had just joined it as a body and merged into it. Little terrorist groups drew up lists of people to be shot, and no one questioned their actions so long as they confined themselves to people who were not affiliated to the Right. So far as I was able to discover, all the Black Squads which carried out the shootings wore Falangist markings. Thus, whoever bears the prime responsibility for García Lorca's death—and this is not a matter which can be solved to-day—there seems no reason why it should not have taken place at a Falangist centre such as Víznar. The only point to be decided was—had it?

As it happened, I was able to obtain a strong corroboration of the statement of the grave diggers. A friend put me in touch with a person who claimed to have spoken to a man who had been present. Lorca, this person said, had been driven straight from Rosales' house to the Falangist depot near Víznar. Then at dawn he had been taken to the *barranco* or ravine close by and shot.

"Not everyone," said this man, "would tell you this, but I am a person who has never meddled in politics or criticised the regime, so I see no harm in repeating what I know. Among ourselves we don't talk of these things, but we haven't forgotten them. They lie at the bottom of our minds and many people who have done things they had better not have done are racked by fear and contrition. Those most deeply implicated find themselves cold shouldered or have to put up with hints and pointed allusions, and some have fallen ill or gone mad through brooding on it. And now it seems that Heaven is punishing Spain for the evil her sons have committed. On both sides, of course, on both sides—not only on ours."

The next step clearly was to go out to Víznar and see what ever was to be seen there. Before doing this, however, we decided to drive to Fuente Vaqueros, the village where Lorca had been born and brought up. It lay some dozen miles away on the *vega* or irrigated plain, on the edge of an estate which had once been Godoy's and was now the Duke of Wellington's.

It was a beautiful drive. Clear, swift-running irrigation channels, islanded with watercress like a Dowland stream: plantations of thin, mast-like poplars: barns for drying tobacco. The village, which was connected with Granada by a tram-line, was low, white and dusty: through the middle of it ran a broad thoroughfare, the *plaza*, planted with pollarded trees, at one end of which stood the usual group of unemployed labourers, staring in front of them with wooden expressions. Mules, or ox carts, pigs, goats, children—the whole place was one great farm, smelling of the soil and of its round of labours.

The house where Federico had lived was one of the largest in the village: a white, two-storied building with balconies, a roof of brown tile and a concealed garden behind. Its unpretentious simplicity gave it a charm often lacking in more ambitious mansions. Next to it stood the church, long, low, colour-washed, with a miniature tower—the image of a toy church in a child's picture book. Unfortunately, like so many other Spanish churches, it had been defaced by the Falangist symbols and clap-trap set up over the porch. After this there was nothing more to be seen, so when we had paid our respects to the poet's aunt and cousin, who lived close by, we set off on our return journey, over roads deeply rutted by ox carts, between flat fields and the grey poles of poplar trees.

Federico lived at Fuente Vaqueros till 1912, when his parents moved to a house on the outskirts of Granada. We visited this house too. It was a *casa de campo* set among small fields, orchards and irrigation channels: white and grave and secret, like all the old houses of Granada, with two cypresses and a vine arbour in front of the door. Since his mother and sister left for America, it has lain empty.

We were now ready to visit the burial ground at Víznar. As soon as we had finished lunch we took a taxi at the Puerta Real. Since our expedition required speed and secrecy—for a visit to one of these caches was a delicate affair, possibly dangerous had we been Spaniards—it was important that we should have a taxi driver who would not show too much curiosity in our movements. But to our dismay we found that the man we had chosen was not only alert and intelligent, but a strong supporter of the regime: he had been a driver to some important general during the war and, though not a Falangist, spoke with high respect of Franco. We should have to find some way of eluding his vigilance.

The car left the main road and began to climb in sharp twists and curves between corn terraces and olive trees. Soon we reached the village, or hamlet rather, with its tall white houses crowding round the church and a few large plane trees.

"Where shall I stop?" asked the chauffeur.

"Here in the square," I answered. "I want to visit the cemetery, where a friend of mine is buried."

Silent with astonishment the chauffeur got out and sent someone to fetch the woman who kept the key.

"I'll come with you," he said. But when he found that the cemetery lay some way off the road, he turned back reluctantly to guard his car.

We followed a narrow path along the edge of one of the *bancales* or stone-walled terraces. Drooping, feminine olive trees, corn and beans in flower and below us on the left the green flat plain, with Fuente Vaqueros in the distance. Here and there the frail tint of apricot blossom or a red-budded pomegranate tree.

The old woman who accompanied us prattled away without ceasing. Her mother, she told us, had always had a great devotion to the dead. Night and day she had kept a lamp burning for them in the cemetery and even when it rained, and even when snow fell, she would go there to tend it. "*Ay, Dios mio,*" she used to say, "if it is wet and cold for us, isn't it colder and wetter for them? There they lie, *los pobrecillos,* out in that place with nothing to comfort them." Then when she was dying, when she was about to set out on her last journey and join them, she had said to her daughter, "*Ay, hija mia,* how can I bear to die? For when I am gone, who will tend the lamp in the cemetery, who will look after the poor dead?" And so she, her daughter, had answered, "I will tend the lamp and look after the dead, please God, as long as I live." And her mother, hearing that, had died in peace.

She informed us that though she had worked at the factory at a wage of 1 peseta a day, she had never failed to find time to visit the cemetery and pray there. To her it was more than the church, more than the saints. She felt such pity for those poor dead, lying there so far from the village and its animation. Even when there was no oil to keep the lamp burning, she managed to find it. And all the time, as she walked, she kept sighing and turning her beads and muttering snatches of prayer, among which one caught a great many *Ay Ay's* and *Madre mia's* and *Pobrecillos.*

Soon we saw the cemetery below us, a little high-walled enclosure like a cattle pen. Inside was a commotion of mounds and hollows, with here and there a few cheap wooden crosses and artificial wreaths, mostly broken and dilapidated: the rubbish heap of a country where the only things ever thrown away as useless are dead bodies.

The woman apologised: this was a poor village—the rich were taken for burial to Granada. And at once she began to pray, interjecting her mumblings with exclamations of how cold it was here on winter evenings and yet what a small sacrifice this was to make to the Lord.

The time had come for us to say what we wanted.

"Listen," I said. "We have come here in search of the grave of a man who was shot as a Red during the first days of the war. Can you help us?"

She did not answer, so I repeated my request.

"There are three or four buried here," she muttered and led the way to the place. Then, as we stood reading the names on the crosses, the impulse to talk became too great for her and she told us their story.

One day some Civil Guards had brought these men here in manacles and had shot them against the wall. But as soon as they had left, one of the men, who had only been wounded, had begun to creep away. Along the hill he had gone, under the olive trees, dragging himself on his hands and knees and leaving a trail of blood behind him on the ground. But someone had seen him and given word to the Guards, and they had brought him back and shot him, this time dead. Ay, such a pity! The whole village had wept as though he were their own. Later they heard that a pardon had come for him. But of what use, *Dios mio*, were pardons to him now? Then, after many years, two women had come to visit his grave. Tall women, beautifully dressed, in black from head to foot, and they had wept a great deal. And after they had finished weeping, they had prayed and had asked her to pray too.

I now felt that the moment had come to put my cards on the table.

"My friend is not buried here," I said, "but in the trenches in the *barranco*. Do you know where that is?"

"In the *pozos* or pits, you mean. Ay, ay, who doesn't know? But since those days no one has dared to go there."

"Will you explain to me how I can find them?"

"They're quite close. I'll take you."

We were leaving the cemetery when a man appeared, wearing a brass-studded bandolier slung diagonally across his chest. He introduced himself as the *regidor* of the village municipality and asked, very politely, what our business was. I replied that I was looking for the grave of a friend who had been shot during the war. I wished, before returning to my country, to say a few prayers over it.

"Have you found it?" he asked.

"Not yet. It seems that he is buried in the *pozos*."

The man did not speak for some moments. Then:

"If you wish to go there," he said, "that is your affair. But you must excuse me if I do not accompany you. The consejo has no jurisdiction in such matters."

"I shall only be there a few minutes," I said to reassure him.

"The fewer the better. *Vaya Usted con Dios*."

"We set off. After following the path for some time we came up onto the road beyond the village.

"Where does this road lead?" I asked.

"To the spring which is just beyond the *barranco*," replied the woman. "There it stops. That is why it is called the *Camino de la Fuente*. In the days before the war it used to be the village *paseo:* people walked along it on Sunday evenings and took the air. They drank a little water from the spring, for this water is famous all round these parts and very fattening, and the children played there. But now no one goes along it—no one."

The last patch of cultivation was coming to an end and the

road began to plunge into the mountains. On our left, just below it, stood a largish red house, ugly and new, built apparently as a summer villa. It was known, our guide told us, as La Colonia. Before the military rising it had been a sort of Brown House for the Falangists of Granada, where they had met and received training. They had also brought their girls here and danced. Then, when the rising had broken out, it had been put to different uses. Every night three or four lorries had roared up the road with their load of prisoners and had deposited them here. A Falangist priest was waiting to confess them and the parish priest was fetched as well: poor man, he had to be present—that was the regulation. Then they were taken down to the ravine to be —— you understand, some by the light of the lorries' headlamps and some at dawn. Women too. The *Escuadra Negra* (here the woman lowered her voice), the Black Squad stuck at nothing.

"And who dug the graves?"

"In the basement of the house they kept prisoners for work of that sort and later on, so it was said, they shot them too. *Ay, Dios mio*, what terrible things were done! To think that Christian men should do such terrible things!"

From where we stood we could see the road twisting like a snake in front of us. It ran into a ravine—the *barranco*—came out of it and ended. All round us were bare shaly slopes, dotted with occasional dry bushes. Below lay the green *vega* and its villages, among them that where Federico had been born, and in front, rising sheer above us, a mountain of harsh grey rock, its summit crowned with stunted pines and pointed rock pinnacles. On one of these had been placed an iron cross.

A few minutes more and we had reached the bridge over the ravine. As we drew near it, the woman, who had ceased her chatter, began to mumble prayers and tell her beads with increasing energy. A little path led up the wide of the dry watercourse and there, fifty yards on, was the place. It was a gentle slope of blue clay, scattered with rushes and thin sedge grasses, a deposit from the freshets that ran when the *barranco* was in spate. The entire area was pitted with low hollows and mounds, at the head of each of which had been placed a small stone. I began to count them, but gave it up when I saw that the number ran into hundreds.

"They buried them here," said the woman, "in shallow pits and then pushed earth over them. What a thing to do! Weren't they all sons of God and Christians who crossed themselves as we do?"

And she began to pray aloud in a low tone, "Holy and Immaculate Virgin, be with us now and in the hour of our death. . . . Be with us now and in the hour of our death."

As I stood there on the pitted clay, I heard a sound and saw that our car had followed us and was drawn up below. The chauffeur had got out and, to the evident alarm of the woman, was climbing the path towards us. However, when he saw us standing motionless with bared heads, he stopped and removed his hat too.

I waited, trying to fix the scene in my mind. In front rose the red, shaly side of the *barranco*—just one little sample of the interminable, barren mountain slopes of this country: on the right lay the green *vega*, with the Sierra de Elvira rising like a volcanic island out of it. Above, the mountain. Such had been the poet's last view, as the dawn rose in brightening circles in the sky and the cockcrows floated up from the plain like their own echoes. I picked a blue grape hyacinth, the only flower growing there among the rushes, and came away.

> *Ay amor*
> *que se fué y no vino!*
>
> . . . . . .
>
> *Ay amor*
> *que se fué por el aire!*

267

WALTER STARKIE

Don Gypsy

A SELECTION FROM *Don Gypsy*

Some men are Gypsies by inclination, ready to take to the open road with the caravan, where there is music and adventure among a strange people. This absurd concept has loyal followers, hidden around the world, in mid-Manhattan, in The City, in New Delhi. There is a cult of vicarious followers of the Gypsies, well-developed among the busnés, or non-Gypsies, and many a Western man has fervently studied the Romany language and customs, and even gone to live among the people for a time.

The man who thus associates with the Gypsies in spirit or in fact is called a Romany Rye. George Borrow, whose dedication to selling Bibles in many lands never quite surpassed his

268

interest in the Gypsies, is the undisputed English chief of these followers—so dominant a man and author, in fact, that there is a small but well-read clique of his followers, Borrovians, perhaps fewer in this than in the last century, but victims of the zest of a remarkable man who always followed the open road.

Borrow has had a worthy successor, a century later, an Irishman named Walter Starkie.

Starkie has been university professor (Dublin), Abbey Theatre director, philologist, musician, and author of many books. As a Romany Rye he has lived with the Spanish people, Gypsy and non-Gypsy, traveling among them with his fiddle and singing their songs—when not lecturing at universities or administering British cultural undertakings.

In this selection, Dr. Starkie describes a fragment of Gypsy life as he saw it in the last good years, in the 1930's, before the Spanish Civil War.

AT LAST after emerging out of the rugged mountain scenery I descended into a fertile valley full of fruit trees in bloom, then up again into further mountain scenery. Towards evening I saw beneath me a great expanse of flat country shut in by low mountains. From where I was the land looked like a fen and it was crevassed and dotted here and there with small knolls. When I descended I found that it was a miniature highland country composed of loam, which Nature had carved out into *mesetas* reminding me of New Mexico and Arizona but without the wide, limitless expanses. The scenery around Guadix is freakish and Nature must have wished to play a joke with the lumps of loam as a child would with plasticine.

269

It was dark by the time I reached the village of Purullena where I put up for the night in a cave recommended to me by a friend in Granada. It belonged to a jovial *mayoral*, or coachman, who had a splendid repertory of *javeras* and *caleseras* collected in long years of omnibus jolting over the mountain road to Granada.

When I reached Guadix next I took up my abode in a workman's inn where a bed cost 1.50 pesetas. For my dinner I ate *chivo* (kid) and tomatoes watered down by excellent red wine which only cost ten *céntimos* a tumbler. The landlady—a fat homely matron—insisted upon including another favourite Andalusian delicacy: *perdices sin güeso* (boneless partridge). I expected a bird, but all I found on my plate was a potato in its jacket. Take a potato, roast it, rub it with garlic, add salt and pepper and you have a boneless partridge—a most satisfying meal for a poor street-player, for it only costs ten *céntimos*.

My main purpose in visiting Guadix was to see the cave-dwelling Gypsies of the "Cañada de los Gitanos," so I set out on my explorations at night-time. During the day the Gypsies in Guadix may be seen in the narrow streets of the town and in the cafés plying their trade of bootblack. My first companion was one called Quitoli—an ugly, cross-eyed, squat-figured man with an unlimited capacity for drink. He was not the companion I should have chosen had I been a free agent, but once he attached himself to me I could not get rid of him. I admit that I was to blame, for I encouraged him at first in the hope that he would give me information about his race, and to loosen his tongue I stood him many *chatos*. Consequently he became loud-mouthed and quarrelsome with everyone. My method of street and tavern-playing is to be as discreet and unobtrusive as possible. I like to slip silently into the café, have a pennyworth or so of wine at the counter, address a few greetings and remarks about the weather to the habitués, giving all the while many a sidelong glance at the bar-tender in white coat or the waiter to see if he looks like a promising patron. But as soon as Quitoli had linked himself to me he became a discreditable confederate, whose co-operation gave me unenviable prominence. He drank three to my one, for while I was playing he would stand at the counter. And when I had finished fiddling he would take all the credit for my performance to himself and swagger—begging at the same time *chatos* from anyone who was fool enough to stand them. I cursed him a hundred times secretly when I saw him draw down general disapproval upon himself, for ultimately I should become unpopular too, as everyone considered me his partner. I made up my mind to escape from him, and so when I saw him installed at the counter in a bar I darted out of the door and away down the street as fast as I could walk, but in vain, for with a whoop he lurched after me shouting so loudly that people looked out of doorways to see what was the cause of the row.

"Eh, compañero! surely you do not want to give me the slip; you are a stranger here and I want to guide you."

I followed him, cursing my fate. It was unwise to fight with him, for he would excite the attention of the whole street. At last I persuaded him to turn his steps in the direction of the "Cañada de los Gitanos," or Gypsy quarter. After passing through various streets we reached a rabbit-warren of caves. At night the mountain cones, honey-combed with caverns up to the summit, were the most fantastic sight imaginable. The cones looked as if they were volcanoes germinating from within and bursting out of the loam here and there in countless, tiny pin-eyes of flame. It is said that half the inhabitants of the town live in those underground dwellings. Many of the caves are even more luxurious than those of the Sacro Monte, for they have windows and bricked-up entrances. We, however, passed by the rich caves and wended our way to the remote Gypsy caverns which are as primitive as the dwellings of the Red Indians at Taos or Acoma.

At night the *cañada* of the Gypsies is a mysterious place, for there are few lights and the earth is most uneven. Occasionally, dark figures brushed past me and I heard voices at one moment seemingly from the sky, at another from the bowels of the earth. A ghostly place it was and I began to regret that I had entrusted myself to the drunken sot Quitoli. He lurched and stumbled, cursing and shouting, and his voice echoed in the silent night. He led me up and down, round and round as in a labyrinth. We climbed slippery paths that winded up the cone-shaped hills from cave to cave. Some of the caves were closed and there was no sign of life within: others were wide open and the glaring light illuminated the brown clay of the hill and the straggling, zig-zag trail linking the cavern to its neighbour. In one big cave we saw a forge. A Gypsy was beating the metal on the anvil, singing in a hoarse voice a *martinete* as he worked. The banging of the hammer on the anvil echoes through the whole hill and re-called to my mind the singing of Antonio Camacho. Quitoli would not let me halt at the forge to listen and shouted—

"Vamos a buscar el sarmiento" (We'll look out for an olive branch).

"What do we want with an olive branch?"

"Haven't you a thirst on you? An olive branch is the sign of a tavern."

On we stumbled through the night, up the steep trails until we came to a cave which was more like a robber's den than a tavern. A gloomy, smoky hole it was. Dark caverns branched off the ill-lit, central room which was thronged with dishev-elled Gypsies. An old man behind a counter poured us out two tiny glasses of wine. Quitoli, after a few minutes' confabula-tion with the Gypsies, exclaimed to me: "Hay un velatorio" (There's a wake on).

"Where?" said I eagerly.

"Over in a cave yonder: come, let us be off. It will be a good *juerga*. They are 'waking' a child. We shall have plenty of *jaleo* and laughter."

"Laughter," said I increduously. Either Quitoli is lacking in respect for the dead or else he is so completely drunk that he does not know what he is saying. How could Gypsies who are always obsessed by thoughts of death ever laugh at a "wake"? I thought of the countless *coplas* which describe the lamentations of the *Calés* when the corpse is enveloped in "the green bird," as the poor in Andalusia used to call the shroud which was supplied at charity funerals. However, I followed Quitoli, groping my way as fast as I could in the dark.

All at once behind the hill I heard the sound of clapping and singing. A crowd of Gypsies were gathered outside a cave half-way up a neighboring knoll. When we reached the cave we found it all ablaze with lights. Some of the Gypsies carried lighted candles, but they took care never to touch the wax with their hands, for that, I was told, is very unlucky, and so they had wrapped paper around the ends of the candles. Quitoli had been right. There certainly was *jaleo*. I thought at first a frenzied *zambra* was going on in honour of some cave-dweller who had won the first prize in the National Lottery. The men danced and capered: the women danced and clapped their hands. I heard the sound of *bandurrias* and guitars at the back of the cave. Around the entrance men were gathered together in a group and most of them were drinking out of wineskins and *porrones*. Inside the cave in the centre of the *fiesta* was a coffin with the lid off. Inside lay the body of a tiny child. At first I thought the child was asleep, for its cheeks were not pale but flushed with colour. But I was told that it was the custom to paint the cheeks of a dead infant and redden its lips to simulate life. The body was wrapped from head to toe in red and blue ribbons, which had been wound round and round the shroud in spirals. The coffin was decorated in flowers and surrounded with candles.

The air was heavy with the smell of sweat, molten wax and the aroma of flowers. I stood petrified, gazing at the pathetic, statuesque little face unconscious of all this grotesque orgy of shouting, stamping and dancing. A man jostled me out of the way and held aloft a flask of aniseed brandy. After swallowing some he held the flask out over the little corpse and sprayed the face. It trickled in a glistening stream down the painted cheeks. Then there were shouts of "Olé!": men and women capered and jumped like demons at a Witches' Sabbath. One woman was wriggling her body in a continual *meneo* and waving her arms. So wild was she that I thought she was preparing for a bacchanalian dance. Her hair had fallen over her sweating face, her black scarf had become untied and floated after her and her feet kept beating a devil's tattoo on the clay floor.

"Who is that witch?" said I to Quitoli.

"That is the mother of the dead infant."

"Why does she behave in such a way? Why does she not cry out her agony for her dead child?"

"The child is up there," replied Quitoli, pointing up at the stars. "Don't pity the child—it already has wings sprouting from its little shoulders. Come here, Cagancho: hand me the flask: I want to baptize the child."

Saying this, he seized the flask and sprayed not only the corpse but all of us who were close by.

As soon as it was possible, I disappeared from the "wake," but it was no easy task because Quitoli shadowed me everywhere. However, I managed finally to escape from his clutches with the help of another *Gitano*.

"Leave Quitoli to me," said he: "he'll leave you alone or

else I'll call the *arcarde de los Gitanos* (the mayor of the Gypsies) to deal with him."

Fortunately, I did not need the services of the mayor, for Quitoli was spirited away from me on some errand and I was free to go back to my *fonda*. As I descended the slope from the cave the grey, ghostly light of dawn came gently stealing over the scene, and the air was misty as if veils of gauze had been drawn down over the caves.

What a contrast that *velatori* had been to others I had seen on my wanderings, when the mother keening her dead child shrieked her helpless despair. Gypsies are as a rule very demonstrative in their grief—they throw themselves upon the coffin, they bang their heads against the walls, they exaggerate the expression of their sorrow. I remember once, in Hungary, how the son of a Gypsy *primás* stood over the open grave of his father and tried to cast himself, violin and all, on to the coffin when it was lowered into the earth. In Sicily I have seen in a cottage in the interior of the island similar scenes of tragedy. The women tore tufts of their hair and cast them upon the corpse: some sang rambling songs and chanted in monotonous voice the virtues of the deceased. For days men and women sat muffled up and motionless in the darkened cottage. And fresh bread and water too was left for the deceased beside the coffin, and a light to guide his spirit, when it returned to partake of the meal of the dead. The custom of dancing, singing and performing music for the dead is general among Gypsies. It serves to quiet the spirit and prevent it from wreaking any vengeance on the living. In Roumania it is even customary to pierce holes in the coffin so that the dead may hear the dirges sung by the paid women weepers.

At first I explained for myself the orgy of gaiety in honour of the dead child by the old adage—"Those whom the gods love die young." Had Quitoli not said—"Don't pity the child:

275

she's gone to heaven and has become an angel." But when I questioned a gnarled, old Romanichal he explained the orgy thus—"Why shouldn't they jump for joy and shout and dance? The child was lucky to die so early. Have we *Calés* so much to be thankful for in life? What a deal of sorrow and suffering that child has escaped."

In the following days I spent most of my time in the "Cañada de los Gitanos." Through the good offices of "the Mayor" of the Gypsies, I was welcomed by the Romanichals, but I certainly did not make money by my minstrelsy. In fact I ceased to be *juglar* and became for the moment Romany Rye—that is to say, I carried a good store of pennies and half-pennies in my pockets as reward for dances, *coplas* and sayings. The mayor of the Gypsies in Guadix is a Gypsy him-self—a certain Juan Bermudez Heredia, by trade a bootblack. He is a most respected citizen of the town and has won the confidence of Romanichals and gorgios alike. His post is an official one, for he serves as a liaison between the Gypsies and the authorities. Such a post is an interesting survival of the ancient days when Gypsies were tried by judges chosen from their own race. Juan Bermudez possesses an ascendancy over the cave-dwellers, for he is an upright man of strong char-acter. He can settle private squabbles and calm those fierce vendettas which are always breaking out between one clan and another. His appointment would seem to contradict the old saying of the *Calés:* "Isna, calorró, terelas e abiyar a gachimbastá sos sina es busnés" (Alas, O Gypsy, you have to go before judges who are gorgios).

The cave-dwellers in the "Cañada" were a great contrast to those in the Sacro Monte at Granada. Whereas the latter are capitalists, full of the sophisticated ideas which the world of *Flamenco* has given them, the former are simple and un-affected to any great extent by modern civilization. They have not advanced from the background into the front of the picture as have the *Gitanos* of the Sacro Monte. They are grasping and money-grabbing, but only in a small way. The Romanichals of Granada beg for *duros* where those of Guadix only beg for "perras gordas." If the latter are corrupted at all it is because the "Cañada" is part of the modern town. It is surprising how primitive those Gypsies have remained. They reminded me by their irresponsible, childlike natures of the inhabitants of the "Street of the Spoons" at Cluj in Transylvania. As a stranger I awakened mere curiosity, but when I talked Caló and fiddled in the caves I created a sensation. Soon the cave where I was playing no longer sufficed to contain the audience, so I stood outside and fiddled to the crowd clustered together on the ground below. They were not an attractive audience: the women cackled with irrepressible laughter: the men gave hoarse whoops; the dogs barked. My music did one good thing: it spurred the women on to dance for me and recite *coplas*. Alas, those *coplas* were not such as a modest pure-minded gorgio woman would recite. Many of the Rabelaisian words escaped me, but when I heard the roars of laughter I asked one called "El Rápido" to explain them. The most outspoken was Serafina, a married woman dressed in coarse blue and wearing a pink *dikló* over her hair. She had five small children gambolling in the dust at her feet and she was expecting a sixth in a few months' time.

"Give Serafina some money," shouted another woman. "Certainly," said I. "Here are two 'perras gordas.' "

"You haven't given me a tiny one for the baby," said Serafina.

"What baby?" said I.

"She's cambrí" (pregnant), interjected the other woman.

"Well, here's another penny."

But Serafina was not yet satisfied: she wanted more.

"Come on, Señor; give me something for the father of the child. He deserves it."

"Don't give it to her, Señor," said the other woman. "Don't or she'll be wanting to sleep with you."

"God forbid," said I, showing embarrassment.

There was a chorus of laughter from all the women and they made remarks about my well-fed appearance and my fair complexion. I heard the muttered words *friscales* and *garibolo*, but I have never been able to discover their meaning. I am sure that they had some picaresque significance, for all the women laughed again and Serafina came up nearer to me and became more provocative.

"Here," said she, "is a young *romí* whose eyes are falling out of her head from looking at you. I'm afraid your eye will make her cambrí." She then pushed up to me a tall, young woman, saying—"Meet La Coroca, Señor—the best-looking woman in the 'Cañada.' She has a taste for men and she likes a good, fat 'Busnó' even better than the 'Calés.' Don't you, Isabela? Anyhow, Señor, won't you give her your young jaw-bone?"

There was a huge roar of laughter at this remark and a young girl added—"La Coroca would not be satisfied with a jaw-bone—she doesn't like bones."

"What do you all mean by the jaw-bone? I don't understand you," said I puzzled.

"Well, I'll tell you," replied Serafina. "The 'Calés' believe that at the beginning of the world God made the 'Busnó' out of slime: then he made a woman out of the 'Busnó's' spare rib. Later on he found that the world was so dull with these two 'Busnés' and their children that he said to himself—'I must liven things up.' So one night, when the man was sleeping in his cave, God goes and takes a bit of his jaw-bone and in a twinkling of an eye he makes out of it a stiff and sturdy 'Calorró' alive and kicking."

Serafina after this long description paused for breath and I was able to observe "La Coroca"; she was a tall, good-looking

Gitana, wearing a white *dikló* on her head and silver bracelets on her arms, but her feet and legs were bare. Without saying a word she began to dance for me, all the time humming a tune. The rest of the women and children stood round in a ring and clapped the rhythm. The dance, I must say, was even more suggestive than the conversation of Serafina. The tune was very simple.

After dancing in the ancient *zorongo* style she varied her movements by what is called the *zarandeo*—a horizontal, cinder-sifting undulation, similar to that which I had seen in Tetuan and Tangier, but much more primitive and negroid. Among the nomad Gypsies in the East there is a similar dance called the *tanyana*, in which there is a continuous undulatory movement. "La Coroca" gave such a *zarandeo*, or whatever else it is called, to her dancing that I cried out to her the classic phrase—"Tienes mucha miel en las caderas" (You have plenty of honey in your hips).

As soon as she had finished her seductive performance a ragged but very pretty girl (she could not have been more than sixteen or seventeen) beckoned me aside and said she wanted to dance for me, but she would not do it before all the people. "Come later to my cave up yonder," said she: "my sisters will sing and I'll dance for you."

As soon as the hubbub had died down and the way was free, I went up to the girl's cave—it was the forge where I had seen the smith working and singing on the night of my arrival in Guadix. The smith was not there, so I asked the girl where he was.

"You mean my husband," answered she. "He's away, that's why I asked you. He would beat me if he saw me dance for you."

Her sisters—little girls of thirteen and fourteen—corroborated her statement—"Yes, Juan Eleria is very jealous: he only married Triné last year." Then the two little minxes began to sing in a monotonous rhythmic voice a song with the refrain "Chirindín, chirindín, chirindero"—

> *"Chirindín, chirindín, chirindero!*
> *en la feria su mare*
> *le va compar un mortero;*
> *chirindín, chirindín, chirindero!*
> *pa que maje er peregil*
> *y sargan los cardos güenos."*

> (*"To the fair his mother goes*
> *to buy him a fine, big mortar,*
> *chirindín, chirindín, chirindero!*
> *that he may pound and grind the parsley*
> *and thistles may grow in plenty."*)

I was unable to find out whether it was a nonsense *copla* or whether the words of the refrain had special significance. From the way the girls shouted the refrain and Triné danced I should say it was a piece of erotic symbolism. The dance was of the same undulatory type as the one performed by "La Coroca," for Triné "cinder sifted" and rolled her eyes as well as her waist, while the other two sang at the top of their voices. They told me that the song *chirindín* was very often danced at "wakes" and at baptismal *fiestas*.

I was going to ask them to repeat their performance and I held out a silver peseta as reward, when suddenly a grim young Gypsy appeared and shouted a volley of curses at Triné. With a loud cry she fled into the cave and hid in one of the dark holes off the main central room. Juan Eleria, for that was his name, without a word followed her. A few seconds later we heard screams and resounding smacks.

"What has happened?" said I alarmed.

"He is jealous," said the girls, "and when he is in that state there is no stopping him. He always beats Triné."

Juan Eleria soon came out smiling and rubbing his hands. "I have given her a little dose," said he. "After all I am the best *curandero* when she is in that mood. Kicking about her legs, dancing 'el molinete,' was she? A woman is like a mule—the more you beat her, the better she loves you; she knows she's got one man who'll break her in, and quickly too. So now, Señor, all finishes in glory. By the way, I think you offered her some money. What about it now? Why not hand it over to me?"

I handed the peseta to him without demur and we parted the best of friends. Triné appeared without a trace of anger or sorrow on her face. She was now submissive and took her place beside Juan Eleria without a glance in my direction.

WALDO FRANK

Man and Woman

A SELECTION FROM *Virgin Spain*

*The Spanish character has perplexed Spaniards themselves.
At least a dozen first-class attempts at national self-analysis
have been made by Spaniards—by Altamira, Castro, Marañón,
Sánchez Albornoz, Ortega y Gasset, among others—each
emphasizing, as it turns out, different aspects of the Spanish
inheritance and temperament. All of them, taken together,
provide a description, but not an explanation, of their con-
tradictory race.*

*Few Americans or English, despite the number of books
which these people have written about Spain, have ventured
into the tangled paths of Spanish character. V. S. Pritchett,
the English critic, made a successful foray, in a book which he*

282

wisely entitled, The Spanish Temper—*for his series of sketches, valid and illuminating, state external manifestations but tell little of causes and relations.*

Irving Babbitt once dashed at the subject of "Spain" in an article, but he tripped over several hurdles, most of which involved a repetitious confusion about the "Oriental" qualities of the Spaniards.

Among the writings of Americans, Waldo Frank's Virgin Spain *remains the best account of the Spanish psyche. Frank is frequently exasperating, often wrong in his conclusions, and sometimes confused, but his knowledge of Spain is considerable, and, at times, his style is up to his content.*

His special achievement has been what may be called "national cultural portraits," or psychological analyses of national groups, long before such a practice was appreciated by the literate American public. His writing in this vein has been much more favorably received abroad, by the portrayed, than by Frank's compatriots—evidence, perhaps, that Frank knows what he is writing about.

Because he wrote early about Latin America, and with wisdom, Frank is better known there than many other North American authors. He knew Spain before he knew Latin America, having lived in Spain during the 1920's, and thereby evolving his mystique about the peninsula and the Spanish soul: Virgin Spain.

QUEEN ISABEL may rest in peace. She had her will although she would not recognize its way. Her conscious will was to make Spain one: it became the unconscious will of every Spaniard. Her concept of the State of Spain has become the universal Spanish state of mind. Here was Spain, this sea of elements tossing and titanic. Here was the Spaniard, pressed by the amorphous world in which he lived to establish unity within himself: to become a person, in defense from the chaos that was Spain. In his will to create Spain, he could not change the theater of his action. He must create Spain *within himself*. The first stage of his endeavor was that of the intense crystallizations which made Spain's *siglos de oro*. These saints and sinners are not fragments: they are entire forms of Spanish energy. And the elements which they personify exist in every Spanish soul. If, therefore, Spain was to be unified within each Spaniard, La Celestina must be equated with Saint Teresa, Quixote and Amadís with Lazarillo and the Cid. . . . Although the energic sum of all these forces might in each individual soul add up to zero!

To the intensely individual Spaniard, Spain became more and more subjective: until at last the boundary to the outer world was lost. Politics, war and church became subjective. The Spaniard saw the world only in terms of himself. This is why he strove to make the State the mentor of conscience: this is why he strove to make the domains of the State a sort of spiritual body. To inculcate faith by Inquisition; to establish truth by the sword; to drive dissenters in spirit from the soil—these were the mad and logical acts of a man who beheld the world in his own image. Willing to create a Spain, each Spaniard remained the anarchic personal creature whose separatism Strabo had noted and Rome endured.

The tragedy of Spain—her reaching of success! First her energy broke up into dominant forms of will: then she equated these forms into the equilibrium she desired. And no energy was left! All of her opponent tensions merge to rest in every Spanish soul. The titanic efforts toward conquest, toward art, toward God which have made Spain great balanced each other at the end. The energy is not gone, not weakened: it is equated. And the result is sleep. . . .

The Spaniard elected a form of achievement and a form of truth which he could reach: and as he reached it, he stopped moving. Truth became the Church of Rome: he attained that truth and rejected every other. His ideal of unity was homogeneity: the simple fusion in every Spaniard of thought and faith, according to a fixed ideal. To this end he impoverished the elements of his psychic world into sharp antitheses: these he balanced against each other: the result was indeed simplicity, homogeneity, a neutralization of energy summing to zero.

The Spaniard of the past two centuries is not decadent: neither is he weak. There is as great force in him as in the days when his still unfused power conquered half Europe, discovered America and poured the vision of Cervantes, Rojas, Calderón and Velázquez upon the world. But now all this energy is *locked* on its own willed equation. Its original dualisms are not dead; they are controlled and neutralized. The equilibrium is complete: and what energy is left from it the Spaniard must expend in holding the equation. There is no energy unemployed: and it is precisely the excess energy of man, the energy that is unable to find its goal within the organism, which creates intellect and which creates creation.

Had he been less heroic in his will, or more objective in his way to it, the Spaniard would not have become this cripple: this giant shattered by his success, this giant imprisoned in the reality of his ideal.

The most willful of men, he appeared will-less. For his power of will went to dominate himself—and to hold his dominion. So that no power was left wherewith to dominate the world. The unity of Spain exists, subjectively and multiplied by millions. In consequence the Spaniard is not adhesive: he is too complete: the motive toward adhesiveness is the sense of incompletion. The most secret impulse of the Frenchman or the Jew has its social dimension. No Jew can people Zion in solitude. No French mystic or philosopher is an anchorite. Pascal and Descartes are Catholic: Paul Cézanne strives to create a new museum art. The rebel in France is a rebel against monarchs. But the Spaniard is an empire and a god unto himself. The perfected Spanish person makes permanent the social Spanish chaos.

The most intellectual of men, he appeared unintelligent. He lived so wholly within his Idea, that no energy is left for further ideation. Creative intelligence is the birth of conflict between the personal will and life: it is born of the pause between impulse and response and of the excess energy which remains after the instinctive action. In the Spaniard, this excess energy was small: he was too self-sufficient to know richly the pauses between will and deed; and in the relativity of values which springs from a chaotic or incompleted conscience he was poor. Having achieved his Idea, he was weak in intellect: having created his imagined world, he was weak in imagination.

Therefore he understood vaguely the causes of his incompetence, and struggled weakly against them. His contemporary literature, up to the latest generation, was strong in plaint: wanting in self-knowledge and constructiveness. Weak, also, in the creative imagination, it was strong in fantasy. The Spanish mind had become like the mind of a child. The child's intellect is not inferior to the man's: it is merely too preoccupied within itself to have achieved the power of association and of objective experience which comes with maturity and which begets analysis and imagination. The child is credulous, because its belief is subjective fantasy and finds no opponent in the real world. Also, the child is cruel because it cannot imagine pain in others; it is anti-social because it has not associated its life with the life around it. The Spaniard was still the victim of the infantile beliefs of medieval Europe. He accepted the literal Heaven and Hell, having no imagination strong enough to make them real, and in consequence to reject them. He was cruel. And his separatism, his want of the adhesive impulse made him a ready victim to tyranny in government. Unable to organize a social body, he accepted the simple body of the King or the alien body of the Church of Rome.

He has the virtues of his state. His personal development brings him a personal integrity, a true personal pride unknown in Europe. He has natural dignity. Whatever his rank, he is a *caballero:* a true microcosm of the Spanish nation. There is no artifice in him. He is clean, self-controlled and independent. In his veins lives the impulse of heroism; in his mind is the knowledge and the acceptance of heroism's price. Cowardice, compromise, hypocrisy are traits more common in more social races. And cant requires no word in *castellano.* Even the Spanish thief is sincere: the tradition of the pícaro has not died. And the power of endurance, of sacrifice, of devotion is developed in the average Spaniard beyond the dream of the romantic north.

The once furious and unleashed elements of the Spanish soul, woven into this counterpoint of rest, made a quiet music. It is natural that the Spaniard's love of music and gift for music should be supreme. This art of vigorous abstracted balance, so subjective, so ruthlessly legal, is the symbol of the Spanish nature. And as with his classic *canto hondo,* the effect in counterpoise and control is almost that of silence. By the same token he is a great dancer: his dance is a synthesis of movements equated to rest. And he loves the drama: where the torrential forces of mankind are fused into a unitary form.

The world nurses two myths concerning Spain. The first, that she is decadent, Spain believed herself, and thereby proved, if other proof were lacking, her failure in self-knowledge. The other myth is that Spain is romantic.

The first myth rests upon ignorance of psychological mechanics. The second is a confusion of words. The philology of the term *romance* is clear. In the formative eras of modern Europe, the Latin dialects which were to become French, Italian, Castilian, Portuguese, Galician, Provençal, etc., were lumped as the *romance* to distinguish them from the pure tongue of Latin. They were popular vernaculars and despite the early instance of such men as Dante and Petrarch, or the Arcipreste de Hita, they were not deemed worthy vehicles of exalted thought. The writer whose ideas were holy or philosophic was supposed to clothe them in Latin. Only if he treated of such vulgar subjects as earthly love, might he employ the vulgar language. By association, *romance* was transferred from the tongue to the subject for which it was disposed: a story of profane love or profane adventure became *romance;* and becoming so, remained trivial and vulgar. The essential attitude of the Spaniard toward the subjects of romance was, however, the very contrary of what we mean by romantic.

Now came the hour of confusion. The knights of Portugal and Spain fought for God, for Mohammed, for the King: for anything but what we call *romantic* reasons. The Iberian north is Celt and is contiguous with the Celtic cultures of Britain and of France. The Iberian knight went northward out of Spain; and when he returned he had become what today we call a "nordic." He was sentimental, tender, monogamous, and chaste. He was the very converse of the old Spanish knight, Arab or pagan-Christian, whose canny materialism speaks so clear in the *Poema del Cid*. He was, indeed, Tristan, Arthur, Lancelot, or Amadís of Gaul. The books that were written about him were published in romance: so that the qualities of passionate devotion which in Spain have been confined to the religious—to subjects too high for romance— became romantic.

288

The romance, therefore, is of the south: the romantic is of the north; and they negate each other. It is the German metaphysicians who invented the romanticism of Calderón; it is Byron and the French aesthetes who created romantic Spain. But the best efforts of Schlegel, Goethe, Mérimée, Gautier, Byron have failed to make the Spanish man or woman in the least romantic.

She is serene and she is incurious. Her Anglo-Saxon sister would call her inactive, even as the *Parisienne* would find her dull. Since sexual adventurousness is normally the result of intellectual curiosity—sensual stimulation by ideas—she is chaste and dispassionate. But if her lack of amorousness is due to her lack of thinking, her serenity and her external inactivity are due to her tremendous power. Women are most clamorous for "rights" in lands where culturally they have counted least. Witness England or the United States, where for all her liberties woman is spiritually sterile. In contrast witness France, whose women were the subtle partners of all deep events; or matriarchal Spain, in which suffragists before the vote was given them were as rare as they would have been superfluous.

The Spanish woman is a pragmatist in love. Love to her is the means of raising children in the grace of Christ. No less sensual, no less amorous woman exists in Europe. As a girl she is lovely: a crisp expectancy makes her flesh sweet and rounds her darkling eyes. She looks to marriage as the highest and most powerful career. Once she is mated, the natural coquetry of Spring falls from her like a season: she is instantly sedate, full-fleshed, maternal. She has no instinct for the game of love. Sexual virtuosity in woman is a slow process nurtured at the expense of the maternal passion. This diversion is rare in Spain. The French or American woman's sexual science is an undeciphered, an irrelevant perversion to the woman of Spain who wears upon her head an invisible crown of matriarchal power.

For she is powerful: this discreet female in a land of furiously dreaming males! Events have sobered her and made her worldly-wise. Her man is the theater of opponent passions, ideals, hungers equating into nothing. She is the compensatory act. She is steady, unemotional, unmystical, canny. She distrusts excess—even of maternal service. Her man has made magic of such words as State, God, Honor. Hers the task to materialize these words which in his mouth bespeak inaction. The family, the garden, the morrow; these become her Word.

The woman of Spain leans on the Church of Rome. No small part this of her dominance in a land incapable of social institutions. Spain with her separatist nature, her inadhesiveness, could never have created Rome: but Rome has gone far toward giving Spain that minimum of organic body which the millions of individual "Spains"—her men—required. The Spanish woman by her massed support makes the Church Spanish.

If the Church belongs to the woman, ruling Spain through her, she has remained outside the exhaustive activities of her husband. The Spanish woman has been untouched by metaphysics: her heroine, Santa Teresa de Jesús, is an ennobled *house-cleaner*, a glorified matron of Christ. The Spaniard's wife has not, like him, been split into intricate traits of will and of expression: nor in the sequel need she spend herself to win back unity from an inner chaos. She is naturally whole: she is the foe of even the fairest anarchies of the spirit. There is in her a heroic amplitude that recalls the poised women of the Hebrews. She is the savior of Spain, for she is the Responder to Spain's excesses of action and inaction.

The land has become a matriarchy—by default. The Spaniard has been too busy establishing theodicy on earth to rule

Spain well: at last too involved in the equating of his em-
battled impulse to rule Spain at all. Imperceptibly, unofficially,
woman has taken hold. She allows man many liberties—trivial
liberties of the sort she would call romantic, if she knew the
word. He may "govern," vote, own; he may fight; he
may drink, gamble, whore. He may act indeed the perfect
child thinking himself the center of the world because of his
exultant vices (of which politics and journalism are the most
absurd). Meantime, she with her compass, Christ, and her
wheel, the priest, steers the slow ship of Spain. In her disposal
are the education of her children, intellectual and moral, the
molding of those customs which go deeper than statute. In
her hands is the family, and the family is Spain. She is the true
controller of finance. It is a common thing in Spain for the
man to own the money of his wife, and for the wife to dis-
tribute the money of her husband. In the peasant classes she is
arbiter of culture and thought: in the middle classes she is
economic judge: in the noble classes the lineage descends
through her in equality with her husband.

The nature of Spain calls imperatively for the dominance
of woman. Woman's mind is individualistic, and Spain is a
congeries of consonant parts rather than an organism. Woman
builds her familial molecule from the Spanish atoms: she erects
a great simplicity in which her man can dwell.

Spain is a dark soul. Sun is a flame in her land, and her land
is a storm of color. But the soul of Spain is neither sun nor
storm. It is neither gaiety nor grief. It is a dark contentment,
midway held between ecstasy and sleep.

Outside the tremor and traffic of spiritual movement, Spain
is moved like a somnambulant. Her body moves: but within
her shut eyes there was a vision truer than her stirring: a vision
stirless and composed.

Her mood has been dark and stagnant. Yet it was pleasant,

for it was not pain. Her soul was caressed passively by this rhythmic swing between the extremes of action: as if the long ages of Spain's agitation had bred this sensuous delight in their denial.

Within her heroic memory, within her heroic land, Spain wandered for long unobtrusively and scatheless. She did not forget nor remember. Upon the surface of her life, intellect pricked, passion stirred, action clamored. But her depths were limpid in a dark and dreamless slumber. . . .

SACHEVERELL SITWELL

A Sitwell in Spain

A SELECTION FROM *Spain*

The mighty cathedral of Burgos is of the essence of Old
Castile; Sevilla's famous feria or spring festival is at the center
of the life of southern Spain. There are few authors—leaving aside, perhaps, the other Sitwells—who have the knowledge, the wit, and the style to treat these diverse aspects of
Spain with Sacheverell Sitwell's rich mastery of content and
form.

Sacheverell Sitwell made his first journey to Spain in 1919,
when he was twenty-two. The journey which is recounted in
Spain was made in 1947 and 1948. A connoisseur of all the
arts, a skilled practitioner of several, Sitwell has written:
"Probably no other land in the civilized world has so violent

293

*a personality, so strong a flavour, as that of Spain." This emi-
nently civilized Englishman has captured that personality,
strength, and flavor.*

AND it is Sunday morning still, or rather, the hour has
drifted on into afternoon, and by the time the bluebell spires
of Burgos (they are the golden dried husks and not the living
flowers) are to be seen far away coming out of the plain it is
so late as to rouse apprehension as to the possibility of luncheon. Half-past three, or nearer four o'clock, but here in Spain
there is no need to hurry. Previous visits during twenty-five
years, or longer, which on occasion had necessitated the spend-
ing of several nights in discomfort and misery, left no pleasant
anticipation of the hotels in Burgos, but there is a new hotel
with a diningroom in Castilian style full at that late hour of
travellers and citizens just settling down to luncheon. Upon
the way to the hotel through the narrow twisting streets we
came to the oddly shaped, arcaded Plaza Mayor, so typical of
a Spanish town, with a statute of Carlos III in the centre, in
whose goat-like features, being nostalgically inclined and unable to forget early an old experience, we may catch an echo
of the palace of Caserta and the Bay of Naples.[1] In the hotel
there were excellent *langostinos*, Spanish olives and anchovies
in hot pastry, followed by a *tortilla*, and much else besides.
The frescoed diningroom, unpretentious and agreeable, was
in the vernacular Spanish style, doubly agreeable after the
international hotels of San Sebastián. And this is as it should

---

[1] Carlos III was King of the Two Sicilies (1734–1759) before succeeding to the throne of Spain (1759–1788).

be; for Burgos after its fashion is the most Spanish town in Spain, a statement which will be furiously contradicted by those persons who possess their own ideas and theories as to what is Spain and what is Spanish; and I do not say that Burgos is my own favourite, my personal tastes run, perhaps, to quite different extremes and other manners, but it will not be denied that for a certain kind of flamboyant late Gothic, entirely unlike our own contemporary Perpendicular, Burgos is a city without rival in the world. In point of architecture this is in a sense the indigenous speech of Spain, though compound of foreign verbs and particles, so that in order to treat of it as it deserves we resume all our impressions of Burgos into one, and for the sake of freshness and clearness of outline are to imagine that we are seeing the capital of Old Castile for the first time. Let it, also, be the first occasion on which we are entering a Spanish cathedral and the first building typically Spanish that we have met in Spain.

This most profuse and elaborate of Spanish cathedrals, with its twin spires of open stonework and its octagonal central lantern flowering into eight more floreated and pointed turrets, has been built into the steep slope of a hill as though for semi-protection or in order to take root there. The pair of great spires are cusped and ornamented, and have a curious analogy to the masts of medieval ships, particularly in the look-out balconies just below their summits, the effect of the thick stone trellis or diaper in which the spires are encased being to suggest that this is in order to protect the mast-poles from being snapped or broken. But this entire upper ornamentation of the exterior is of German origin. The plan of the cathedral, however, is French, and underneath all the ornamentation it is a great thirteenth century French church, which explains our remark that the speech of the Spaniards in architecture is full of foreign verbs and particles. Burgos cathedral, we say in conclusion before plunging into its chill interior, is not impressively mammoth-like in dimension: rather it is small compared with other ecclesiastical monsters, and entirely overlaid, inside and out, with ornament.

The interior could not be more demonstrably and undeniably Spanish or more typical of Spain. Those persons who have seen nothing of the sort before will be amazed at the superb ironwork, the towering wrought iron screens and grills, or *rejas*, and at the railed-in processional way leading from the choir to the high altar. The *coro*, itself, with its hundred and more carved stalls of box and walnut and its great lecterns and illuminated choir books, resembles as ever a musty old music room and library in one. At the far or east end of the cathedral, behind its own *reja* or wrought iron railing, lies the chapel of the Condestable, or to give but his bare name and two of his titles, Don Pedro Hernández de Velasco, Conde de Haro and Hereditary Constable of Castile. The double tomb of this nobleman and his wife, Doña Mencía de Mendoza, of Carrara marble carved by a sculptor from Genoa, though fine and splendid, is perhaps hardly worthy of so extravagant a chapel in this land of tombs. It is the work of Hans and Simon of Cologne, father and son, the German architects who built the central lantern of the cathedral and the twin open spires, and all the panoply of Spanish heraldry is displayed upon the walls. There are pages, in pairs, holding up shields-of-arms, and lions erect on their hind legs, so curled and glossy of mane that they resemble living golden fleeces, and so high upon the wall that all we can distinguish is that they are holding stone cartwheels enclosing sacred initials or monograms in their front paws. High over our heads is the open-traceried, eight-pointed star-vault or *cimborrio* of the ceiling, a design not unlike a white passion flower or clematis from the blanched colour of the stone.

But there is more to see in the cathedral. The chapel of the Condestable has its own sacristy and treasury; and a beadle in a gown of green velvet will unlock room after room along the cloisters. The silks and brocades, the silver pyxes and monstrances, massy plate, coral ornaments, jewelled necklaces, carved ivories, and precious stones of a Spanish cathedral will daze and bewilder the eyes. There are but few kinds of sightseeing so rewarding, and withal so tiring, as these earliest attempts at museum arrangement in the modern world. It is better, perhaps, to save our energies for the chapel of Santa Tecla, with its *media naranja* (half-orange) dome treated with polychrome decorations applied to the stone ground, and the work of a member of the Churriguera family. This is a quiet and modest example of the exuberant style that spread to Mexico. It is tactful to its setting in this Gothic cathedral, but interests by reason of the wild and unprecedented units or motifs of its ornament. Perhaps the polyglot character and history of this typically and supremely Spanish cathedral are now apparent.

Hans and Simon of Cologne, who must have settled the cathedral on its course of ornament, had a number of craftsmen, workers in metal and carvers in wood and stone, to carry out the details, and it was work which extended over two or three generations. Among them were Germans and Burgundians. But we have still to see the *escalera dorada*, a double staircase with gilded balusters by a French ironsmith, that descends into the body of the north transept from the slope of the hill outside and is the work of Diego de Silóee. The stair is an architectural conceit serving no useful purpose, but more must be said about this individual with the odd surname, and about his father, Gil de Silóee, who was one of the very greatest of the wandering artists of the later Middle Ages.

In order to establish his curious identity we have to return for a moment to Hans of Cologne, the architect of the twin spires and of the lantern, for he was brought to Spain by a Jewish bishop of Burgos, Alonso de Cartagena. It appears that

Gil de Silóee, as well as Hans of Cologne, owed his arrival in Spain to Alonso de Cartagena, who had been born a Jew, and that Gil de Silóee himself was a Jew, for his father was a merchant of Nuremberg called Samuel and his mother's name was Miriam, in the light of which knowledge it may be wondered whether Hans of Cologne was not Jewish also. In the second generation Diego de Silóee certainly, and it is probable Simon of Cologne, were born in Burgos, and in the instance of the Silóees, father and son, we have the only considerable artists of Jewish origin to appear in Europe before the twentieth century, and with Gil de Silóee, it may be, the greatest artist in the plastic arts that the Jewish race has produced. This, too, in that short interregnum before the Jews with the Moors were expelled from Spain; but if, as could be advanced with some little force of probability, Hans of Cologne, his son Simon, and grandson Francisco, were Jews also, then the work of these two families becomes, perhaps, more interesting even than their skill deserves and we have to look at Burgos cathedral in the light of that ambiguous origin and it becomes something unique, indeed, in Christian annals.

But Gil de Silóee has to be seen at the Cartuja de Miraflores, two or three miles outside Burgos, a royal foundation built by Hans and Simon of Cologne. The chapel is contemporary with Eton College chapel and the chapel of King's College, Cambridge, to the former of which, save that it is built of golden not of grey stone, its exterior bears a certain resemblance, and it contains the tomb of Don Juan II and Isabella of Portugal, whose grandmother was the Plantagenet Philippa of Lancaster, daughter of John of Gaunt. The tomb is a marble octagon; in fact, it is eight-pointed like the great lanterns or *cimborrio* of the cathedral or the eight-pointed passion flower or clematis of the chapel of the Condestable. It is, therefore, sixteen-sided, with the king and his queen lying with crowned heads, in robes of incredible richness, the

Queen holding an open prayer-book in her hand, the cornices and sides of this star octagon being ornamented with allegorical figures of prophets and evangelists, with two lions each to the eight angles, sixteen in all, upholding coats-of-arms, and carvings of birds and quadrupeds, of leaves and branches. You can climb some wooden steps and look down over the wrought iron railings upon this pair of effigies. They are, indeed, most beautiful, not least in the back of the wimple of the Queen's headdress, the handling of which, now, seems to us unlike any other work of the Middle Ages, due perhaps to the pent-up imagery in Gil de Silóee because of his Eastern blood. We can only repeat our previous conviction, stated in another place, that this king and queen lying, crown on head, in robes of ceremony, form the most entire masterpiece of late Gothic sculpture, and that for its special qualities there is nothing to equal it in other lands. Even persons of the most levelling political tendencies must be awed and silenced by this witness to the splendours and miseries of old Spain. Upon the wall opposite is the wall tomb, also by Gil de Silóee, of the young Infante Alfonso, at whose early death the future Queen Isabella becomes heiress to the throne. The Infante is kneeling at a priedieu under an elaborate arched canopy, and at the sides there are carvings of children playing in the tendrils of a vine and picking grapes. The astonishing golden complexity and elaboration of the *retablo* rising behind the high altar is also by the same sculptor. Like many another Spanish *retablo*, it sparkles and glitters with the gold of Mexico, and if this be the first *retablo* to be seen we may carry away little more than the impression of the crucifix and of the figure of a pelican feeding its young with its own blood. All of these monuments, these tombs and this *retablo*, are due to Isabel la Católica and to the new-found wealth of Spain. But it is time to come out of the chapel of the Cartuja into the golden sunset, and by way once more of the crockets and pinnacles of Burgos, its late Gothic buildings in the failing light as prolix and repetitive of ornament as a wood of blue-bells, we arrived after many hours at the capital, nearly in the middle of the night.

A light grey rain was falling a day or two later when we left Madrid, not so much falling perhaps as implicit or sus-pended in the lead-grey air. It had been tropically hot for the time of year, hot enough to have luncheon and dinner out of doors in the garden of the hotel, a little oasis of white columns, of palms and pine trees, surrounded on three sides by trams, but where an owl hooted late at night when the trams were intermittent and the jazz-band had done. The road out of Madrid starts from the Puente de Toledo, one of the most fantastic and magnificent creations of decadent archi-tecture, a bridge that is splendid and Spanish in scale but positively Aztec in ornament, and that could lead over the lagoons, the *chinampas*, or floating gardens, to the stepped pyramids and to Montezuma's palace. At one time it traversed a dreary slum of new tenements and shacks built out of petrol tins. Later comes Aranjuez and its green groves, its splashing waters and its nightingales. The treeless plain resumes; and presently, under a bluer sky, we reach the deep red soil and the vineyards of Manzanares, where, in the words of Richard Ford, "the red blood of the vine issues from this valley of stones." We are in the midst of La Mancha, among the bare hills and windmills of Cervantes. Next comes Valdepeñas, with more vineyards and a still redder soil. There follow a rocky gorge and the mountains of the Sierra Morena. The rockrose is in flower upon the hillside, first one and then hundreds of white rockroses, as far as the eye can see, and the rarer crimson-pink or it may be magenta. Lower down, as we near the plain, there are asphodels and soon dwarf palm (palmito), the acanthus, and the aspidistra. A huge peony, alone of its kind, is in flower down in the valley. The first cactuses and prickly pears appear. This is Andalucía. Is it only in imagination that there seems to be a mist or haze out of Africa hanging over the plain? But the heat is deep and tremendous. The sky is unfathomable and of intense blue. When we stop late in the afternoon at the Albergue de Bailén, and the blue flags are in flower, the sun awnings are let down to shade the white-washed pillars and the semicircular diningroom is cool though full of travellers bound, like ourselves, for *las fiestas de Sevilla.*

Some hours later we are in the suburbs of Córdoba, and coming to the Roman bridge over the Guadalquivir turn aside up the little hill to the battlemented walls of the cathedral or, we would have it, the mosque, la Mezquita, as it is still called today. It is late, nearly dark, and the doors are locked; but one gate is yet open into the court of orange trees, and the lovely, spicy, drowsy smell of the orange blossom, after all that has happened during these many years of war, is an intoxication and a draught of magic. In that moment one felt that one might not have lived to know that scent again. Impossible not to stand quite still and motionless and breathe it in. A pyramid of the red-gold fruit lies heaped in a corner under a Moorish archway. It was worth while coming all the way from London in order to breathe for this one instant in the orange grove. And the mosque was opened for us, which looked, in that darkening hour, even more beautiful and mysterious than I had remembered it. But a mosque that is ten centuries old must not be hurried. We leave its forest of columns and horseshoe arches, the Moorish stalactites and honey-cells, for another time, and crossing the bridge with its many arches stop for petrol by an age-old water well, a fountain to which the women come with their pitchers, where horses and mules are watered now that dark has fallen, where not so long ago, when the women were veiled, there must have been men in gowns and turbans, and long strings of camels. For that is the secret of the orange blossom. Those are perfumes of Arabia. And for a couple of hours more, through the night, there came that breath of orange blossom from time to time and the deep croaking of the frogs. The "dew-dropping South" of Mercutio was eternal and unaltered; and so it continued, balmy and spice-laden out of the dark leaves, until the red glare of a distant town announced Seville; and after enquiry in the dusty suburbs we drove past the fair ground, with its high masts and arc lamps, and along the flank of the famous Tobacco Factory, no longer used for that purpose, to where the hotel, with innumerable motorcars drawing up and departing, stood enmeshed, as it were, in a perfect cocoon of tramlines.

To awaken in Seville is, in itself, something of a sensation, as though the syllables of that magical name had been ringing in one's ears, through all the other noises, all night long. And coming out of the hotel how hot it was! How narrow the pavement! How shrill the motorhorns and the clanging of the trams. But here was the cathedral, its golden parapets stained with lichen or even nodding with weeds in that cloudless sky. And in a moment or two we are in the Plaza de San Fernando, where formerly, in the cloisters of the Franciscan convent, stood the Roman statue of the *Comendador* in his toga, in fact the statue of the supper scene in Don Giovanni. Since last I saw Seville this square of San Fernando has been converted into the most beautiful of rose gardens. The rose bushes in the middle of April were in full bloom, a most wonderful vision after the long and pitiless winter, roses high and low and in every variety of form and colour, some few of them, no doubt, new triumphs of Señor Pedro Dot and the rosarians of Catalonia, and many of them more scented than the new English roses. They were beautiful in full sun and not less lovely when the rose beds were in shade under the tall palms.

But, continuing on our way, where is there a street of shops more fascinating than the Sierpes, as narrow as the Mercería in Venice and, like that, motorless, without wheeled traffic, but so much more interesting than the Mercería owing to the goods in the shop windows: the high tortoise-shell combs and mantillas, and fans painted with scenes of bull fights and serenades or the processions of Holy Week, with further on the posters of bull fights and coloured postcards of matadors in the tobacconists' shops, the confectioner at the far end of the Sierpes with the bonbon boxes in his window formed in the shape of the cowled figures of the different *cofradías* of the Semana Santa; at about which spot in the Sierpes, towards noon, are gathered the *aficionados* of the bull ring in their short jackets, stiff-brimmed Córdoban hats, black or grey, and carrying their long, thin sticks or wands, sticks which are peeled of their bark in alternate rings of black and white, tapering to a point, and with a forked end where they rest their thumbs. The *majos,* or most of them, are countrymen come into Seville for the bull fights, and they are meeting their friends at the wineshops in the Sierpes, a sign that it is midday and that soon the shop shutters will be noisily let down.

At the hotel a mule carriage and pair was waiting at the door, for its owner had come to call upon us, and it was in this same carriage, with its coachman and footman on the box in grey Córdoban hats and liveries of grey cloth with brown facings, that later in the evening, after a long and necessary siesta, we drove through the Parque de María Luisa and down the Paseo de las Delicias, names that breathe or whisper of the tall acacias, the roses, camellias, and orange trees, of what must be the most beautiful public park in Europe. Indeed, this drive becomes in memory one of the most lovely experiences I have had for many years, not least because of the anachronism of the mule team, not an anachronism really, because there were few other vehicles but mule- or horse-drawn carriages, but there was an indescribable air of excitement even down the languorous and scented avenues, a hurrying in one direction; and here we saw the first of the many horsemen of the Feria, but forbear to describe them, because, as warned at the time, they will appear in all their finery tomorrow. The Paseo de las Delicias, which lies along the bank of the Guadalquivir, now comes out from the shade of its trees into a huge plain, known, appropriately, as the Tablada, and we see the scene towards which all this concourse of persons has been riding or driving, the white-washed walls and enclosures of the Venta de Antequera.

For it is the eve of the Feria of Seville and the great festivities will begin tomorrow. The fighting bulls have been driven this morning, or the night before, from the *ganaderías* and are now penned or paddocked, each enclosure bearing the breeder's name above it. Thirty or forty bulls, enough for a week's entertainment, are in the three or four enclosures, each with a bullock or two, a cowbell round its neck, for company, and in order to avoid monotony. The huge beasts are coloured either black or brown and seem hardly conscious of the great crowd come to watch them. To the stranger they may look alike, but the *aficionados* can discuss their heredity not only in physical appearance but in movement and action. The strains of the different breeders have their qualities and peculiarities and are known for their particular temperaments and methods of attack, in light of which they are being examined by the onlookers for their physical condition, while the ignorant majority are only come to look at each other and at the animals that are doomed to die.

It is the Venta, in a sense the first of the ceremonies of the Feria, and the grandstand above the pens is crowded with the rank and fashion of Madrid and Seville, drinking sherry or eating ices to the strains of a band. Young men and women on horseback, in Andalucian costume—but it is even painful to stare at them in the direct rays of the setting sun—are pressing their way through the crowd. Many will stay and dine here, and look down on the bulls that are lying out like shadows in a false moonlight; but we drive back along the Paseo de las Delicias into Seville behind the jangling mule team. The sun is setting, the church bells are ringing; tomorrow will be the Feria.

It has been settled that at midday we are to drive round the fairground. The mule carriage is at the door, but today both grooms and mules are in their splendour: blue and yellow cords are cockades (the colours of the owner); rosettes of blue and yellow on the trappings and the harness; blue and yellow hammercloths; while our host himself has put on a grey Córdoban hat for the occasion. And so, along the length of the Tobacco Factory, with its Baroque statues trumpeting fame upon the skyline, to the Feria. The fairground is nearby, on the Prado de San Sebastián, but "it is not so much a fair as an outing or festival," lasting three days, and in which the entire population, high and low, participate. A huge cattle fair is the immediate excuse for the Feria, and the present year (1947) being the centenary, the celebrations have been doubled and extended to six days, with a bull fight every afternoon. Passing the fountains, which will be illuminated this evening, the scene of the Feria is a quadruple avenue, three or four hundred yards long, and bordered on both sides of its four lengths with *casetas*, which are pavilions or open summerhouses, "the origin of which is to be traced to the tents put up by the cattle dealers, long ago, in order to sleep beside their herds." No motorcars are allowed upon the two middle avenues, which are only open for carriages and persons on horseback.

Within a moment our mule carriage is moving no quicker than at walking pace. The heat is tremendous, such as it may have been seventy or eighty years ago in Hyde Park or the Champs Elysées during the age of the carriage and the crinoline at the height of summer, and such as I do not remember, of its

kind, since childhood, since in fact I last drove among the other
carriages on Sunday morning along the Esplanade. I believe
this must be the sensation of all persons who see the Feria for
the first time, as we did, at midday, when the great concourse
of persons is driving or riding round. We shall discover that it
is due, principally, to the Gypsy dresses worn by the young
women. It is this that makes the scene like a vision of the early
or middle part of the last century, though it is only necessary
to be reminded of the riders or the mule carriages to know
that it has nothing to do with that dead world of the Bois de
Boulogne or Rotten Row. For this is a sight that is to be seen
nowhere else in the world today; and it must be described
slowly and, as it were, at walking pace.

There are many different sorts of dresses. All are not dressed
alike. The young women of the sidewalks are wearing
flounced skirts that touch the ground, of blue or pink or red
cotton, patterned with different sizes of white dots. All day,
yesterday, we had noticed such dresses being carried home
from the dressmakers, over one arm of an owner or dress-
maker, and had stopped and tried to examine them. It was a
revelation of how many effects can be made with a white ring
or circle. But there are dresses of white flounces too, edged
with a blue or red cording, like the moonlit equivalent to those
patterns of mock suns. And, as well, there are the different
shapes and forms of flounces, crinolines, if we call them that,
of three or four or five or more tiers or storeys. The young
women in these full skirts walk bare-headed, with a scarf or
handkerchief at their necks, their glossy hair kept well in place,
always with the traditional flower behind the ear. There are
little girls of three or four years old dressed in even more detail than their cousins or elder sisters; sometimes with a long
train behind that sweeps the ground. And we are looking continually, delighted at every turn, for fresh ideas and colours, as
for instance to see a green dress or one of saffron yellow,

306

which did not happen till the third morning of the Feria, when a flowered crinoline of daffodil yellow made an appearance, was lost in the crowd, but quickly recognized again.

At this hour of the morning the *casetas* are half empty. The crowd is on foot or on horseback. Upon the pair of outer avenues, where it is allowed, we even pass motorcars carrying three or four young girls draped in their full skirts upon the bonnet and the mudguards. But this is in bad taste. It is one of the few faults of the Feria, and is corrected, quickly, by much jangling and a mule carriage of more substantial make, drawn by a "six-in-hand," with a middle-aged man in short black coat and Córdoban hat holding the reins. This beautiful equipage seems to sail forward upon the admiring glances of the onlookers. But, rounding the corner, we are on the outer side of our avenue and can see in every detail the splendid cavaliers and their ladies as they ride towards us and pass by. Taking the young women first, there are the two sorts, those who go pillion and those who ride alone. The pillion riders, precariously with an arm round their partner's waist or holding to the horse's tail, wear the flounced skirts of the pedestrians. Their brothers, or lovers, ride one arm akimbo, which accentuates their thin waists. Many are wearing elaborate and fanciful leather trousers, in which we can see the origin of the cowboys' leggings and of the Mexican *charro* costume. The young women ride pillion with an amazing grace, the beauty of their bare heads and arms in that violent sunlight being as animal as the steeds they share. Every young woman is beautiful to look at, some of the girls being real visions of Spanish beauty with their camellia skins and black hair and eyes. But not all are dark, and there are young girls riding pillion, in green or white crinolines, with fair hair, bareheaded like the rest, and glowing in the midday sun.

It is wonderful to watch a cavalier, arm akimbo, riding towards us, Spanish-fashion, and then to wait and admire the young woman upon the crupper holding lightly to his waist. But the other sort of riders, the true Amazons, are yet more enthralling, those who ride by themselves, astride, not hatless, and wearing more than one type of costume; in fact, one form of dress is worn the first day of the Feria, and we are told that tomorrow they will be wearing another costume and a different form of headdress. The first—for we will take both together, as they are to be seen on later mornings—consists of a leather apron and divided skirt, a white shirt like a man's, a short jacket, and one of the hard-brimmed Córdoban hats. It is a feminine version of what the men are wearing, with the addition perhaps of a rose behind the ear. The thin waist, the level shoulders and hard outline of the hat, worn at a charming angle above a rounded face, such are the attractions of this riding dress, which is infinitely varied in detail and which suits the Spanish type of good looks to perfection.

The other form of costume belongs, as it were, to another tradition; the skirt or trousers, it matters not which, are not so aggressively in imitation of the masculine; the jacket is short, and without the leather apron or leggings is more revealing of the figure; the hair is worn at the back in a snood or chignon, while the hat is a round black one, resembling the crown, without the wings, of the matador's three-cornered cap or tricorne. This must, undoubtedly, be its inspiration, and nothing more in the popular tradition of Spain could be imagined than a young woman on horseback in one of these round black hats, or on foot, and wearing, not a snood, but a *mantilla de madroños*, which is a scarlet or magenta net with wide meshes worked with bobbles. The soft complexions of the young girls are ravishing to behold, and to compare with the carnation or camellia behind the ear, to which we must add the peculiar beauties of the Spanish horsemanship that allow of so graceful a seat and, where the women riders are concerned, could have been conceived of especially in order to be admired.

But the heat is such that the leather and the painted wood-work feel, by now, like fire. The mules are halted, and after a drink of sherry we drive back to the hotel for luncheon and to take a siesta for the greater part of the afternoon. But at that hour there is nothing else to do in Seville—nothing until about half-past five, when you hear people starting off for the bull fight. Then it is quieter still, and the air is more languorous and somnolent than ever. Perhaps I enjoyed as much as anything else in Seville those hours when the noisier part of the population was at the bull fight. In the shuttered room one's mind filled so easily with nostalgia longings. I would lie there thinking of many things, for another hour or more, until, from all over the town, there would come the sound of castanets, snapping and crackling, hundreds of pairs of them, some fast, some slow; and going to the window I would see the pavements and even the street itself full of a great crowd of persons all converging in this one direction, towards the Feria, a multitude mainly of young women and children, and all playing their castanets as they walk along.

This would be the signal to begin moving towards the coloured fountains and the lights, which go off as we come near to them at the same moment that there is a flicker of lightning and that people standing at the cheap jewellery stalls, close by, look up for rain. But it is better to see the Feria in the sunset —leave it when the lights go on—and come back again. For it is a marvellous sight at this hour. The *casetas* are filling up; dancing has begun, but we will not listen to the music till tonight. We are only aware of it, and of the growing and increasing sparkle upon the air. Instead, we turn down one of the side avenues to the *barracas*, which are the roundabouts and merry-go-rounds of the fair. Here is a stall where they are selling an extraordinary spun concoction, of the consistency of cottonwool, dipping a stick or straw into the frothing, churning mass, drawing it forth with a shock or head of the sugary cottonwool attached, and handing it out as quickly as made, like a sweet cocoon. The sellers of shrimps and *langostinos* are doing a quick trade. There are stalls, too, where coloured drinks, *agraz* or *horchata de chufas,* are sold. But the merry-go-rounds and mountain railways, the miniature motorcars and "witching waves" are no different from those of any other fair. Not so the mountebanks, the like of whom may be extinct in every other country, and who maintain the centuries-old tradition of the actor coming in front of the curtain to advertise the play, with a cracked voice this evening, and through a megaphone. His speech is interminable, and the heat in the crowd such that it is impossible to stand still and listen.

Besides, this is only a few feet away from the open-air restaurants or eating places of the Gitanas. They have established themselves and put up their booths along one entire side of the pavement. The setting is a line of cabins or small *casetas,* a half or a quarter the size of those upon the main avenues, and with chairs and tables arranged in front of them. Unexpectedly, there are white linen cloths upon the tables, but the Gitanas are awarded a prize every year for the cleanest and prettiest arranged of their *casetas.* Even in this noisiest part of the Feria, next to the loud-speakers and steam organs, they manage to assert themselves above the din. It has, in fact, spurred them into frenzy.

The younger and more alluring of the Gitanas have come right forward in front of their own tables, into the edges of the crowd, where they stand like bathers in a heavy surf, nearly carried away, and having to struggle in order to get back to the thresholds of their flowering caves or grots. They will come out and pursue you, and be borne along for a little, smiling and cajoling with all the battery of their bright glances, with red lips and fingernails, even and superb white teeth, and smoothed back hair. They are small in height, with the crowns of their heads well below your shoulder, probably no more than fourteen or fifteen years old, and with the rounded faces of their race. In fact, their tawny darkness is extraordinary; and in the background, as if this is not enough, the older women with their snake-like locks—could serpents be as ebony and glossy as a raven's wing—stand in the open door-ways, lifting the cauldron lids or stirring, half-hidden in the steam. They have turned this corner of the fair into a nomad encampment, and their unbelievably dark skins at this hour of the evening in the fading light betray the Indian origin of their nation. The old women are in a fury too, and the whole scene of these booths or cabins decorated with flowers and branches is something entirely and absolutely of the Gypsies. There is no other race who have the power to create a nationality and a nomad background by merely cooking something and stand-ing in a door. They have only to do this and it becomes at once the fortune tellers' tent and the cave of the sorceress.

There is the savour of their world apart in the fumes of their cooking, which has the Oriental pungency and is, at once, an enticement and an alarm. They are frying things in oil and can be seen cooking as though frenzied. Excellent their food is said to be, but not suited to this hot night and to the noise and hubbub. It is to be noticed, moreover, that here they have the entire air of Gypsies, but that they have nearly lost it in their Gypsy surburb of Triana. It must fire their blood to be once more in the smoke and uproar of the encampment. At Rou-manian cattle fairs there are these identical open-air restau-rants, with roofs of leaves and branches, which are the pleasure gardens of the fair, and that evoke some of the imagery of Rimbaud's *Les Illuminations*. On a particular occasion, upon the plain between Sinaia and Bucharest, they lined sides of an alley-way, and held some hundreds of persons sitting in the shade, eating their midday meal; the meat was grilling on the charcoal embers, while here and there among the diners musi-cians wandered, violin in hand, playing popular tunes. There was the same Eastern pungency in the air that I recognized at the Feria, and I now wish more than ever that I had seen the great horse fairs in Moldavia, that last for as long as three days, and had walked late at night by the open-air eating booths. Neither fair, it is true, would allow much time for thinking of the other. Here, in Seville, the cries of the mountebanks, the din of the roundabouts, above all the blare of the steam organs, make the night low-hung and lurid, for all the lights are now switched on, the lines of lamps all lit-up fountains, and we leave the Feria for an hour or two in order to have our dinner.

It was always midnight or after when we returned, a phrase that holds in itself the sensation of the Feria, by which I mean the memory and feeling of the six days it lasted, for it seemed to be a world or experience apart and to go on for ever. At half-past twelve or one o'clock, then, we return by the changing fountains, down the flood-lit avenues, under the festooned arches. A great cowd is still arriving, playing castanets as they walk along, and when we stop in front of the *casetas* there is music coming from nearly every one of them. There are *casetas* belonging to clubs or associations, others that are shared by groups of families, or owned by individuals. They can be of all sizes: as large as a restaurant or quite small; but most are upon the scale of the pierrot's booths upon the sands, with room, that is to say, for a piano and a row of chairs. The chairs are pushed back against the walls, and in the middle is the dancing floor. Many of the *casetas* have had climbing rose trees or flowering creepers trained upon their walls; they have been decorated with posters of bull fights or hung with paintings and family photographs, and furnished, so as to give them the semblance of little rooms. One of the fascinations of the Feria is to pass by such a *caseta* at a moment when an entire family in all its generations—but it may well be two or three families and their friends, one whole side of a little street, or all the inhabitants of some whitewashed court—are resting, exhausted, the older ones sitting staring in front of them, with the smaller children crawling at their feet or asleep upon their knees, awkward upon their chairs as are housewives and small shopkeepers who have to stand all day and, as it were, caught or imprisoned in this cell or interior of their own choice with the enlarged photographs upon the walls and the family piano in the middle of the floor. It is one or two o'clock in the morning, but not one of the smaller children has been put to bed. There is no one left in the house to look after them and they must stay at the Feria till the whole family go home.

Meanwhile the crackle and fire of the castanets is continual and strains of music come from every direction for as far as the lights glitter and the night sky is lit up from the fair. There is this accompaniment of the castanets playing in the crowd as they walk up and down, and the music of the *casetas* as you stand and watch for a moment and move on. There are mechanical pianos which are too loud and drown the music from next door, but at least the music, or nine-tenths of it, is Spanish. There is no "jazz" or "swing." It is, mainly, clapping of hands, and the guitar, *Flamenco* music, good or bad, but on a night like this such is the intoxication from light and sound that the whole body of music becomes lifted and inspired. They are dancing the *sevillana* to an accompaniment of castanets and clicking fingers, to the clapping of hands and the grinding of a guitar, perhaps six or eight young women dancing at once, the older teaching the younger, even little girls of five or six years old in their long-trained crinoline skirts joining in, and one of the younger men of the family standing by, without warning, and taking up the rigid posture of the dance. The *seguidilla* is admired largely for the gracefulness of arms and hands, for the feet do not move much; it is the lascivious grace of the upper part of the body that it is judged by, and by the languorous movements of the wrists. If we would search for an image for the hand and fingers of a dancer in the *seguidilla* it would be that her hands resemble the head of a cobra, or of some other serpent, as it sways its head to hypnotize, and prepares to strike; or that it is like a peacock's head and crest upon that long neck, when the peacock is displaying and makes the snake-like movements of its dance. As a spectacle to watch upon a hot night, and as an expression of the heat, the *seguidilla* is an invention of genius. In which other city of the world or upon what occasion is it possible to watch fifty or a hundred *seguidillas* being danced at one time, and without pause? Only in Seville, and only during the Feria. There is no other population born to this dance, as are the Sevillanas, no other inhabitants who fall naturally into those attitudes or who can wear those flounced dresses so becomingly, being heirs and descendants of the Gaditanian dancers, who "were known" in antiquity "for their agility of body," and Dr. Lemprière of the *Classical Dictionary*, delighting at the shock, adds, "their incontinency"; but, in fact, the evidence of early Greek travellers points to the inhabitants of Andalucía as running great herds of bulls upon the swamps and plains and to their women as excelling in the dance. The castanets, we are to suppose, come down directly from antiquity, from pre-Roman antiquity, and were borrowed, in all probability, from the temple dancers of the Carthaginians, who, in their turn, had taken them from their ancestors in Tyre and Sidon. This Phoenician heredity or influence is to be seen in so many things that are typically Spanish: in the dance of the Seises before the high altar of Seville cathedral and, contrasting the sacred and profane, in the high combs and mantillas of the Spanish ladies, after the bull fight, as they move about in the American bar of the hotel.

In order the better to appreciate the marvellous spectacle of the Feria it was a good plan to go away from it for half an hour, and so, upon one of the last nights, we went to walk in the Barrio de Santa Cruz, a whitewashed labyrinth of narrow alleys lying in a semipiternal moonlight of its own, with doorways, hidden patios, iron well heads, and some of the oldest palaces of Seville. At one end of this there is a garden, touching upon the lovely gardens of the Alcázar, and like those breathing of the orange blossom, and here—it was between one and two o'clock in the morning, in that moonlight begotten of so many whitewashed walls—we heard the sound of voices, and in the tiled space around a fountain found a group of young men and two young women; one unslung his guitar, the others clapped hands rhythmically, there was the crackle of castanets, and the younger of the two girls began to dance the *seguidilla*. This done, they talked excitedly, and she danced again, another form of *seguidilla* with ballet steps, to no tune, only the clapping of hands and the strumming of the guitar. Once again, and yet once more, she danced; a cool air moved among the overhanging branches; the loveliness of this ancient city, the soft and balmy breath of the orange blossom—something I had not known for so many years since the jasmine-laden airs of the Tunisian gardens; airs so pungent and redolent of jasmine that they amounted, almost, to a jasmine civilization, made this scented early hour of the morning, this music, and this dancing into an unbelievably beautiful experience; and all the time, not far away, the night sky was lit with the Feria, and you could hear a continuous, distant roaring, now and then individual voices of strains of music, and the crackling fire and rattle of, perhaps, ten thousand pairs of castanets. It produced an excitement and a beauty that were indescribable. The Feria was beckoning, and we must return.

HONOR TRACY

In the Land
of Sherry

A SELECTION FROM *Silk Hats and No Breakfast*

*Sherry is unique, not only among Spanish wines, but among
the wines of the world. There are good, rough red wines produced in central and northern Spain which owe no apologies to
their Italian and French brothers, but no one with taste would
push competition further between Spanish and non-Spanish
wines. But sherry has no competitor. It derives, and can derive,
from only one region in the world, a tiny area of a few thousands of acres centering on the white city of Jerez de la Frontera. The reasons for the uniqueness of sherry are beyond the*

control of commerce: the special quality of the soil and sun and moisture of these hillsides of Andalucía, together with a process of production different from that followed in making any other wine, converts the pale grapes into a variety of fragrant tastes: jerez.

Sherry has no vintage years, for many vintages are combined in a long, not perpetual but at least centennial, blending through the solera, *or mother cask. From each harvest is added selected new must (wine before fermentation) to the pre-existent wine of similar type and quality; thus there is a constant renewal of the distillation from the scraggly vines which grow here and there where the Mediterranean joins the Atlantic.*

The techniques of cooperage, corkage, and sale of sherry have been mastered in recent centuries, perhaps two or three, although the wine was produced a millennium—or two—earlier in Andalucía. The English gave sherry its fame outside Spain, buying it in such large quantities that they ended up buying a good part of the bodegas *and the vineyards. Sometimes they merely married the owner's daughter, and thus they and their children became part of Andalucía and Jerez, and the land took its pleasant revenge on the men from the chilly island who persisted in corrupting* jerez *into "sherry" and seco —"dry"—into "sack."*

Jerez is a city of enormous bodegas *and white buildings, and the streets are lined with orange trees. The bullfights are good, the sun is strong, and the wind blows stiffly up from Cádiz among the vineyards on the hills of white earth.*

In the following episode from an amusing and useful if badly titled book, Miss Honor Tracy, an accomplished Irish writer, tells a little about Jerez and the world of sherry, and also something about the kind of Americans who invaded Spain under the Spanish-American alliance of 1953 and after: the military people and the base-builders.

IN one of the narrow lanes that led to the Castillo there now appeared an enormous American motor-car driving the on-coming mules and carts backwards before it and causing the inhabitants to leap to the wall for safety. It was followed in reverent silence by a little crowd of boys and men. As I came up it stopped, and a round head covered with straw-coloured bristles poked out of a window.

"Hey! You're not Spanish."

The head went on to explain that it had seen the Church of Santa María, which was pretty, though, it guessed, not really worth the ride from Jerez, and inquired what else it ought to see before turning around. Hopefully I indicated the Castillo, but the head guessed it didn't care for crumby old castles; it wanted Art. But I was a stranger there myself. Then the head withdrew for consultation with another head, shaped like an egg this time and as smooth, and once more emerged.

"Hey! We're going on back to Jerez. Don't you want to ride with us?"

A handsome offer, and gratefully accepted, for there were still a couple of hours before the bus would leave and I was beginning to feel like something left in the oven. The car squeezed its way to the Plaza de España, where there was room to turn for the descent of the hill: the Americans having introduced themselves as Bill and Joe, we crept off down the lane again with the driver giving way now and again to exas-perated comment.

"Why don't they widen the goddam street?"

"Wake up, Sambo! Want me to run you down?"

The pair were interesting as the first Americans, except for holiday-makers, that I had come across on my journey. To hear some Spaniards talk, you would fancy the country was under an American occupation; and the supplement of a New York paper I had seen in London, devoted to the wonderful job that was being done there, had led me to fear the worst. But the Americans in Spain turned out to be much like the churches burned in the Civil War, seldom or never where you happened to be, although thick as flies (it would be asserted) in territory some way off. But here at last were Bill and Joe, engaged on work so vital to the preservation of Western values that they could not bring themselves to divulge its nature, beyond darkly stating they were at present on Survey.

At the foot of the hill there was a café and Bill guessed we better have a drink, since it would be all of thirty-five minutes before we could get another. The place was empty at this hour except for two youths who were buying a bottle of cordial and another, smaller one which contained a dark fluid obviously potent. "Hey, Sambo, kay esta?" genially shouted Bill, and explained then to me it was his habit to talk to everyone he met, so that he could get the feel of the country. Smiling, the youth offered him the bottle in the graceful Spanish invitation which is not meant to be taken up, any more than the English "How do you do?" calls for details of our physical condition. Bill took the bottle, and pouring himself a liberal dose, drank it down, pulling a face as he did so. "Lemme," said Joe, and repeated the performance. Mournfully, the boys watched their little Sunday treat dwindling away.

"Go on. Take some. You'll hurt their feelings," Bill urged me.

"Ugh! we better have some brandy quick and take the goddam taste away," said Joe.

On the way back to Jerez, as their beautiful car sailed over the bumpy road, they discussed with good-humoured toleration the shortcomings of the Spanish race, its discourtesy, savagery, sloth, inefficiency and, in particular, its failure to appreciate the United States.

That evening the fountain played in the Square of the Catholic Rulers because it was Sunday.

"Simpática, la fuente, no?" the waiter asked.

The word was well chosen. It was indeed *simpático* to see how the precious water was squandered. The part that water, or the lack of it, plays in the life of Spaniards can hardly be exaggerated. It is a favourite topic of conversation, like the weather in England; the people of Madrid would formerly argue the merits of their water systems as a constant theme, and a good approach to a stranger whom you wish to draw out is to ask about the water in the *pueblo*, a matter on which he will hold forth with fluency. Fierce passions are roused, the most relentless village feuds begun, by someone taking more than his due share of the supply of irrigation. But to make the Sunday evening more pleasant, the noble people of Jerez de la Frontera were throwing it into the air as gaily and nonchalantly as if they lived in the Lake District, or still had the Moors to teach them how to look after it.

"Muy simpática," I agreed. He watched it a little while longer, smiling to himself, and then went to fetch my beer. Fifteen minutes elapsed and then he came back with it: another fifteen, and he brought olives and anchovies.

"It all takes time," he explained.

There was a bond between us because the evening before he had dropped a key in the dark and I had helped him to find it: so easily are good relations established in Andalusia.

It was about eight o'clock and the town, in all its finery, was strolling up and down the square under the stolid palm trees with purple climbers hugging their stems. Everyone had put on a brave show, down to the babies in arms who in spotless muslin and silk sashes looked as if they had just been snipped off a Christmas tree. The town had a fine air of patrician calm about it, and a flavour of the nineteenth century. Now and again an elegant carriage and pair would go bowling by, driven by a liveried coachman with confident ease as if he were unaware that other means of travel had yet been thought of. Whole families were piling into the town *fiacres*, lugubriously hooded and drawn by feeble, despondent horses; or a solitary rider would make his way through the crowded place on a high-stepping Andalusian mount.

A more contemporary note was struck by a cinema near at hand, whose loudspeaker was blaring its head off although the doors would not open for another hour. The poster announcing the Hollywood film to be shown that night had a sticker on it marked "Authorized for Adults" and it was discouraging to see, therefore, that nobody in the queue looked more than fourteen years old. With immense, self-sacrificing care a sort of clerical watch committee views all the films and classifies them in appropriate groups (Forbidden to All, Authorized for Adults of Sound Moral Education Only, Authorized for All Adults, Tolerated, Permitted to All, etc.), and it is a grievous thing that many young people should regard its work merely as a guide to the more rewarding entertainments.

All at once in the square three youths came bounding along, followed by a troop of little boys, all shouting and laughing and panting with excitement. One of them had a wounded swallow in his hand, and this he threw into the air like a paper dart, when it went a little way, faltered and dropped to the earth. After it tore the gang to snatch it up and hurl it again, round and round the gardens. Sometimes the youth would vary the entertainment by tossing it up and down and catching it like a ball, while it fluttered and cheeped in his hand. No one displayed anything but a sweet indifference except when the little creature fell on a bed of flowers and a keeper hurried forward with lifted stick to complain of the boys trampling over it.

In Spain it often happens at the very moment when one feels most admiring and appreciative that some incident of the kind will intervene to shatter the mood. No people should be so magnificent and so repulsive at once. The horrid impression now was created less by the action of the youths, for there are cruel boys anywhere, than by the acquiescence of the public at large. Nothing was more illuminating: and there came into my mind, as contrast, a to-do of the evening before. Passing the lovely old Church of San Miguel I had dropped in for a moment, although my veil was at home and the usual notice was up in the porch about the modesty expected of the Christian Woman. In one of the chapels Benediction was just being said and everyone turned eagerly round for a good look at the newcomer. At the sight of my bare head a little wave of agitation swept over the worshippers, like a breeze passing over a field of corn. Flustered whispering took place: people gesticulated reproachfully towards their own coverings: a little miss of eighteen or so jumped up from her knees and came to me with a handkerchief in her hand which she shook commandingly in front of my eyes. The air was full of disapproval and hostility, the attention of the entire assembly switched from their devotions to me; and to avoid causing further distress I went away. A small infringement of custom was profoundly troubling to the popular mind: the torment of a helpless little bird left it unmoved.

I paid for the beer and went away for a quiet walk in the country. In a few minutes Jerez was left behind and under a fiery sunset a sweep of bare, tawny hills went rolling away as far as the eye could see. White cabins were dotted about in the folds of them and as darkness began to fall their little lights came out and merrily twinkled. Each side of the winding dusty paths the round spiky leaves of the prickly pear turned black against a sky of persian green. Not a sound was to be heard but the cicadas twanging away in their thickets like so many diminutive guitars or the distant barking of a dog. Very few people were still about, a grizzled countryman returning from the fields, girls setting out for the town, two women trotting along on one mule. A great peace lay over those wide dusky spaces, and at last I went tranquilly home by the light of the stars to a pitiless Spanish dinner and an implacable Spanish bed.

In the morning I was awakened by the merry hum of a market which had established itself in the *plaza* outside the hotel. Beautiful water-jars of classic form and baked of pale clay, many of a size to hold a small child, were arranged in orderly rows while here and there, comfortably propped against the larger ones, a vendor slept. Women swarmed about the wheel-barrows piled with tomatoes and eggs or haggled amiably for little bunches of flowers. Terrified hens peered out of the wicker baskets in which they were compressed or lay on the ground in heaps, tied leg to leg. A pure white mule stepped delicately through the rubbish on the ground with a pannier of white daisies swaying on each side of its back. The air was full of the vivacious greetings of Spaniards who have not met each other for twenty-four hours, and of laughter and friendly altercation.

In the hotel itself, although it was long after nine, all was peace and quiet: the night watchman, still on duty, dozed by the switchboard. I took coffee at the bar of a nearby café in company with a number of men, grave and preoccupied as senators, all of whom were beginning their day with a glass of brandy. About a yard from where I stood was a basin with running water fixed to the wall, and here a magnificent old countryman, with high cheek-bones and side-whiskers under his stiff Andalusian hat, was apparently washing his hands; but when I turned for a better look at him I saw that in fact he was relieving himself. The immense dignity, the utter unconcern, with which he performed this necessary act in a crowded public room left a most favourable impression.

When breakfast was over, I went to visit one or two of the sherry lodges. The first was a small one, with the pleasant family air of long-established concerns, and stood in beautiful grounds with trim grass and gay beds of flowers. On one of the chimneys a stork perched on one leg, guarding her nest with the peculiar air of importance that storks always have at such times: an importance all the more comical since, as the guide informed me, she had built her nest so incompetently that they had pushed a support underneath it to save the eggs from falling down the chimney.

This guide was a man of vivid personality who used the English tongue in a most original way. Much of his spare time, he told me, was spent in studying it. He had a romantic passion for the England he had never seen, which he thought must be due to a drop of English blood from an ancestor. He showed everything there was, the presses and the special nailed shoes for treading the grapes and the great casks piled one on the other in the *criaderas* or nurseries awaiting their time to enter the *solera*, all ranged in high, airy barns; but fascinating as his information was, or such of it as I could understand, more pleasing still was the lovely joy and pride he took in it all, his sense of the absolute worth of what was being done. His eyes glowed with an inward light as he spoke of the great wines slowly maturing here before they went forth to ease the pains of humanity: his vocabulary, his idiom, grew richer and stranger yet: the most miserable teetotaller alive must have yielded in time to the warmth of his persuasion and I, an old believer, was entirely carried away by it.

This happy confidence is to be found in all the *bodegas* of Jerez and spills over into their printed advertisements, which become little hymns of devotion and praise. "Sherry! joy to the sorrowful, strength to the weak!" will run the preamble to a list of types and prices and there is true feeling in it, far removed from the synthetic enthusiasm of other manufacturers. It is difficult to read unmoved the booklet on sherry published by Jerez Industrial, of whose flavour the following passage may give some idea:

> "Fino: the colour of sunlight: "topaz" is the metaphor used since 1836. Tastes of almonds. Pungent aroma. Fino Sherry is so sensitive that it responds to the arrival of Spring even in the bottle. On its surface appears the tenuous yeast-like *flor*, in other words, the wine flowers as though it still had roots in the vineyard: indeed, the experts say that the appearance of this "flower" occurs at the precise time when the mother vine first puts out green shoots. This must be Nature's most involved and romantic love-call!"

Similar phrases are trippling off the tongue of my companion one after the other. The tour ended in a gay little private bar where stood a row of bottles which visitors are welcome, and indeed expected, to sample one after the other: it is seldom they leave the premise in the same condition as they enter. Having another call to make I contented myself with one glass only: for such is the power of this glorious liquid that, given a chance, it gently expunges all thought of duty and purpose, focusing the mind instead on the delights of meditation and the importance of inactivity.

It was fortunate that I did so, for at the next place of call things were differently managed. This one was Gonzalez Byass which, with Domecq, is the largest and most important of the sixty-two lodges in Jerez. The visit opened quietly: I had no personal introduction here and was asked to fill out a form, much as if I were trying to see a Civil Servant in London. After a wait of some time in a formidably business-like room, a spare, melancholy gentleman appeared and announced in a fading voice that he was ready to take me round. Once again I saw the presses, the *criaderas*, the machines for bottling, corking, ticketing, while the guide sadly explained their uses or delivered a lecture on the history of the firm. I was on the point of begging him to desist and to unburden himself instead of the private sorrow which seemed to weigh upon him when we came to a barn in which were stored great casks of wine ready matured, and here we were joined by a man with a long, slender pipe in his hand.

"Tio Pepe," said the guide dismally, halting in front of one of the casks and signalling to the man with the pipe.

Quick as lightning, he plunged it into the butt, filled two glasses and stepped back to watch the effect they made. I took this to be the culmination of the tour and, handing back the empty glass, turned vaguely in the direction of the door.

"This way, please!" said the guide. He walked on a few paces and stopped in front of another cask. "Apóstoles," he said, signalling. Again the glasses were filled and emptied and the guide, now showing a few early signs of animation, seemed distressed that I would not have another. "You should have taken more of the Tio Pepe perhaps; English people always seem to prefer the dry," he mused.

"Matúsalem," he said a few moments later, and signalled.

In this instructive and enlivening fashion we toured the cellar and at each brief halt the spirits of the guide rose a little higher. By the time we had crowned the various succession of *copitas* with a glass of Insuperable brandy, he was as gay as a lark. Sherry was the answer that never failed. Visitors came, serious people from all over the world, asking factual questions and making notes in little books, only to leave treading on air and laughing like children. Once, indeed, an American lady had arrived at ten in the morning and never opened her mouth except to swallow four glasses of the Insuperable one after the other before departing, speechless and immovable to the end, but that experience was never repeated. Within these walls, he told me, a note of reverence creeping into his voice, grief and pain were left behind. At this moment I was overcome by a fit of coughing and he rushed me back to the Insuperable barrel. It was the one sure remedy in such cases. In fact, the best cure for a cough, and one much used by Spaniards, was four fingers of brandy and one of hot coffee in a glass: he got me to repeat this after him to make certain I had the proper proportions right:

"*Cuatro* dedos de coñac. *Un* dedo de café!"

Through a golden haze I inspected the notable sights that remained. There was a circular grange built by Eiffel to house the famous *Solera* of 1847 with the *escudos* of the Spanish provinces and of foreign countries painted on the butts: the collection of casks dedicated to the great or autographed by them in white chalk; the museum of dusty, cobwebbed casks dating from the foundation of 1835: and many other curious and interesting things of which alas! my relaxed and contented brain failed to make a proper note and for which later on I searched my memory in vain.

In one of the granges were twelve plump barrels of Olorosa named each after an apostle, and in the middle of them a giant one for Christ Himself: El Cristo del Gran Poder, perhaps. The habit Spaniards have of naming their good things in this way is an attractive one, showing a truly grateful and pious spirit, and the expressions on the guide's face as he gazed devotedly upon the casks was beautiful to see. As in the first *bodega*, here too was the sense of people dedicated to the service of mankind: here too the family atmosphere, the well-kept gardens where Tio Pepe, a little white donkey, gravely drew his cart down the path, the smiling workmen; and here the same warm and generous welcome to the stranger. With one last lyrical flight the guide, whose now beaming face paid sherry a tribute more eloquent than any words could do, left me at the gates.

The walk home was a curious affair. Although the sun beat down as fiercely as ever the sky was strangely overcast and threatening, and I called out to a peasant riding by on a mule that it looked like thundery weather. He replied oddly, with a loud laugh, by asking if I had enjoyed the *bodegas*.

Yes; but what had that to do with it?

"You have your sun-glasses on," he explained and, still guffawing, rode away.

I snatched them off in confusion. On the impressive walls of the Alcazar was a notice to young people to refrain, out of respect for culture, from throwing stones at them: just now a bunch of girls and boys were stoning away with all their might and for some reason it seemed divinely witty of them. I stood there feebly laughing and, when they stared, unwisely attempted to share the joke: at which they stared all the harder and I was forced to conclude they had no sense of humour. After I had gone some way it occurred to me that I had addressed them in French, but I decided against going back. Not content with reeling to and fro, the houses and buildings had a subtly altered appearance, deliberately misleading as I thought, and in no time I was lost in a tangle of lanes and alleys until at last I stumbled on the Calle Pérez Galdós: where the contrast between the miserable street named for Spain's greatest novelist and those grandiose avenues all over the country called after a certain fat adventurer plunged me into a sudden, deep woe. Indeed, I was on the point of tears; but then it struck me that I was simply drunk. Pig drunk in the middle of the day and in full view of respectable Spanish families. Those sherry-makers lured honest people into their caves and gave them a lot of fine talk about involved and romantic love-calls, and all the while they were scheming to make them tipsy and send them out to act the buffoon. My face now working indignantly, I hailed a *fiacre* and drove to Los Cisnes for the largest, most solid meal that money could buy. Gazpacho there was, cold as a mountain lake, with dishes of bread, onion, pimiento and cucumber to throw in it, an Algerian omelet, roasted sucking-pig, a great bowl of figs, apricots and cherries and splendid Turkish coffee, for less than ten shillings. A little steadied, I went home and floated, or possibly flew, up the stairs to bed and slept until ten of the evening.

MacKINLEY HELM

Salamanca

A SELECTION FROM *Spring in Spain*

The golden stone of the churches and palaces and university buildings of Salamanca casts a glow upon the city and gives it a special warmth, although it is only a few miles from frigid Ávila and in nearly as barren a situation on the wind-swept plain. Perhaps there are other sources of the glister. The university still lives and its buildings are monuments to the distant golden age of the intellect when the University of Salamanca, founded in the thirteenth century, ranked with the world's earliest and greatest. And the wealth of Spain's golden century is traced in delicate stone carving on the faces of scores of buildings, in the style of architecture called plateresque because the stone is worked as intricately as the silversmith shapes his metal.

One is thankful that so much remains after centuries of poverty and neglect and war; the city is precious and rather sad. The university exists, but it was greater in almost any other century; the Irish students and priests are gone from their college and from the river, where they ice-skated in the rare, cold winters when the Tormes froze; the ducal palaces are abandoned, or full of poor squatters.

But the tone of Salamanca is gay, or at least vital. The plaza, one of the most beautiful in Europe, is crowded; the shops are busy; there are the students, and the strong hope that among them may be other Unamunos and others like Fray Luis de León, bold philosophers who taught and suffered for the freedom to teach.

Toledo is a national monument, and Ávila, too; there are working cities like Barcelona and Madrid, and sunny cities like Sevilla and Valencia. But Spain has only one Salamanca, only one medieval university city, only one place where such a delicious incident as MacKinley Helm describes in this selection, written in 1952, could occur.

MacKinley Helm lives in New England and writes of many matters—biography, travel, art, history, and literature.

Salamanca monumental! Ascending and descending three hills which reach a considerable height above the meandering Tormes, Salamanca has been compared to Rome. She is a *Roma in parvo.* And so elegant and well ordered are her monuments and plazas and convents and palaces, and so maturely and sagely has she ministered through them to the mind's necessities, that writers have called her the Spanish Athens.

If you find yourself in an open place at the top of San Isidoro, the central hill named for an eminently respectable scholar, a Visigothic archbishop, you can see—and could reach in a moment by foot—superb illustrations of the history of Christian architecture in Spain. The Romanesque epoch survives in several parish churches, though the French destroyed still a greater number. The old cathedral is transitional Gothic. The "new" cathedral and the Ursuline convent are Gothic. The Spanish Renaissance style is seen in the Dominican convent, the university, the Palacio de Monterrey, and the Irish college. And since Salamanca was the workshop of José Churriguera, sire of the wonderful baroque cities of central Mexico, you can see the Counter Reformation at work in his sumptuous clothing of the faultless Jesuit college and in the reredos of St. Stephen's. Salamanca's generations of building come to an end with the church and convent of the Augustinian *madres*, a step short of rococo.

Opulent beyond belief, then, for so small a city, Salamanca is also satisfactorily colorful, with its cool, weathered gray and warm golden limestone. Its warmth, deriving otherwise from intangible factors, would have been greatly enhanced, we felt, by the Mexican sun. Since the weather was cold and rainspotted during most of our visit, we might have missed the feeling of warmth altogether but for an encounter with a delightful outlander who made us feel at home where we had no acquaintance.

Leaning out of corridor windows on the afternoon train in which we left Ávila, my wife and Anita and I were saying good-by to the friends who had taken lunch at the hotel with us on the last day of our visit—or perhaps more specifically, we were accepting an invitation to return the next year to fish trout in the Tormes River—when a deep-toned voice said behind us, "Surely it's nice to hear the good Saxon language spoken by fishermen after all these long months from home."

The childhood tutor of one of our Ávila friends was an Irishman, and perhaps for the reason that I had been hearing fragments of English spoken with an Irish accent, my ear now caught the speaker's oblique intention as well as the not altogether unfamiliar inflection. Without turning my head to look at the owner of the cheerful, rich voice, I said to my friend on the platform, in tones intended to be clear to the stranger, "Did you notice, Mario, that the *señor* behind me was careful not to say *Anglo*-Saxon? What will you bet there's an Irishman here?"

A spill of hearty masculine laughter poured from the narrow corridor into my ears, and now for the first time glancing backward, I saw the fine open face of one of the grandest men in all Ireland. It was a big clove-pink pink face, the skin somewhat verrucose and lined deeply from laughter, the frame of hair gray and springy. The Oxford gray suit in which the man's broad-shouldered, athletic bulk was encased was set off by a white clerical collar—not the tight choker affected by American clergy, but a comfortable Anglican collar, loose and round, designed to give ease to the pleasures of conversation and eating.

I introduced myself to his reverence, a gesture his broad smile invited, and presented him to my traveling companions and to our friends on the platform. Introducing himself, in turn, as the rector of the Irish college, he invited our Ávila friends to come and see him in Salamanca. Knowing the college, our friends were pleased to commend us to the care of its rector, and soon we were off for the university city in a shower of benedictions and a flutter of scarves—sad, not a little, to leave the warm hospitality of the coldly reputed Ávila de Santa Teresa.

We stood by in the corridor while our little electric train huffed and puffed up the grade above the western towers of Ávila and paused briefly (was this stop designed as a tribute or

333

merely for breathing?) near the spot where Santa Teresa, about six years old, was intercepted on her uncharted journey to preach to the Moors. Then, when we had seen the last of the stout granite walls, at the turn of the grade, our new friend introduced us to two Irish bishops and told us the story of the Irish college.

One of our friends had said, upon meeting the rector, "*Si, si, el colegio del arzobispo, lo conozco*, I know it." Known in university circles as the Archbishop's college because the lavish Renaissance structure it partly occupies was built by Alonso de Fonseca, member of an immensely rich Spanish family and Salamanca's sole wearer of the cardinal's hat in the Toledo cathedral, the Irish college was one of several boarding schools founded on the Spanish peninsula, in the first Protestant Queen Elizabeth's era, for the education of the sons of the English-speaking Catholic nobility. The young men sent out to Spain in Queen Elizabeth's day were pledged to return to their homes and, if need be, meet persecution. A third part of the first group of Irishmen's transplanted sons did go back to Ireland, according to collegiate annals, and met death as martyrs. But so many Irish youths remained securely in Spain and bred so industriously with the local young women that it is said (said the rector) that every third person you meet in Castile has an Irish ancestor.

I inquired of my lord bishops, two witty and learned and distinguished gentlemen, whether, in view of this their impending first visit, they would care to hear George Borrow's account of the Archbishop's college in the 1830's. Like Borrow, I explained, we were of Protestant family, though I assured their lordships that we had not come, like Borrow, to insinuate the Protestant Bible into university precincts. I was amiably invited to read from a volume at hand in my book box, and I read the following passage:

"My sojourn at Salamanca was rendered particularly pleasant [wrote Borrow] by the kind attentions and continual acts of hospitality which I experienced from the inmates of the Irish College, to the rector of which I bore a letter of recommendation. . . . It will be long before I forget these Irish, more especially their head, Dr. Gartland, a genuine scion of the good Hibernian tree, an accomplished scholar, and a courteous and high minded gentleman. Though fully aware who I was, he held out the hand of friendship to the wandering heretic missionary, although by so doing he exposed himself to the rancorous remarks of the narrow minded native clergy, who, in their ugly shovel hats and long cloaks, glared at me askance as I passed by their whispering groups beneath the piazzas of the Plaza. But when did the fear of consequences cause an Irishman to shrink from the exercise of the duties of hospitality? However attached to his religion—and who is so attached to the Romish creed as the Irishman?—I am convinced that not all the authority of the Pope or the Cardinals would induce him to close his doors on Luther himself, were that respectable personage at present alive and in need of food and refuge."

"Delightful, delightful," the rector exclaimed when the chuckling subsided, "yet I am overcome with mortification. I am unable to extend to you and your wife and the *señorita* the hospitality shown by my predecessor, that genuine scion of the Hibernian tree. The college being no longer frequented, we could not do so much, at this time, as to give Martin Luther himself an Irish potato."

It so happened, however, that we were all putting up at a hotel in the Plaza of the Poet Iglesias and we engaged ourselves to meet after dinner and damn the English together over coffee and brandy. On that cheerful occasion, I recited Borrow's toast to the Irish: "Honor to Ireland . . . her fields have long been the greenest in the world; her daughters the fairest; her sons the bravest and most eloquent. May they never cease to be so."

The Fuero de Salamanca, the first of the great Spanish civil codes, speaks of several twelfth-century Romanesque churches. Of these there remain, besides the church at San Marcos, the San Cristóbal, San Julián, Santo Tomás, and San Juan de Barbalos parish churches, each with its own weathered quality. The church of Santiago, a delightful example of Romanesque and Mudéjar, still adorns the district where Arabized Christians lived under the patronage of Alfonso's Catholicized Moorish consort.

Temporarily reserving the Gothic, we skipped from the Burgundian age straight to Carlos V and the Renaissance period. The University of Salamanca is older than its Renaissance fabric by more than two centuries. Its establishment goes back to about A.D. 1220, in the reign of Alfonso IX of León, known to his Moslem opposite, Ibn Khaldūn, as the Slobberer because he foamed at the mouth when he felt he was slighted. This Alfonso intended to leave his kingdom to his daughters by Queen Teresa, his cousin, in spite of the fact that the Pope made them bastards by annulling their mother's marriage. His second wife, Berengaria (a mere second cousin), had a different idea, however, and adroitly united her husband's throne of León and her own throne of Castile under her son, Don Fernando. This was the St. Ferdinand, or San Fernando, whose life and work we had almost daily encountered from our first landing in Spain, and it was a pleasure to get back to an account of his origins: of which a pertinent fact, in this context, seemed to be that he was pronounced wholly legitimate though the Pope had unkindly refused to recognize Berengaria's marriage to his father, the much married Slobberer.

Whatever is known of the early history of the Royal and

Pontifical University of Salamanca has been found in a holograph letter of this son of the founder. San Fernando himself went on to enlarge his father's foundation and set up a scholastic tribunal to govern it in a disciplined manner. Alfonso the Wise, San Fernando's son and successor, built a great library, inaugurated a school of astronomical studies, and instituted the Socratic "Plan," the democratic procedures which thereafter distinguished Salamanca from Bologna and Paris, where the teaching was essentially aristocratic in method.

The sixteenth-century façade of the university building is the most imposing example of Plateresque architecture in Spain, though the Casa de la Salina of the Fonseca family is not far behind it. The street front of the university, as it gives upon the open Patio de las Escuelas, looks like a tapestry woven for the Catholic Kings who are honored in it, so refined is the carving, and the cloister and grand staircase behind it add up to opulence. Whether the intellectual life of the university still reflects the splendor of the cloister and library, I was not able to judge. Academic society is no longer one of my preoccupations. But I have a friend who says the university has undoubtedly suffered from the general decline of critical scholarship in the last fifteen years.

"What has caused the decline?" I inquired. "The exodus of your republican intellectuals?"

"Such as who?" he replied. "Have any of them been setting the world on fire?"

I had to say I thought not. Few of the scholars in exile have lived up to their early promise, perhaps by reason of their transplantation. On the other hand, the boys and girls who flocked into the Plaza Mayor after classes looked as bright and attractive as the young people on the campus of any coeducational American college. A visiting lecturer told me that he found them mature and serious. And to judge by the large number of bookshops, books are being sold in considerable quantity. Science, a bookseller informed me, outsells the humanities. . . .

And now the reader who has followed the ins and outs of my Churrigueresque theme in preceding chapters may like to accompany me, as the weather clears up, to two or three cheerful churches and convents built or refurbished in the baroque era. If others prefer to sit in a sheltered spot in the plaza and drink some good Spanish brandy, I promise to join them there presently with a curious story.

Two baroque monuments which remain to be seen—the French, have I said, destroyed half the city in the time of Napoleon—are the church of San Esteban and its arrogant rival, the Jesuit Clerecía. The former, St. Stephen's, was begun, to be sure, in a pre-baroque century. Juan de Álava, later the master builder of the so-called "new" cathedral, was the author of its original plan, and that plan, as you can see in both church and cloister, called for a spacious treatment of the peculiarly Spanish Renaissance style of which Álava was an inventive creator. His patron was Fray Juan Álvarez de Toledo, a young son of the "Great" Duke of Alba, and since money was never an object in that fabulous family, the architect was encouraged to dream expansively and build expensively.

The principal entrance to St. Stephen's Church is let into a great arch of triumph sealed by an inner wall of carved stone —strictly speaking, a narthex. The façade takes the form of a gigantic altar-piece of which the Biblical tableaux and statues and grotesques and medallions are wrought in limestone of at least four tones of rose color ranging from pale pink to red. When you see these rich rosy sculptures in the afternoon sun, you think the wall must be set with thousands of transparent gems.

"But," I hear you say, "we thought we had finished with Renaissance Salamanca. Where is your friend Churriguera and the baroque era?"

I reply, "Step inside."

Down at the end of the long lofty nave, beyond the choir where the friars sang their office in an ampler moment of history, you will see the great baroque masterpiece of my friend Churriguera. It appears, at first glance, to depend from the sky.

Perhaps you must see to believe it; though if you have seen Mexican churches like that of San Agustín in a dusty pueblo also called Salamanca, you will have an idea which you need only to blow up to incredible size to approach St. Stephen's baroque reality. Six immense twisted (salomónica) columns, entwined with carved vine branches and tendrils and clusters of grapes, shelter a huge tabernacle. The tableau in the tall altarpiece represents the stoning and death of St. Stephen. The niches between the columns contain monumental figures of miscellaneous saints in extreme baroque posture. For the first time in Spain, I felt satisfied that I had, with my own eyes, seen the original source of the extravagant Mexican high-baroque architecture called Churrigueresque. I had seen resplendent examples of its flamboyant grace in Granada. Salamanca was where it had come from.

The Xurigeras, as the family was originally known, had come from Madrid. The father, José, who kept a shop for carving *retablos* to order, had five sons who became artists and architects. José's namesake, José de Churriguera, the most famous of the five brothers, had at least three sons who became practicing architects. Since this race of talented Churrigueras did much of their work as a team, it is not always possible to separate their individual styles and declare arbitrarily who did what.

José de Churriguera went to Salamanca at the end of the seventeenth century, accompanied by his sons and brothers, and simply took over the municipal—and some of the national —architectural problems. But here is a poser: not all of the

Churriguera solutions are Churrigueresque! Few of the works of the brothers and uncles and nephews are as flamboyant as the St. Stephen *retablo*. When José de Churriguera was commissioned, for instance, to plan and build a complete village, he turned out a plan with a church and a plaza in a neoclassical style that would have pleased Felipe II, the patron of the severe Juan de Herrera. The baroque twists and turns of ornamented design which liven up the traditional surfaces—the interiors especially—of earlier structures, as in Anadalusia, were multiplied and magnified by Churriguera disciples until, out in Mexico, the ornament all but swallows up the original forms.

The Jesuits tried three times before they felt they had at last found a plan that would satisfy their sense of the truly magnificent and also stare down the church of San Esteban which they proposed to confront a short lane's length to the north. The townspeople said that the Jesuits meant to put out the eyes of the Dominican Friars, and I expect the Jesuit Fathers felt they had succeeded in doing just that.

The college and collegiate church were originally planned in the seventeenth century by Juan Gómez de Mora, whose stately but rather cold drawings for the cathedral of Mexico City were sent out to the New World and discarded; but in more than a century of proceeding by trial and effect, Gómez de Mora's already somewhat qualified "House of Austria" style—Doña Margarita of Austria was underwriting the project with gold from America—was altered in an overtly baroque direction. There are Spanish critics who think the completed work, as one sees it today, to be the most flawless example of the Spanish baroque in the country, and in respect to the patio in particular, I should be inclined to agree. This galleried cloister is an exciting example of the fluidity, mobility, and the elegance of baroque design. In its time, the whole work stood as a Jesuit challenge to Protestantism to unveil its bare bones in front of the glory and splendor of the Catholic religion.

Of further examples of Salamanca's nearly inexhaustible architectural treasures I shall speak of only one—though I should like to visit again the Franciscans' six rococo altars. Standing in front of the Casa de las Conchas, the House of the Shells, across the Calle de la Compañía from the Jesuit college, I was once more transported to Mexico, where the shell, the symbol of St. James the Apostle, appears over and over again in the architecture of the colonial period; as in churches with a narthex fluted and veined to give the illusion of a gigantic scallop shell. The façade of the Casa de las Conchas in Salamanca is "appliquéd" with hundreds of shells carved seriatim from the pink limestone. The palace is entered through a doorway decorated with the lions and fleurs-de-lis of the Gothic escutcheon of the family to which the Catholic Queen's physician belonged, and the patio to which one is thus introduced is a rarely well preserved example of the so-called mixtilinear style, the gallery above the arcade being supported by truncated Gothic arches.

I am reluctant to pass over the convent of the Augustinian *madres* with its sumptuous display of Italian neoclassical marbles and its priceless Ribera altarpiece, one of the undoubted masterpieces of Spanish baroque painting—no male mortal can report on the cloisters!—and I should also like to pause at the Palacio de Monterrey, the home of the seventh Conde de Monterrey, Viceroy of Naples and founder of the convent of Augustinian ladies. Now one of the unnumbered palaces of the dukes of Alba, its windows and frivolous loggias look down upon the plaza of the austere Augustinian ladies. In such a setting, its theatrical decorations of masks and skulls and decadent Romanesque arches are purely delicious. But I have promised to tell a tale in the plaza. . . .

The story that I have to relate of the great eighteenth-century plaza of Salamanca goes back to a day in Ávila when someone spoke to me, with a wry smile, of a sculptured portrait of the royal ancestor of one of our fellow-guests at the house of the countess. This ancestral portrait of Alfonso the Wise had been, until lately, one of a series of war-like and kingly likenesses carved on marble medallions placed, in Renaissance style, on one of the lateral walls of the plaza.

"How is it that you speak of the portrait as a thing of the past?" I inquired. "Was the plaza defaced in the Civil War? What has happened?"

"You will see," said my friend. "When you enter the Plaza Mayor from the Plaza del Poeta Iglesias, where you will be staying, turn right and walk to the end of the entrance arcade. On the right-hand arcade, the arcade of the House of the Kings, you will see the medallions of the warrior-kings of León and Castile. Go on until you reach San Fernando and then see who comes next."

So one morning in Salamanca I entered the plaza just before lunch, turned right, and then left, and found on the spandrels between the arches of the ornate Casa de los Reyes the round marble plaques which my Ávila friend had mentioned so drolly. There were lots of Alfonsos: El Bravo, the Valiant, who recovered Toledo from the Moslem invaders; and the Great and the Chaste and the Battler. I was approaching my goal with the Slobberer—Alfonso IX, the university founder. Then came San Fernando—I was getting warmer—and honest to God! Displacing Alfonso the Wise, ancestor of one of today's ducal Pretenders, and looking grand and complacent, the small *generalísimo*, regent of All the Spains in our time, kept an eye on the plaza from the next granite spandrel.

I sat down at the nearest sidewalk table and ordered brandy and coffee. Dispatching Buttons for paper, I wrote a note to my friend: "The Plaza Mayor—I see what you mean. Next time I go to Toledo I shall examine El Greco's repainted

'Apostles' more closely. Perhaps one of them will be wearing a wholly new face."

While I sat amazed in the sun, I grew aware of three strangers whose affairs all became, before the sun set that day, involved in a Spanish ultraist drama. At a table just at my elbow sat a blonde Spanish girl, pretty, feminine, vibrant, with a dark English boy of a look and a countenance midway between Byron's and Shelley's—the *dégagé* air of Shelley and Byron's clean profile. The young people spoke mostly in French, though the girl had some English; more English words, perhaps, than the English boy had in Spanish. I noticed that both wore bright gold wedding rings and I supposed at first that they were on their honeymoon and had yet to learn each other's vocabulary. But some exceptional urgency, both of voice and manner, soon caught my attention, and short of removing myself to a more distant table, I could hardly escape overhearing scraps of their conversation.

They were married all right, it turned out, Lord Byron-Shelley and the blonde Spanish girl, and quite lately married—but not at all to each other. They had just met; actually just met in the plaza.

"I knew, you know, as soon as I saw you," said the English boy.

"What did you know? Not that you could . . ." said the girl.

"Oh, I don't mean *that*," said the boy. "I never thought I could just ask you to—*you* know. I mean that I knew right away that I had to *know* you."

"*Pero que bárbaro!*" said the girl. "What you ask is impossible." (Whatever it was that he asked, he had asked before I came into the picture: but it was not hard to guess what it was that he asked.)

"Why impossible? You can see that it's impossible for me not to *want* you."

343

"But I *don't* see," said the girl. "Spanish men, yes, they are so—patriotic. They always make all women seem wanted. That's what we women live on, the pretension, at least, of being desired. But you English are not so flirtatious. You frighten me now because you are not frivolous, are you?" She used the nice word *folâtre*. "You are quite serious." (This was not a question.)

"I am deadly in earnest," said the young man. "You merely consume me."

I felt as though I were surreptitiously reading a letter. Resolving to fold it up halfway through and put it back in its envelope, I tinkled my brandy glass with a spoon and summoned the waiter. And while I waited for the waiter to return with the brandy, I watched an elderly clergyman amble awkwardly over the uneven paving stones of the plaza.

The old gentleman was wearing a faded soutane and a shabby, lackluster flat beaver hat. He would walk a few steps, rock on his heels, and go on, up and down, up and down in the sun. I saw that his shoes, though run-down at the heels and in need of a cobbler, shone with a high homemade polish. I saw that his hands, joined behind his back at the waist, were encased in new black silk gloves. I saw all this while the young people were talking.

"Tell me about the little old priest who walks up and down, up and down in the sun," I said to the waiter when he came back with my brandy.

"He is *loco*," said the waiter, tapping his forehead. "Just *loco*—but perfectly harmless. He comes to the plaza whenever the sun comes out and just walks up and down."

"Please ask him to take a *café exprès* as my guest," I commanded; adding—I don't know why; perhaps because the waiter looked doubtful; perhaps because I still felt disengaged—"at some other table, please, out in the sun."

The waiter shrugged his shoulders. "As you please, *señor*," he said, "but don't forget that the old man is cuckoo."

344

The padre looked up in annoyance when the waiter tapped his shoulder: in annoyance and dread. Poor old fellow, I thought, he probably expects to be thrown off the premises. But then I saw his face take on a look of surprise. He cupped a black-gloved hand to his ear, looked across at me sharply, smiled a toothless smile, and sat down at one of the tables, perhaps three tables distant.

When the waiter returned with his coffee, the padre tore the thin paper wrappings from two or three packets of sugar and plunged the coarse lumps into the small steaming cup. He acknowledged my treat with a bow and a blessing and I acknowledged the blessing with a lift of my hat.

The conversation at the table beside me had meanwhile continued—rapid, urgent, improvised out of passion. The blonde girl's thin face looked strained.

"I don't see how I can, I don't see how I can," she repeated. "I have my ticket."

I gathered she had been visiting in Valladolid and was now on her way home in Madrid. She had merely stopped off between morning and afternoon trains to renew her acquaintance with the university city. She was not rich or poor; she had to be practical.

"So have I to be practical," said the boy. "We can change the tickets."

"What excuse could I give to my husband?"

"Oh, any excuse. I too have . . . friends who are waiting for me up in Valladolid. We'll send telegrams."

"But you don't know Spanish men. I can't just send a telegram. I have to *say* something."

Sensing that the girl was now within reach, the boy clapped for Buttons and ordered telegraph blanks from the nearest post office station.

"Say you are sick," said the boy.

"Sick in Salamanca? How unlikely!"

"Say you have met an old friend."

"My husband would be here on the very next train. One doesn't meet women friends in strange places."

"Say you missed the train."

"My husband would be in a frenzy."

"But what could he *do?* Would he hurt you?"

"Oh, no, not that. He never actually beats me."

Buttons arrived with the telegraph forms.

"Come along then," the English boy said. "Say you've missed the train, you'll be home in the morning, you're sorry. I'll write it."

"I had better write it myself, in case anything happens."

"Right you are! Here's my pen."

"Don't watch me so closely, you make me nervous," said the blonde girl, writing slowly. "Don't touch me. I shan't be able to make the letters come clear if you touch me."

"You ask," said the boy, "for more than desire permits me— *querida*, my love, my dear love." He touched her cheek. Her eyes shone. . . .

"*Muchas gracias*," said the padre, rocking now on his heels in front of my table, "*y vaya Usted con Dios.*"

"Adios, *señor*," I replied. "Till we meet."

Walk, stop, rock, walk, stop, rock, and soon the old man disappeared from the plaza. After taking a turn with the colorful pageant of students and teachers and shopgirls and office men now parading the plaza, I too wandered out through the gate and returned to our lodgings. I had seen too much, heard too much—imagined too much—for my comfort.

After lunch and siesta, I wandered over the Rua Mayor, a street lined with bookshops, and up the street to the arbored Plaza Anaya to visit the two interwoven cathedrals. Having to wait a few moments for the doors to be opened, I had time to admire again the stone sculptures of the western façade, the lovely "Adoration" by Juan Rodríguez, with its solicitous magi and worshiping shepherds. The verger who opened the

door was my slave (he announced) and I advanced behind
him into the dusky interior of the "new" cathedral—the
twelfth-century cathedral next door is only four hundred
years older—and held my breath to behold the slim columns
which seemed rather to drop from the roof in search of the
floor than to spring from the earth to support the high vaulting. Meretricious, perhaps, this evasion of architectural function, yet the effect suited the disturbed mood that midday had
wrought in me in the Plaza Mayor, a mood which a very good
lunch had not yet shaken off. The cathedral heightened my
feeling that life is precarious. The mad priest, the risky love-
making, now the unstable columns: all one. And so immediate
were the priest and the lovers to my unquiet senses that I
wondered the verger did not exclaim to see them beside me as
we moved through the shadows.

"Can this church be the work of men's hands?" I inquired in
silence. I still could tingle at the thought of the Gothic rise
and leap of the Seville cathedral and still melt to recall the
rosy white reaches of mirthful Granada. Yet I declared in-
stantaneously to my unseen companions that this was now my
favorite church in the world: warm in its high-roofed magnificence; splendid in the gilt vaulting, the gold rosettes sprinkled
everywhere upon the warm gray walls; ironic and humorous
in its fantastic animals coursing over the sculptured stone
cornice.

"Come now," I said to the lovers, "forget your anxieties
just for a moment. See the dangling columns. Attend to the
choir which blocks up the main aisle. See how the sculptor
has forced stone to yield to the chisel as though it were wood
in the hands of a whittler."

Her telegram sent, the die cast, the blonde Spanish girl just
might, for a moment, have listened: though she would have
replied, as she clung to the hand of Lord Byron-Shelley, that
they of Castile thought the old church more chic.

347

We stepped down a steep step, the verger and I—did I put out my hand to steady a tottering padre wearing a faded soutane and new black silk gloves?—and passed through an old door to the neighboring church. The twelfth-century cathedral, to my mind, was not more chic, as they say; it was merely quainter.

"See how the saints and bishops and donors await the Last Judgment in their mausoleums and chapels," the verger whispered. They waited precariously. Their effigies, one and all, lay aslope on their sides, the better to expose their expectant carved features to a posterity troubled by sin and damnation. . . .

I never lost my three ghostly companions until the verger began to describe the terrors of student life in the Middle Ages. Then I was temporarily turned in on myself; caused to call up the pleasant years of my own graduate studies while the verger reenacted the trial of endurance which preceded the awarding of a doctor's degree in old Salamanca. He showed me the chapel of Santa Barbara where the candidate spent the last twenty-four hours, from sunrise to sunrise, before his examination at the hands of practiced theological doctors. He could read, review, annotate. He prayed much and ate little. Sleep he might not, a constant attendant watching, from outside the chapel, to see that he didn't. At the end of the vigil, he sat at the foot of the bier of a recumbent bishop, his feet pressed against the soles of the feet of the bishop—the verger sat thus and then seated me there—and then for twelve hours he defended his thesis.

If the test tried the souls of intrepid scholars, the rewards for passing it were wholly Gargantuan. If you pleased the professors, you were carried shoulder-high through the streets of the city, flags flying, bells ringing, balconies draped and crowded, and you ate and drank for four days at the public expense. When I stood away from the bishop at the end of the verger's portrayal, my three friends had vanished. They had disappeared while I was stuffing myself with the academicians.

The sky was clearing after a shower as I stepped out into the Plaza Anaya and headed, like an idle student, for the principal square. The waiters at cafés exposed to the westering sun were now setting out tables in anticipation of their proper share of the daily commerce. It was not yet quite six o'clock when I seated myself at a marble-topped table that promised a half-hour's warmth before evening. In the restful solitude of the first fifteen minutes, I surveyed the monarch of Spanish plazas from a new angle. Here, then, complete and now nearly empty of pedestrian traffic, was Alberto Churriguera's realization of a royal dream of the finest plaza in Europe—grand, immense, homogeneous.

I had read that Alberto's task was not easy: local pride cherished the acres of palsied palaces and stinking slums that had to give way before the king's dream came true. The old Count de Grajal, whose palace, I took it, had stood about where I now sat, had carried his case to the courts; kept it there for ten years. The tower of the Palacio de Grajal, he said, was the last jewel of his line. But wall by wall the arcades had gone up. First, the royal pavilion in 1729; that was the block with the portrait medallions placed on the spandrels; then the arcades of San Martín with the principal entrance; then the western aspect was laid out and built up after the death of the count and the architect. Lastly, the lordly Casas Consistoriales, where I had encountered the mad priest and the lovers. Was that only this morning?

The thought was a clear case of transference, for the padre now bore down upon me from the Puerta de San Martín, a thin cloak drawn over his moss-colored cassock, and the blonde girl and her English companion sauntered down from the north, hand-in-hand, dreamy-eyed. The lovers sat within earshot at a table laid out in the small patch of sun and I noticed they wore the clothes they had on at midday—the girl a smart gray suit and white blouse, the boy a blue city suit and blue collar.

It was past the time for the train to Madrid, I considered. Time enough for sending the telegrams, but not very much more. The English boy, poor northern lover, had he made no beginning? Was he waiting for darkness to mantle his passion?

The padre stopped at my table and rocked on his heels. It was chillier now, and his expectant pale face looked like a piece of old altar linen in need of a mender. My waiter lounged out from his post at the café window as I rose to salute the old gentleman. Like the waiter in front of the Casas Consistoriales at noon, he tapped his head and silently spoke the word *loco*. I nodded, as if to say "quite all right," and invited the padre to join me.

"When I was a boy in the seminary," said the padre, the customary polite phrases spoken, "this was a great place. Twenty thousand people packed into the plaza and yet space enough was left for the bullfights. And the religious processions! You should have seen the banners and tapestries, *señor*, the choristers ankle-deep in rose petals. Oh, those were great days!"

I expressed myself as so bold as to ask leave to wonder what the old priest did *now* (he didn't *seem* crazy). He replied that he lived in retirement at the charity hospital, for alas he had no one to mind him.

"You are a stranger here?" he inquired. "No one has told you?"

I shook my head. The padre looked this way and that way and bent his head over his cup of sweet coffee.

"I live in dishonor, *señor*," he said, touching his lips with a gloved index finger. "I live ignominiously."

350

"Good heavens!" I thought. "What have I got into?"

I could not make the inquiries the case seemed to demand without shouting out loud in my Mexican Spanish; so that if it was a confidence that was now looming up, I was unsure how to keep it. I decided to make my lips say *porqué* in silence.

"Did you say why?" asked the padre. "It was because of my miracle. I was thrown out of my parish because of a miracle."

His voice grew louder, caught the ears of the lovers, who now turned to listen.

"Tell me," I said, using an inferential short phrase I had learned from a Spanish telephone operator.

"Did you say *tell* you? Don't you want me to show you?"

Show me a miracle? Right here in the plaza? I replied, "Why not?" with an affirmative nod.

The padre drew off his gloves and held out his thin hands. In the center of each wrinkled palm was a dreadful red scar, as from deeply burned flesh or a cancerous wound.

"Oh, never!" I said.

"Wait, *señor*," said the padre. "You have seen only half. My people were leaving my parish to visit a Virgin who wept fresh tears on Fridays. I prayed to Our Lord and he came to me as he came to St. Francis. See my feet!"

The old gentleman loosened the laces of one of his well-polished boots, drew it off, rolled down a clean white wool stocking.

"I know, padre," I cried. "The wounds of St. Francis!"

"Of course, the Stigmata. But they wouldn't believe me. The deans and the bishops, they wouldn't believe me."

The Spanish girl gasped. She turned pale. She cried out. She clasped her hands to her face.

"It's a sign. Holy Mother of God, it's a sign! I must leave

you." And clutching her purse to her breast, she darted out of the plaza.

The waiter, momentarily called from his post by augmenting custom, rushed up to see what was happening.

"Padre, padre, put your shoe on," he ordered. "You know what will happen, they will take you away. *Loco, loco!*" he shouted.

Lord Byron-Shelley tossed the waiter a couple of cartwheels of silver.

"You're all crazy," he said, as he hurried away.

ROBERT GRAVES

"Why I Live in Majorca"

A SELECTION FROM *5 Pens in Hand*

The Balearic Islands form a region of Spain which has the benign climate that unwary foreigners associate with all of Spain. If the islands improve upon the climate of much of the mainland, they share with a part of the latter the rich history and qualities of popular character which make Catalonia and the Catalans exceptional in an exceptional country.

Robert Graves is the most talented of the English authors— and the authors in English—who have made their home in Spain. He moved to Mallorca in 1929 and has since lived there,

353

*except during the Spanish Civil War and World War II,
when he was obliged to leave. Poet, historical novelist, critic,
classical scholar, translator, biographer, and autobiographer—
the names state some of the dimensions of his complex talent.
His Irish-German inheritance, his experiences in World War I,
his attachment to antiquity, these may be counted among the
factors which have provided Graves with special attitudes
toward the twentieth century. He is, in fact, although now
the holder of the Poetry chair at Oxford, a man from England
who renounced living in England. But rejection is not retreat,
and in Spain, in Mallorca, Robert Graves pursued his high art
amid the people of a land he loves.*

I CHOSE Majorca as my home, a quarter of a century ago,
because its climate had the reputation of being better than
any other in Europe. And because I was assured, correctly
it proved, that I should be able to live there on a quarter of
the income needed in England. And because it was large
enough—some 1,300 square miles—not to make me feel claus-
trophobic. Then from all Majorca I chose Deyá, a small fishing
and olive-producing village on the mountainous north-west
coast of the island—the rest is mostly plain or rolling country
—where I found everything I wanted as a background to my
work as a writer: sun, sea, mountains, spring-water, shady
trees, no politics, and a few civilized luxuries such as electric
light and a bus service to Palma, the capital. It was also fairly
mosquito-free, being some four hundred feet above sea level.

Let me add frankly that I came away from England after a
painful domestic crisis. But that was merely the provocation
—I had already decided against living permanently in England

354

when it suddenly dawned on me that the country was grossly overcrowded, its optimum population being about eight million, as in Tudor times. Particularly the new fashion of ribbon-building, which extended even small towns for a mile or two into the country, warned me to be off; so did the growing mechanization of agriculture. I wanted to go where town was still town; and country, country; and where the horse plough was not yet an anachronism. There were other desiderata, naturally, such as good wine, good neighbours, and not too great a distance from the Greenwich meridian.

Come to think of it, the first person who recommended Majorca to me was Gertrude Stein. I went to see Gertrude in Haute Savoie, after saying my good-bye to the white cliffs of Dover, and though her country seemed rich, hospitable and mountainous, the sea lay too far away and the winter would have been a little severe for me. I did not fancy the continuous brooding presence of "Madame" Mont Blanc. There was nothing really to prevent me from going wherever I liked, because a pen is the only essential luggage a writer need take —a typewriter even would be a luxury—but I had never travelled for the sake of travelling and wanted to get settled as soon as possible. Gertrude, who always talked sense, assured me that the Majorcans were cheerful, clean and friendly people, culturally Southern French, and agriculturally still in the eighteenth century. She added that there would be no catch at all—if I liked Paradise, Majorca was Paradise. But she preferred herself to spend most of her year in Paris. On consulting the atlas, I saw that Majorca lay almost dead on the Greenwich meridian, in the centre of the most consistent fair-weather area in Europe, and that it had one mountain at least as high as any in England. So off I went, and Gertrude proved to have been right: there *was* no catch, unless for people who carried their own hell with them.

After a few months at Deyá, I fetched my books and furniture from England, and then stayed six more years without so much as visiting the mainland. In 1929, Spain had been under the Dictatorship of Primo de Rivera; a year or two later this gave way peacefully to the Republic—but the village took no notice, except to add a strip of Republican purple to the red and yellow Spanish flag at the Casa Consistorial—and when, in July, 1936, the Revolution broke out, nobody thought that it would affect Majorca. The most recent fighting in the island had taken place during a peasants' war around 1450, and the last invasion in 1229, when King James of Aragon and his knights drove out the Moors. Now the Captain-General and the Civil Governor made up their minds that Majorca must, as usual, pick the winning side; and therefore, after a certain hesitation, declared for General Franco. Minorca and Iviza, the two neighbouring islands, remained loyal to the Republican Government. Aircraft from Minorca soon flew over us and began dropping leaflets and hand-made bombs. Presently, Italian and German armed forces intervened on Franco's side, and since this was to be a dress-rehearsal for World War II, all British residents were advised to leave at once by warship to avoid international incidents.

I found that rather hard. By now I had built my own house at Deyá and, if the Spaniards had been left to themselves, would not have been obliged to move. Spaniards are always faultlessly polite to foreign residents who behave themselves and keep out of politics, but General Franco needed foreign support, especially when Negrín, the Premier, began buying arms from Russia; and soon Palma became the base from which young Mussolini and his bomb-happy friends daily demolished Barcelona. The Non-Intervention Committee announced themselves satisfied that there were no Italians on the island; and I cannot prove that there were, because I had already gone off at an hour's notice, with a small handbag, aboard H.M.S. *Grenville*.

During those first seven years in Majorca, life had been far less civilized than it is now. Beef, butter and cow's milk were not easily obtained; but there was plenty of fresh fruit throughout the year: a sequence of oranges, loquats, cherries, apricots, peaches, plums, strawberries, apples, pears, first figs, grapes, figs, pomegranates and oranges again. So, with black coffee and cheap black tobacco, and a very sound heady wine from the village of Binisalem, and brandy at three pesetas a bottle, all was well. Wages for masons and other manual workers were the equivalent of four dollars weekly, and they worked a ten-hour day; full domestic service cost about twenty cents a day. Gertrude had not misled me about the islanders, who were (and still are) excessively honest and friendly, and soon accepted me with all my foibles, as part of the landscape. They did not resent my being a Protestant and not attending Mass; or building a house on the best site for miles. Some of them wept when I said good-bye.

The Spanish Civil War lasted until 1939, when the World War was clearly imminent, and General Franco's debt to the Axis prevented my return to Deyá. So I wandered disconsolately around Switzerland, France, the United States, and was on a brief visit to England when Hitler invaded Poland. The longer the war lasted, the more vivid grew my dreams of Majorca. I found myself sympathizing with the Children of Israel in the Wilderness who wept saying: "We remember the fish which we did eat in Egypt freely; the cucumbers and the melons and the leeks and the onions and the garlic; but now our soul is dried away." My longings were also for the fruit in my garden; the smell of olive-wood fires; the chatter of card-players in the village café; the buoyant green waters of the cove; the sun-blistered rocks of the Teix mountain; my quiet white-washed study; the night noises of sheep bells, owls, nightingales, frogs, and distant surf. . . .

What was it about Deyá that tugged so strongly at the

heart? I remembered it as a spectacular, but not really a beautiful, place. Nothing of importance had ever happened there, and I had no reason to suppose that anything ever would. The villagers were neither well-educated nor quaint: they had long abandoned the peasant costume that is still worn in other parts of the island, and the village fiestas were not what they had been. No hunting, no racing, no yachting, no organized games of any sort. No ancient monuments of any interest. Not even village politics. And the population had been dwindling for years.

Well, what *was* Deyá like? To refresh my memory I turned to the guidebooks. One Colin Campbell had written in 1719:

> Deyá is a Place belonging to Valdemoça, a Town provided with variety of early and later Fruit, besides great plenty of Oyl and Silk. The Air is here extremely pure. All the Vallies, Hills and Woods round are cover'd with beautiful Groves that afford agreeable Shades . . . Deyá consists in Countrey Houses separated from one another. The many Fountains, Groves and Fruit-trees that are here contribute extremely to the Pleasantness of the Place. The Church is in the middle of a Plain on the Top of a small Hill.

A more lyrical note had been struck by travellers of the present century:

> Deyá is a tiny hamlet perched on the apex of a hill overlooking a garden valley. On the crest is a chapel surrounded by a shabby and delightful little garden in which sleep the dead, among flowers, within sound of the sea, visible through a gap in the mountainous shore. All about the valley other mountains tower, their crests salmon-pink at sunset, solidified flame. . . .

358

The quaint little houses with their roofs of ribbed tiles rise above each other in tiers or groups, but each with its little terraced garden, dotted with almond or orange-trees, and bright with the flowers which seem to assert themselves despite the lack of intentional cultivation. And just as the town itself is a delightful vision from the highway, so the views it commands from its mountain-valley situation are of constant yet ever-changing charm. For here, as in so many other regions of the island, form and colour seem to vary with every hour of the day. . . .

The mountains are so near that they seem about to fall and crush the hamlet. Eagles swing above, and wild canaries dart and trill below. The white road winds along the side of the mountain on the opposite side of the valley like a ribbon, curving in and out among the trees. Foliage is everywhere, reaching to the rose and white summits, and down to the hidden river. Through the soft air yellow butterflies float, mingled with drifting almond-petals. After sunset the valley is filled with a translucent effulgence of colour—amethyst, mauve, blue, and creeping shadows which die to purple night. . . .

These extracts were interesting to me mainly because they showed the strange, hallucinatory power that Deyá exerts on foreign visitors. Campbell saw the church and the country houses, but did not see the village; his successors saw the village, but neither the church nor the country houses. Campbell imagined a plain, where there is only a steeply-terraced valley with nowhere a broad enough level place for a tennis-court; his successors heard the trilling of wild canaries—there are none on the island—festooned barren precipices with foliage, crowned them with eagles' eyries, and credited the houses of Deyá with non-existent gardens. Germans have written even more extravagantly about the place. This hallucination may have something to do with the moon. The church is said to be built on the site of an Iberian shrine of the Moon-goddess, and I am prepared to swear that nowhere in Europe is moonlight so strong as in Deyá; one can even match colours by it. And moonlight is notorious for its derangement of the wits.

All sorts of holiday-makers came to Deyá in those seven years: painters, professors of literature, dipsomaniacs, pianists, perverts, priests, geologists, Buddhists, run-away couples, vegetarians, Seventh Day Adventists, but especially painters. (Some wit had said that the name "Deyá" is a corruption of *El Pueblo de ya pintado*—"The village of what has already been painted"—because every artist pitched his camp-stool in exactly the same spot). All went away a little dafter than they came. The painters splashed their canvases with cobalt, viridian, vermilion, and a dirty olive-green, though the prevailing colours of the landscape are grey, smoke-blue, a translucent grey-green, blue-black, biscuit and rust; and the sea is never cobalt. They painted the crooked olive-trees as though they were elms; and the harsh rocks, as though they were cakes of Castile soap. Seldom less than ten of them stopped at the inn, or rented cottages during the season.

But what was Deyá *really* like? A village of some four hundred inhabitants, and some two hundred solid stone houses, most of them built on the landward side of a rocky hill which occupied the centre of a great fold of mountains. The coastroad encircled Deyá, but touched the outlying houses only. A church with a squat tower and a small cypressed cemetery crowned the hill; no houses at all were built between it and the sea, half a mile away. A torrent, dry during the summer, ran half-way round the village and down a narrow gorge until it emptied into a cove, with a beach of sand and pebbles. Apart from the small port of Sóller, six miles up the coast, this was one of the very few inlets along the island's ironbound north-western coast. No car could get down to the cove from the village, and the fisherman's path was a rough one indeed: a four-hundred-foot descent from the coast-road, first through olive groves and then through a scrub of lentiscus, spurge, asphodel, caper and wild asparagus.

The fishermen's huts in the cove were used only during the summer months. No refreshments could be obtained there, and one got very hot climbing back after a bathe. The mountains had been laboriously terraced all the way up from sea level to about nine hundred feet. There were lemon and orange groves where irrigation was possible; but only three springs in the village ran all the year round, and the soil was everywhere poor and stony; apart from a few carob-trees that provided wholesome fodder for mules, all the rest was olive-orchard. And the olives were not the well-behaved, bushy-topped, stately variety one finds in Italy, France, and California; but twisted, bossed, hacked-about grotesque, often growing from cracks in the live rock, never watered, never manured, once a year scratched around with a primitive mule-plough, and every seven years trimmed of their biggest branches. They were almost indestructible: a good many had been planted by the Moors, more than seven hundred years before. "Pamper an olive-tree," the villagers used to say, "and spoil the fruit."

In the Spring some of the olive terraces could be persuaded to raise a sparse crop of broad beans. These, with figs, served to feed the black pigs which were ceremoniously killed at Martinmas, and turned into red and black sausages; each household had its pig, and the sausage must last until the following Martinmas. Above the olive-trees rose an unterraced belt of stunted ever-green oak, where charcoal-burners worked all summer, pigs routed in the autumn, wild peonies flowered at Easter, and wild cats, martens, and civets maintained a precarious existence. Above that, towered sheer precipices streaked with rusty ochre, and above those the bald limestone brow of the Teix.

At last the World War ended; but for ten years I had been unable to communicate with my village friends—because Spain had remained officially pro-Axis, and I did not intend to embarrass them. Nor had I been able to send them money. But after V.E. Day, tension relaxed. I heard that my house was still standing unplundered; and, in 1946, the Spanish Embassy allowed me to return. No airlines were running, no boats, the Franco-Spanish frontier was tightly closed. But an R.A.F. friend of mine had just helped to start an air-taxi service, so that made movement possible.

Back in the village, I had to double-kiss a whole row of male and female cheeks, and tears were shed as at my departure. Though I had meanwhile acquired a wife and three small children, it seemed as if I had been absent only a few weeks, except for the immensity of the tangerine bushes in the garden, and loquat-trees already bearing fruit where I had once carelessly tossed away loquat pits. Of course, children had grown up, and a few old people had died; but families remained intact. In England, very few of our friends still had the same husbands and wives as before the War; at Deyá one marries, after a seven-year courtship, and remains truly married for keeps. Everything I had left behind had been looked after—linen, silver, books and documents—though the moths had got into my socks; and if I felt so inclined, could have sat down at my table, taken a sheet of paper from the drawer and started work again straight away. Deyá certainly rolled out the red carpet for me; my return made everyone hope that prosperity was once again around the corner.

The next three years were, I admit, pretty hard. Spain

had not profited from World War II as from World War I. On the contrary, rationing was now far severer than in England, a family loaf cost as much as a bottle of champagne and effective steps could not yet be taken to suppress the flourishing black market. The flow of tourists remained negligible. There is this to say for tourists: their arrival in bulk tends to relax police regulations, encourage amenities in food and household utensils, and decrease unemployment. And though an excess of visitors sends up prices and wages and fills the towns with ugly advertisements, souvenir shops, cheap jacks, and shady adventurers from everywhere—and at the peak season can actually wear down the tempers of so patient and long-suffering a people as the Majorcans—still, the island has not yet been spoilt even by the massive influx of the recent "Majorca, Isle of Love" period. This is because few Majorcan roads are capable of taking buses and taxis, so tourist traffic is canalized along a limited grid. Visitors who bring their own cars, unless they are jeeps or the equivalent—high-slung and with truck tyres—are advised not to adventure into the real country, except on foot, with rucksacks, down roads white with dust. And when they reach the real country, naturally, they must consent to be coarse feeders, as I was in the old days.

I have now lived here under the Dictatorship, the Republic, and the present régime—but the people do not change. They have always been liberty-loving, though staunchly conservative; highly moral, though confirmed sceptics of ecclesiastical doctrine; with a rooted dislike of physical violence, drunkenness or any breach of good manners—for instance, money-grubbing. In the villages, bills are presented not weekly, nor monthly, nor quarterly, but at the end of the year. The cost of living has, of course, soared steeply. Wages and commodity prices are six times what they were; rents ten to twenty times. And import taxes on foreign manufactures remain severe.

Since the price of a new car is nearly trebled by customs duties, models built in the early 'Twenties, which must look like phantoms to English and American visitors, are still on the roads, and worth good money. Yet, for those who avoid the "Golden Mile" of hotels and villas running west out of Palma, the island remains far cheaper to live in than the South of France, or Italy; and the weather is more dependable.

Once a year we go to England, for a fortnight or three weeks, to remind the children that they are English. Also to greet friends, relatives and publishers; to buy books and whatever else cannot be bought in Majorca; and to compare this year's England with the last. Every visit makes me feel more relieved than before that I listened to Gertrude Stein. Last September we managed, at great expense, to rent a furnished flat in Hampstead, while the owners were on holiday in Spain; but were warned that, since England was suffering from full employment, domestic help could not be got at any price. So there were we buying food, cooking, washing, looking after the children, and sweeping the rooms as in wartime; with no leisure for shopping or visiting as we had intended. This is not a plea for commiseration; but in Majorca our two maids, one charwoman, and our part-time gardener earn, between them, around $12 a week—which is good wages here. When we left the Hampstead flat, and felt obliged to give it a farewell cleaning, we had to borrow a Majorcan maid whom a friend of ours, a Harley Street doctor, had imported. The shine she gave the place!

It is always pleasant to come back to the island, escaping the first frosts, and find several weeks of summer still in hand, with a single blanket on the beds, instead of three and an eiderdown. And then the food. In London, you can now get everything, in theory—including fruit and vegetables out of season from the deep-freeze, and all Continental delicatessen. But who can really *cook*? A recipe from Alice Toklas's *Cook Book* will include, say: a sucking-pig's foot, a chicken liver, a sprig of basil, wild marjoram, a taste of rosemary. Imagine going out to tick off that list in London, even in Soho! But in the Palma market, it would be the most natural thing in the world.

One important characteristic of Majorca, from my point of view, is the relaxing climate; if I live in too bracing an air, my mind revs too fast—I get nervous, lose weight, sleep badly. Another good thing is that nothing newsworthy ever happens here, still, or is allowed to happen, bar seasonal fiestas, traffic accidents, revivalist missions, visits from the U.S. Fleet, an annual pedal-cycle race around the island and (every hundred years or so) the backwash of Civil War from the mainland. For some reason or other, foreign visitors are not encouraged to be aware of any local recreations in Palma, except the Sunday afternoon bullfight, gipsy dancing at expensive night-clubs, betting at the pelota *frontón*, and swimming on beaches inconveniently far from the city—the magnificent Palma sea front is abandoned mainly to coal yards, gas-works, and sewage. They will find no casino, no golf course, and very little tennis. But there is always plenty going on in a quiet way: from trotting races, cock-fighting, league soccer and all-in wrestling, to a symphony orchestra (unexpectedly conducted by a North Korean); Father Tomás's marvellous choir, which specializes in ancient Spanish music; and a Classical Ballet school, directed by a pupil of Pavlova's.

In the villages perfect tranquillity reigns; or you can call it vacancy. The Majorcan countryside is not at all a place to go in search of inspiration; but admirable for people whose minds already teem with ideas that need recording in absolute quiet—poets, mathematicians, musicians, sculptors and such. They are advised not to get involved with the "Golden Mile" clique who, coming here for inspiration, find only cheap brandy, dope, and a temptingly relaxed moral climate among those who also came for inspiration—or perhaps simply to do nothing, or for mischief.

ROBERT GRAVES

As I was saying, the tourist grid covers only a comparatively small area, because of the roads. Quite sizable towns are linked by mere dirt tracks. Villages like Sinéu (once the Roman colony of Simium), in the heart of the wheat-growing and mule-breeding district; Capdepera, with its fantastically crenellated mediaeval fortress; Bañalbufar, famous for its tomato terraces, zigzagging boldly down towards the sea; Búger, a splendid little town on a hill surrounded by a sea of almond and fig-trees; Galilea, an inland village, which in late January seems perched on a mountain of snow—almond blossom, in fact; Orient, the highest hamlet in the island, with its walnut groves and oddly North Welsh appearance; Petra, the sleepy birthplace of the Franciscan missionary Fra Junípero Serra, who represents California in the Hall of Fame—all these are beautiful in their diverse ways, and seldom see a foreigner for weeks on end. Instead, daily tourist excursions are organized to the Valldemosan convent cell where George Sand and Chopin spent their illicit and uncomfortable honeymoon in 1839; to the damp stalacite caves of Manacor and Artá; to the dusty, cypress-lined Calvary of Pollensa; to the Blue Gorge, whose blueness and picturesqueness are loudly commented upon by the guide. No excursions visit the spectacular prehistoric towers (called *talayots*), or even the Iberian village excavated a few years ago, in the Lluchmayor direction, where you can pick up Roman and Bronze Age pottery shards by the basketful. In the remoter parts there are annual village fiestas with spontaneous dancing—not the "folklorical" dances laid on for tourists at Valldemosa and elsewhere—threshing with wooden flails, ploughing with wooden ploughs, ancient handicrafts, the shepherd's flute and tabor, occupational songs. The women still wear their traditional peasant costume of lace head-dresses (or enormous straw hats), long plaits, short-sleeved jackets, and very full skirts.

The Puig Mayor, a rocky peak of some 4,300 feet, is the

haunt of the black vulture, the largest European bird of prey, recognizable by its pointed wings and wedge-shaped tail. Around Galilea and Puigpuñent, young men still hunt game with sling, like their famous ancestors, the Balearic slingers who provided the finest missile troops for both the Roman and the Carthaginian armies. They can knock down partridges on the wing, and seldom miss a rabbit or pine-marten at thirty yards. In two or three villages the mediaeval witch cult remains active, to my personal knowledge. It is based on the red-light quarter of Palma, where the Chief Witch can be seen only by appointment, and an annual Grand Sabbath is supposedly celebrated at Sinéu; however, the town authorities strenuously deny this.

Although hundreds of the most picturesque houses in Palma, some dating from the fifteenth century, were destroyed a year or two ago to make room for a grandiose covered market, thoroughfares lined by office buildings and kitsch-shops, and workmen's tenements, it remains a beautiful city. I can wander happily for hours in the network of narrow flagged lanes behind the Cathedral, or in the direction of the cavalry barracks—Tower of Love Lane, Wind Alley, Ecce Homo Alley, Miracle Passage, Twopence-half-penny Street, and the rest. But the Civic authorities have allowed two noble Renaissance merchant-palaces to be converted, one into a government office, the other into a repair shop. The Lonja, the finest Merchant Guild House in Spain, overlooking Palma harbour, now pretends half-heartedly to be a museum. The roof of one of the finest Cathedrals in Europe is in a dangerous state of disrepair. I should not be surprised to hear casually some day that the twelfth-century Moorish Baths had been removed to make room for a cinema, or a hair-dressing salon.

During school terms we have been living in a Palma flat, because village education is even more inadequate than the sort supplied by the city. At the end of June—also at Christmas and Easter—we move to our house at Deyá. We find Palma life no hardship. The ordinary townsfolk go to bed early, as we do, and never use knives, or coshes, or revolvers. A few noble families remain locked away in their decaying mansions, where hardly a room has been refurnished or a modern convenience introduced since the seventeenth century; but are regarded with pity rather than awe.

No social distinction is acknowledged in Majorca between the rest of the native population: peasants, professional classes, and merchants. Everyone is a gentleman or gentlewoman; because all consider themselves bound by the same high standards of politeness and rectitude implied in the adjective "formal"—which invariably carries a good sense. Informal though I am by nature, I try to pass as a *caballero muy formal:* doing nothing in public to shock my neighbours' susceptibilities. As I always remind friends who write me "for information about your island": "It is not my island, but theirs." I often wish all foreigners would take this simple fact to heart.

The main difficulty about going off the beaten track, besides transport, is food. Some time must always elapse before a foreign stomach gets used to olive oil, frequently rancid, as a substitute for cooking-fat or butter; or a foreign palate to garlic. The peasants' staple fare consists of beans, spinach, raw pork sausages flavoured with red pepper, blood-pudding flavoured with aniseed, coarse bread, rice, onions, tomatoes, and dried figs. Wine is usually tempered with water. At Easter, a popular sweet cake comes decorated with this same raw pork sausage, candied peel, and sardines; and in the coastal villages octopus is sometimes served with chocolate sauce. Foreigners also find an unexpected language difficulty: although politically Majorca forms an integral part of Spain, a great many peasants have not spent long enough at school to learn more than a few words of Spanish. Among themselves, they habitually talk Mallorquin, which is as old a language as English and purer than Catalan and provençal, its nearest relatives.

The Majorcans are a good-looking, sturdy people, and the women walk gracefully. It is a mixed race, the foundation being prehistoric Iberian, with layers of Phoenician, Greek, Roman, Vandal, Moorish, Pisan and Aragonese. A large element is Jewish; since the first century A.D., Jews seem to have constituted the main artisan population of Palma. Both the Romans and Moors let them be; and it was only in 1453 that the Christians drove them by repressive laws to mass-conversion. The Goldsmiths' Guild kept their faith until the time of the Holy Inquisition, when they were forced to choose between emigration, conversion or burning at the stake. There were extensive pogroms among backsliders as late as the eighteenth century.

Education has been our main problem. The Majorcans are marvellously patient and kind to little children, compared with French, English or Americans. The schools, however, are fifty years out of date: the hours being usually from 7.30 in the morning to 7.30 at night, with Spartan school dinners and, as a rule, no organized games. Lessons are learned by heart and all explanations withheld. But we get long summer holidays. For foreigners the only alternative is home tutoring, total or partial; or, at the age of thirteen, when the problem becomes critical, to send the children off to France, England or Switzerland. By then they will, at any rate, have learned Spanish, mathematics of a fairly high standard, and good manners. The rest can be added. Our sixteen-year-old son has settled down comfortably enough at an English public school; but his Majorcan contemporaries whom he greets in the vacations are already men, whereas his form-mates in England are still outsize small boys. Since no career would be open to him

369

in Spain except business, he accepts his fate and sets himself to understand his extraordinary fellow-countrymen. Two more of our children are soon off to school in Switzerland.

Statistics show that only three per cent of the foreign visitors to Majorca ever return. I could not say what percentage of those who go, say, to Dinant or Ostend or the Black Forest, return; but it is probably a good deal higher. Of those who come to live here permanently, and keep their resolution, the percentage must be .00003, or thereabouts; Paradise soon palls. I should confess that we have very few close Spanish friends, apart from village folk, shopkeepers and such. One reason is that we obstinately go to bed at 11 p.m. and get up at 7 a.m., instead of going to bed at 3 a.m. and getting up at 11 a.m., as well-to-do Spaniards must; our meal-times simply cannot be made to correspond with theirs. Other reasons are the extreme formality of most Spanish households, and the apparent lack of any close intellectual bond between husbands and wives.

Both before I left the island at the outbreak of the Revolution, and since my return, I have never had the least trouble with the Spanish authorities. What I write or think is no concern of theirs, so long as I commit no breach of the peace. "To every man his beliefs," they say. Moreover, the grim-looking *guardias civiles*, with their peaked hats and their rifles always at hand, are the kindest-hearted and politest body of police you could hope to meet anywhere. I have often enlisted their tactful aid against drunk, aggressive or impertinent foreigners.

English friends come to visit us at Deyá during the summer holiday—we have a spare cottage to put at their disposal, and a private boat-house, with boat. The interesting thing is that we get to know them very well here; they have no immediate worries, the weather can be depended on, they relax completely, wear no ties or collars or high-heeled shoes, and pay

370

full attention to our questions. When we make our brief raids on London we hardly recognize them; they are so obsessed with the struggle for existence. The Majorcan winter is short —about two and a half months—and, though not severe, because frost only reaches the mountain tops, can be trying: unfortunately the islanders have an ancestral tradition that winter does not exist. This ridiculous belief has affected architecture. Few houses have fireplaces except in the kitchen, most windows and doors fit badly, and one is expected to huddle over a charcoal brazier, or wear several woolen petticoats, if a woman; or freeze, if a man. Or move into a modern hotel, if rich.

Adam and Eve's Paradise was, I agree, more select than ours has become. This year one hundred and twenty British artists, in waves of thirty, are expected at only one of our now numerous Deyá inns and *pensions;* also increased numbers of strangers who claim to have read all my books—which means four or five million words—and are under the mistaken impression that we keep open house, that I like talking about myself, that I am a house-agent and general-inquiry bureau, that I can help them to publish their poems. We may soon have to retreat into the still unexplored hinterland.

ERNEST HEMINGWAY

Death in the Afternoon

A SELECTION FROM *Death in the Afternoon*

*In northern Mexico, a thousand miles from Mexico City and a
mile from the United States, bullfights are held, usually bad
fights in crumbling arenas, while out in the sandy cattle country around the towns men wearing chaps and broad-brimmed
hats ride horseback across the land. The stamp of Spain is on
the earth and on the people. It is also on the land and people to
the north of Mexico, in the Southwest and West, but although
the "Anglos" may live in ranch houses and wear Andalusian
"cowboy" vests to rodeos, the* fiesta brava *was too alien for*

them to absorb it into their culture. It was impossible to think of absorbing it even in some of the Latin American countries such as Argentina and Chile where remoteness, temperate climate, the place of origin in northern Spain of the early settlers made the bullfight unacceptable and eventually illegal.

Southern Spain is the setting for the art at its height; the art of death, unimaginable outside that setting, perhaps in the eighteenth-century ring at Ronda above the gorge of the river, or on the golden sand at Sevilla, with the tower of the Giralda rising beyond the wall of faces in shadow on the opposite side of the ring.

Death in the Afternoon *may be the best of Hemingway. It is certainly the best book about bullfighting in any language.*

AT this point it is necessary that you see a bullfight. If I were to describe one it would not be the one that you would see, since the bullfighters and the bulls are all different, and if I were to explain the possible variations as I went along the chapter would be interminable. There are two sorts of guide books; those that are read before and those that are to be read after and the ones that are to be read after the fact are bound to be incomprehensible to a certain extent before; if the fact is of enough importance in itself. So with any book on mountain ski-ing, sexual intercourse, wing shooting, or any other thing which it is impossible to make come true on paper, or at least impossible to attempt to make more than one version of at a time on paper, it being always an individual experience, there comes a place in the guide book where you must say do not come back until you have ski-ed, had sexual intercourse, shot quail or grouse, or been to the bullfight so that you will know what we are talking about. So from now on it is inferred that you have been to the bullfight.

You went to the bullfight? How was it?

It was disgusting. I couldn't stand it.

All right, we will give you an honorable discharge but no refund.

How did you like it? It was terrible. How do you mean terrible? Just terrible. It was terrible, awful, horrible. Good. You get an honorable discharge, too.

How did it seem to you? I was simply bored to death. All right. You get the hell out of here.

Didn't anybody like the bullfight? Didn't anybody like the bullfight at all? No answer. Did you like it, sir? I did not. Did you like it, madame? Decidedly not.

An old lady in the back of the room: What is he saying? What is that young man asking?

Some one near her: He's asking if any one liked the bullfight.

Old lady: Oh, I thought he was asking if any of us wanted to be bullfighters.

Did you like the bullfight, madame?

Old lady: I liked it very much.

What did you like about it?

Old lady: I liked to see the bulls hit the horses.

Why did you like that?

Old lady: It seemed so sort of homey.

Madame, you are a mystic. You are not among friends here. Let us go to the Café Fornos where we can discuss these matters at leisure.

Old lady: Wherever you wish, sir, provided it is clean and wholesome.

Madame, there is no wholesomer place in the Peninsula.

Old lady: Will we see the bullfighters there?

Madame, the place is packed with them.

Old lady: Then let us be off.

Fornos is a café frequented only by people connected with the bullfights and by whores. There is smoke, hurrying of waiters, noise of glasses and you have the noisy privacy of a big café. We can discuss the fight, if you wish, and the old lady can sit and look at the bullfighters. There are bullfighters at every table and for all tastes and all the other people in the café live off bullfighters in some way or another. A shark rarely has more than four remoras or sucking fish that fasten to him or swim along with him, but a bullfighter, when he is making money, has dozens. The old lady does not care to discuss the bullfight. She liked it; she is now looking at the bullfighters and never discusses things she has enjoyed even with her most intimate friends. We talk about it because there were a number of things you say you did not understand.

When the bull came out did you notice that one of the banderilleros ran across his course trailing a cape and that the bull followed the cape driving at it with one horn? They run him that way always, at the start, to see which horn he favors. The matador, standing behind his shelter, watches the bull run by the trailing cape and notices whether he follows the zig-zagging cape on both his right and his left sides, this showing whether he sees with both eyes and which horn he prefers to hook with. He also notices whether he runs straight or if he has a tendency to cut ground toward the man as he charges. The man who went out with the cape in both hands after the bull had been run, and cited him from in front, standing still as the bull charged, and with his arms moving the cape slowly just ahead of the bull's horns, passing the bull's horns close by his body with a slow movement of the cape, seeming to keep him controlled, in the folds of the cape, bringing him past his body each time as he turned and recharged; doing this five times and then finishing off with a swirl of the cape that turned the man's back on the bull and, by cutting the bull's charge brusquely, fixed him to the spot: that man was the matador and the slow passes that he made were called veronicas and the half pass at the end a media-veronica. Those passes are designed to show the matador's skill and art with the cape, his domination of the bull and also to fix the bull in a certain spot before the entry of the horses. They are called veronicas after St. Veronica who wiped the face of Our Lord with a cloth and are so called because the saint is always represented holding the cloth by the two corners in the position the bullfighter holds the cape for the start of the veronica. The media-veronica that stops the bull at the end of the passes is a recorte. A recorte is any pass with the cape that, by causing the bull to try to turn in less than his own length, stops him brusquely or checks his rush by cutting his course and doubling him on himself.

The banderilleros are never supposed to use both hands on the cape when the bull first comes out. If they use only one hand the cape will be trailed and when they turn it at the end of a run the bull will turn easily and not sharply and brusquely. He will do this because the turn of the long cape gives him an indication of the turn to make and gives him something to follow. With the cape held in both hands the banderillero can snap it away from the bull, flop it brusquely out of his sight and stop him dead, and turn him sharply so that he twists his spinal column, lames himself, has his speed cut, not by being worn down, but by laming, and make him unfit for the rest of the fight. Only the matador is supposed to use two hands on the cape during the early part of the fight. Strictly speaking the banderilleros, who are also called peones, are never supposed to use two hands on the cape except when bringing the bull out from a position he has taken and refused to leave. But in the way bullfighting has developed, or decayed, with emphasis increasingly placed on the manner of execution of the various passes rather than their effect, the banderilleros now do much of the work of preparing the bull for killing that was formerly done by the matador; and matadors without resources or science, whose only ability is their plastic or artistic talent, have their bulls, if these offer the slightest difficulty, prepared, worn down, dominated and everything but killed by the skilled and destructive cape of an experienced banderillero.

It may seem foolish to speak of almost killing such an animal as a fighting bull with a cape. Of course you could not kill, but you can so damage the spinal column, twist the legs and lame the animal and, by abusing its bravery, force it to charge uselessly again and again, each time recorting it ferociously, that you may tire it, lame it, and deprive it of all speed and a great part of its natural forces. We speak of killing a trout with a rod. It is the effort made by the trout that kills it. A catfish arrives at the side of the boat in full possession of all its force and strength. A tarpon, a trout or a salmon will often kill himself fighting the rod and line if you hold him long enough.

It was for this reason that banderilleros were prohibited from caping the bull with both hands. The matador was supposed to do all of the preparation for killing and the killing himself. The picadors were to slow the bull, to change his tempo, and to bring down the carriage of his head. The banderilleros were supposed to run him at the start, to place the banderillas quickly and in such a position as to correct any faults of hooking if they existed, and never to do anything to destroy the strength of the bull, in order that he might come intact into the hands of the matador who was supposed, with the muleta, to correct any tendencies toward hooking to one side or the other, to place him in position for killing, and to kill him from in front, make him lower his head with the red serge of the muleta and killing him with the sword, driving it in high up at the top of the angle between the two shoulder blades.

As the corrida has developed and decayed there has been less emphasis on the form of killing, which was once the whole thing, and more on the cape work, the placing of the banderillas and the work with the muleta. The cape, the banderillas and the muleta have all become ends in themselves rather than means to an end and the bullfight has both lost and gained thereby.

In the old days the bulls were usually bigger than they are now; they were fiercer, more uncertain, heavier and older. They had not been bred down to a smaller size to please the bullfighters and they were fought at the age of four and a half to five years instead of three and a half to four and a half years. Matadors often had from six to twelve years of apprenticeship as banderilleros and as novilleros before becoming formal matadors. They were mature men, knew bulls thoroughly, and faced bulls which were brought to the highest point of physical force, strength, knowledge of how to use their horns and general difficulty and danger. The whole end of the bullfight was the final sword thrust, the actual encounter between the man and the animal, what the Spanish call the moment of truth, and every move in the fight was to prepare the bull for that killing. With such bulls it was not necessary to give emotion for the man to pass the animal as deliberately close to him with the cape as was possible. The cape was used to run the bulls, to protect the picadors, and the passes that were made with it, by our modern standards, were exciting because of the size, strength, weight and fierceness of the animal and the danger the matador ran in making them rather than by the form or the slowness of their execution. It was exciting that the man should pass such a bull at all, that a man should be in the ring with and dominate such an

animal furnished the emotion rather than that he should deliberately, as now, try to pass the points of the horn as
mathematically close to his body as possible without moving
his feet. It is the decadence of the modern bull that has made
modern bullfighting possible. It is a decadent art in every way
and like most decadent things it reaches its fullest flower at its
rottenest point, which is the present.

It is impossible, day in and day out, to fight bulls that are
really bulls, huge, strong, fierce and fast, knowing how to use
their horns and old enough so that they have their full growth,
with the technique that has been developed, starting with Juan
Belmonte, in modern bullfighting. It is too dangerous. Belmonte invented the technique. He was a genius, who could
break the rules of bullfighting and could torear, that is the
only word for all the actions performed by a man with the
bull, as it was known to be impossible to torear. Once he had
done it all bullfighters had to do it, or attempt to do it since
there is no going back in the matter of sensations. Joselito
who was strong (Belmonte was weak), healthy (Belmonte
was sickly), who had an athlete's body, gypsy grace and an
intuitive and acquired knowledge of bulls that was never
surpassed by any bullfighter; Joselito for whom everything
in bullfighting was easy, who lived for bullfighting, and
seemed to have been made and bred almost to the measure-
ment of what a great bullfighter should be, had to learn Belmonte's way of working. Joselito, the heritor of all great
bullfighters, probably the greatest bullfighter that ever lived,
learned to torear as Belmonte did. Belmonte worked that way
because of his lack of stature, his lack of strength, because
of his feeble legs. He did not accept any rules made without
testing whether they might be broken, and he was a genius
and a great artist. The way Belmonte worked was not a
heritage, nor a development; it was a revolution. Joselito
learned it, and during the years of their competition, when

379

they each had around a hundred corridas a year, he used to say, "They say that he, Belmonte, works closer to the bull. It looks as though he does. But that isn't true. I really work closer. But it is more natural so it doesn't look so close."

Anyway, the decadent, the impossible, the almost depraved, style of Belmonte was grafted and grown into the great healthy, intuitive genius of Joselito and in his competition with Juan Belmonte, bullfighting for seven years had a golden age in spite of the fact that it was in the process of being destroyed.

They bred the bulls down in size; they bred down the length of horn; they bred them for suavity in their charges as well as fierceness because Joselito and Belmonte could do finer things with these smaller, easier bulls. They could do fine enough things with any bulls that came out of the torils; they were not helpless with any of them, but with the smaller, easier bulls they were certain to do the wonderful things that the public wanted to see. The big bulls were easy for Joselito although they were difficult for Belmonte. All bulls were easy for Joselito and he had to make his own difficulties. The competition ended when Joselito was killed in the ring on May 16, 1920. Belmonte went on one more year, then retired, and bullfighting was left with the new decadent method, the almost impossible technique, the bred down bulls and, as bullfighters, only the bad ones, the hardy, tough ones who had not been able to learn the new method and so no longer pleased, and a crop of new ones, decadent, sad and sickly enough, who had the method but no knowledge of bulls, no apprenticeship, none of the male courage, faculties or genius of Joselito, and none of the beautiful unhealthy mystery of Belmonte.

The ability of a bullfighter with the muleta is what, in the end, determines his ranking in the profession, for it is the most difficult of all the phases of modern bullfighting to dominate and is the part of the bullfight where the genius of a matador has greatest latitude for expression. It is with the muleta that a reputation is made and it is by the extent of this ability to give a complete, imaginative, artistic and emotional performance with the muleta, granted that he has a good bull, that a bull-fighter is paid much or little. To draw a brave bull in Madrid, have him come in ideal condition to the final act and then, through a limited repertoire, not be able to take advantage of his bravery and nobility to make a brilliant faena finishes a bullfighter's chance of a successful career. For bullfighters are now categoried, classed and paid, strangely enough, not by what they actually do, for the bull may upset their perform-ance, they themselves may be ill, they may not be altogether recovered from a horn wound, or they may simply have off-days; but by what they are capable of doing under most favor-able conditions. If the spectators know the matador is capable of executing a complete, consecutive series of passes with the muleta in which there will be valor, art, understanding and, above all, beauty and great emotion, they will put up with mediocre work, cowardly work, disastrous work because they have the hope sooner or later of seeing the complete faena; the faena that takes a man out of himself and makes him feel immortal while it is proceeding, that gives him an ecstasy, that is, while momentary, as profound as any religious ecstasy; moving all the people in the ring together and in-creasing in emotional intensity, as it proceeds, carrying the bullfighter with it, he playing on the crowd through the bull and being moved as it responds in a growing ecstasy of ordered, formal, passionate, increasing disregard for death that leaves you, when it is over, and the death administered to the animal that has made it possible, as empty, as changed and as sad as any major emotion will leave you.

A bullfighter who can do a great faena is at the top of his profession as long as he is believed capable of still doing it, if the conditions are favorable; but a bullfighter who has shown his inability to do a great faena with the conditions right, who is lacking in artistry and genius with the muleta even though he be brave, honorable, skillful and not lacking in knowledge of his work, will always be one of the day laborers of bull-fighting and paid accordingly.

It is impossible to believe the emotional and spiritual inten-sity and pure, classic beauty that can be produced by a man, an animal and a piece of scarlet serge draped over a stick. If you do not choose to believe it possible and want to regard it all as nonsense you may be able to prove you are right by going to a bullfight in which nothing magical occurs; and there are many of them; enough always so you will be able to prove it to your own satisfaction. But if you should ever see the real thing you would know it. It is an experience that either you will have in your life or you will never have. How-ever, there is no way you can be sure you will ever see a great faena in bullfighting unless you go to many bullfights. But if you ever do see one, finished by a great estocada, you will know it and there will be many things you will forget before it will be gone.

Technically, the muleta is used to defend the man from the charge of the bull, to regulate the carriage of the bull's head, to correct a tendency he may have to hook to one side or the other, to tire him and place him in position for killing and, in killing, to furnish an object for him to charge in place of the man's body as the matador goes in on him with the sword.

The muleta is, in principal, held in the left hand and the sword in the right and passes made with the muleta in the left hand are of greater merit than those made with it in the right since when it is held in the right hand, or in both hands, it is spread wide by the sword and the bull having a larger lure to charge may pass farther from the man's body and also, by the swing of the larger lure, be sent away to a greater distance from recharging; thus allowing the man more time to prepare his next pass.

The greatest pass with the muleta, the most dangerous to make and the most beautiful to see is the natural. In this the man faces the bull with the muleta held in his left hand, the sword in his right, the left arm hanging naturally at his side, the scarlet cloth dropping in a fold over the stick that supports it. . . .

The man walks toward the bull and cites him with the muleta and as he charges the man simply sways with the charge, swinging his left arm ahead of the bull's horns, the man's body following the curve of the charge, the bull's horns opposite his body, the man's feet still, he slowly swings his arm holding the cloth ahead of the bull and pivots, making a turn of a quarter-circle with the bull. If the bull stops the man may cite him again and describe another quarter of a circle with him, and again, and again, and again. I have seen it done six successive times; the man seeming to hold the bull with the muleta as though by magic. If the bull instead of stopping with the charge, and what stops him is a final flick the man gives the lowest end of the cloth at the end of each pass, and the great twist that has been given his spinal column through the curve the matador has forced him to describe in bending him around, turns and recharges, the man may get rid of him by a pase de pecho, or pass past the chest. This is the reverse of the pass natural. Instead of the bull coming from in front and the man moving the muleta slowly before his charge, in the pase de pecho, the bull, having turned, comes from behind or from the side, and the man swings the muleta forward, lets the bull go past the man's chest and sends him away with the sweep of the folds of scarlet cloth. The chest pass is the most impressive when it completes a series of naturals or when it is forced by an unexpected return and charge of the bull and is used by the man to save himself rather than as a planned manoeuvre. The ability to execute a series of naturals and then to finish them off with the chest pass mark a real bullfighter.

First it takes courage to cite the bull for a true natural when there are so many other passes in which the bull-fighter exposes himself less; it takes serenity to await the arrival of the bull with the unspread muleta low in the left hand, knowing that if he does not take the small lure offered he will take the man, then it takes great ability to move the muleta ahead of his charge, keeping him well centred in it, the elbow straight as the arm moves, swinging straight, and to follow the curve with the body without moving the loca-tion of the feet. It is a difficult pass to make properly four times in succession before a mirror in a drawing room without any bull being present and if you make it seven times you will be dizzy enough. There are many bullfighters who never learn to make it presentably at all. To do it well, without contortion, keeping the lines of the figure with the horn of the bull so close to the man's waist that they would only have to move up an inch or two to gore, controlling the bull's charge by the movement of arm and wrist and keeping him centred in the cloth, stopping him with the wrist flick at just the proper moment, repeating this three or four or five times takes a bullfighter and an artist.

The natural can be tricked by doing it with the right hand, the muleta spread wide with the sword and the man gyrating on his feet so that the bull follows a sort of half spin made by man and muleta rather than a slowly moved arm and wrist. There are many passes made with the right hand that are of positive merit, but in almost all the sword with its point pricked into the cloth and the hilt held in the same hand with the stick enlarges the spread of the muleta and by giving it greater extent enables the bullfighter to pass the bull farther from his body if he wishes. He may pass him close, but he has a means of passing him farther away in case of necessity that the man working with the muleta in his left hand does not possess.

Aside from the natural and the pecho, the principal passes with the muleta are the ayudados, passes made with sword pricked into the muleta and the two held in both hands. These passes are either called por alto or por bajo, depending on whether the muleta passes over the bull's horns or is swung below the bull's muzzle.

All passes, and half passes, that is those in which the bull does not completely pass the man, made with the muleta have a definite purpose. Nothing so punishes a bull that is strong and willing to charge as a series of naturals which at the same time that they are twisting and tiring him make him follow the lure and the man with his left horn, training him to take the direction the man wants him to take as he later goes in to kill. A bull whose neck muscles have not been sufficiently tired and who carries his head high, will after a series of ayudados por alto; passes made with the muleta and sword held in both hands and the muleta held high so that the bull drives up after it as he goes by the man; have his muscles tired so the head will be much lower. If he is tired and carries his head too low the matador can bring it up, temporarily, with the same pass if he modifies it and does not wait for the carriage of the head to fall again before he goes in to kill. The low passes, made with a swing and a sharp twist of the muleta, sometimes a slow-drawing swing and flip of the lower part of the cloth, and the quick chops back and forth are for bulls that are still too strong on their feet or difficult to fix in one spot. They are made from in front of bulls that will not pass and the merit of the bullfighter consists of his foot-work in never losing his place at the head of the animal, never retreating more than he needs to, and with the movements of his muleta dominating the animal, making him turn sharply on himself, wearing him down quickly, and fixing him in position.

A bull that will not pass, that is charge from a certain distance with sufficient force so that if the man remains still and moves the muleta properly the bull will pass him entirely, is either a cowardly bull or a bull who has been so used in the fight that he has lost all buoyancy and will no longer attack. A skillful matador can by a few passes that he forces at close range and is careful to keep suave, not turning the bull too much on himself or twisting his legs, make the cowardly bull believe that the muleta is not a punishment; that he will not be hurt if he charges, and convert the cowardly bull into the semblance of a brave bull by giving him confidence. In the same way, by working delicately and wisely, he can light up the bull that has lost his charging ability and bring him out of his defense and into the offensive again. To do this a bullfighter must take great chances as the only way to give a bull confidence, to force him to charge when he is on the defensive and to master him is to work as close to him as you can get, leave him just enough of his own terrain to stand on, as Belmonte puts it, and in provoking the charge from such close range the bullfighter has no way to avoid being caught if he gusses wrong and no time to prepare his passes. His reflexes must be perfect and he must know bulls. If at the same time he is graceful you may be sure that grace is an altogether inherent quality and not a pose. You may be able to pose as the horns approach from a distance, but there is no time to pose when you are between them, or shifting back and forth to a little place of safety at the corner of his neck as by giving him the muleta on one side and then withdrawing it, pricking him with the point of the sword or the muleta stick to make him turn, you wear him down, or light him up when he does not want to charge.

There is a whole school of bullfighting in which grace is developed until it is one essential and the passing of the horn past the man's belly eliminated as far as possible, which was inaugurated and developed by Rafael El Gallo. El Gallo

386

was too great and sensitive an artist to be a complete bull-fighter so he gradually avoided, as much as possible, those parts of the bullfight which had to do with or were capable of bringing on death, either of the man or the bull, but most espe-cially of the man. In this way he developed a way of working with the bull in which grace, picturesqueness, and true beauty of movement replaced and avoided the dangerous classicism of the bullfight as he found it. Juan Belmonte took such of Gallo's inventions as he wanted and combined them with the classic style and then developed the two into his own great revolutionary style. Gallo was much of an inventor as was Belmonte, he had more grace, and if he would have had the cold, passionate, wolf-courage of Belmonte there could never have been a greater bullfighter. The nearest you come to that combination was Joselito, his brother, and his only fault was that everything in bullfighting was so easy for him to do that it was difficult for him to give it the emotion that was always supplied by Belmonte's evident physical inferiority, not only to the animal he was facing but to every one who was working with him and most of those who were watching him. Watch-ing Joselito was like reading about D'Artagnan when you were a boy. You did not worry about him finally because he had too much ability. He was too good, too talented. He had to be killed before the danger ever really showed. Now the essence of the greatest emotional appeal of bullfighting is the feeling of immortality that the bullfighter feels in the middle of a great faena and that he gives to the spectators. He is per-forming a work of art and he is playing with death, bringing it closer, closer, closer, to himself, a death that you know is in the horns because you have the canvas-covered bodies of the horses on the sand to prove it. He gives the feeling of his im-mortality, and, as you watch it, it becomes yours. Then when it belongs to both of you, he proves it with the sword.

BIBLIOGRAPHY

Bone, Gertrude: *Days in Old Spain.* London: Macmillan and Co., Ltd.; 1938. Pp. 139–48.

Borrow, George: *The Bible in Spain* [etc.]. London and New York: Everyman's Library; n. d., 1906. Pp. 112–22, 223–33.

Brenan, Gerald: *The Face of Spain.* London: Turnstile Press; 1950. Pp. 122–46.

Calderón de la Barca, Frances E. I.: *The Attaché in Madrid or, Sketches of the Court of Isabella II.* Tr. from the German. New York: D. Appleton and Company; 1856. Pp. 174–86, 268–73.

Disraeli, Benjamin: *Home Letters Written by the Late Earl of Beaconsfield in 1830 and 1831.* London: John Murray; 1885. Pp. 6–26, 29.

Ellis, Havelock: "The Genius of Spain." *The Nineteenth Century and After,* LI (May 1902). Pp. 753–69.

Frank, Waldo: *Virgin Spain: The Drama of a Great People,* 2nd ed. New York: Duell, Sloan and Pearce; 1942. Pp. 240–51.

Graves, Robert: *5 Pens in Hand.* Garden City, New York: Doubleday and Co.; 1958. Pp. 15–29.

Hay, John: *Castilian Days.* Boston: James R. Osgood and Co.; 1871. Pp. 1–5, 21–6, 78–91, 121–4, 126–30.

Helm, MacKinley: *Spring in Spain.* New York: Harcourt, Brace and Co.; 1952. Pp. 193–7, 199–214.

Hemingway, Ernest: *Death in the Afternoon.* New York and London: Charles Scribner's Sons; 1955. Pp. 63–70, 206–13.

Howells, William Dean: *Familiar Spanish Travels.* New York: Harper and Brothers; 1913. Pp. 197–213.

Huntington, Archer M.: *A Note-Book in Northern Spain.* New York and London: G. P. Putnam's Sons; 1898. Pp. 59–73.

Irving, Washington: *The Alhambra.* New York: G. P. Putnam's Sons,

Repperban Edition; London: n. d. Vol. I, pp. 7–9, 46–52, 53–63, 65–7.

King, Georgiana Goddard: *Heart of Spain*, edited by Agnes Mongan. Cambridge, Mass.: Harvard University Press; 1941. Pp. 67–75.

Longfellow, Samuel, ed.: *Life of Henry Wadsworth Longfellow, with Extracts from His Journals and Correspondence*. Boston and New York: Houghton, Mifflin and Co.; 1886, 1887, 1891. Vol. I, pp. 104–8, 125–8.

Macaulay, Rose: *Fabled Shore: From the Pyrenees to Portugal*. New York: Farrar, Straus and Cudahay, Inc.; n. d. [1951]. Pp. 9–21.

Maugham, Somerset: *Don Fernando, or Variations on Some Spanish Themes*, rev. ed. London: Wm. Heinemann; 1950. Pp. 61–70.

Orwell, George: *Homage to Catalonia*. Introduction by Lionel Trilling. Boston: Beacon Press; 1952. Pp. 15–37.

Sitwell, Sacheverell: *Spain*, 2nd ed. London: B. T. Batsford, Ltd.: 1951. Pp. 3–17.

Starkie, Walter: *Don Gypsy: Adventures with a Fiddle in Southern Spain and Barbary*. New York: E. P. Dutton and Co.; 1937. Pp. 355–67.

Ticknor, George: "George Ticknor's Travels in Spain," edited by George Tyler Northup. *University of Toronto Studies, Philological Series*, No. 2 (Toronto, 1913), pp. 16–26.

Tracy, Honor: *Silk Hats and No Breakfast: Notes on a Spanish Journey*. London: Methuen and Co., Ltd.: 1957. Pp. 51–63.

A Note on the Type

THE TEXT of this book was set on the Linotype in JANSON, a recutting made direct from type cast from matrices long thought to have been made by the Dutchman Anton Janson, who was a practicing type founder in Leipzig during the years 1668–87. However, it has been conclusively demonstrated that these types are actually the work of Nicholas Kis (1650–1702), a Hungarian, who most probably learned his trade from the master Dutch type founder Dirk Voskens. The type is an excellent example of the influential and sturdy Dutch types that prevailed in England up to the time William Caslon developed his own incomparable designs from these Dutch faces.

Composed, printed, and bound by
Kingsport Press, Inc., Kingsport, Tennessee.
Typography and binding design by
VINCENT TORRE

A Note about the Author

THOMAS F. McGANN, who is professor of
Latin American History at the University of
Texas, was born in Cambridge, Massachusetts,
in 1920. He took his B.A., M.A., and Ph.D. at
Harvard, where he was formerly instructor
and assistant professor of history. In addition
to articles in popular and scholarly journals,
Mr. McGann has written *Argentina, the
United States and the Inter-American System:
1880–1914*, and translated and edited two other
books. He lives in Austin with his wife and
four children.

May 1963

DATE DUE	
JAN 26 2012	